An Introduction to Text Processing

The MIT Press, with Peter Denning as general consulting editor, publishes computer science books in the following series:

ACM Doctoral Dissertation Award and Distinguished Dissertation Series

Artificial Intelligence
Patrick Winston, founding editor
J. Michael Brady, Daniel G. Bobrow, and Randall Davis, editors

Charles Babbage Institute Reprint Series for the History of Computing
Martin Campbell-Kelly, editor

Computer Systems
Herb Schwetman, editor

Explorations with Logo
E. Paul Goldenberg, editor

Foundations of Computing
Michael Garey and Albert Meyer, editors

History of Computing
I. Bernard Cohen and William Aspray, editors

Information Systems
Michael Lesk, editor

Logic Programming
Ehud Shapiro, editor; Koichi Furukawa, Fernando Pereira, and David H. D. Warren, associate editors

The MIT Press Electrical Engineering and Computer Science Series

Research Monographs in Parallel and Distributed Processing
Christopher Jesshope and David Klappholz, editors

Scientific and Engineering Computation
Janusz Kowalik, editor

Technical Communication
Ed Barrett, editor

An Introduction to Text
Processing

Peter D. Smith

The MIT Press
Cambridge, Massachusetts
London, England

Many of the designations used by manufacturers and sellers to distinguish their products and services are claimed as trademarks. Where the author was aware of such claims, the designations have been shown in all capitals (for example, VAX) or with initial capitals (for example, WordPerfect).

Printed and bound in the United States of America.

Library of Congress Cataloging-in-Publication Data

Smith, Peter D. (Peter Desmond), 1950–
    An introduction to text processing/Peter D. Smith.

       p.   cm.
    Includes bibliographical references.
    ISBN 0-262-19299-3
    1. Text processing (Computer science) I. Title.
QA76.9.T48S55   1990
005—dc20   90-5696
                              CIP

for Caitlin

Contents

Contents

Preface

This book is a survey of text-oriented applications, techniques and algorithms. Although many of the first applications of computers were in solving numeric problems, there has always been interest in using them for processing text. For example, formatters and editors have been in existence for 30 years; document storage and retrieval techniques were being developed in the 1950s. Recent developments of personal computers and high quality printers have increased interest in text processing software.

A file of text, for example the one containing the source of this book, can be viewed at a number of different levels. At the lowest level it can be treated simply as a stream of characters. At the other extreme it may be regarded as a natural language text with semantic content. This book is divided into five parts each corresponding to a level at which a text file can be processed. Some techniques, for example compression, employ character and symbol based methods. Generally, techniques are categorized according to the simplest view, thus compression is grouped with the character level operations.

In Part I we look at techniques for operating on files as a whole, including ways in which a source file can be created, stored and retrieved. Typically we are concerned with the source text of documents rather than their final formatted or printed form. In chapter 1 we look at document capture and construction. In chapter 2 we examine techniques for document storage and retrieval.

Part II examines character level operations: editing, compression and encryption. In chapter 3 we look at editors, in chapter 4 at text compression and in chapter 5 at encryption. The next level of techniques, described in Part III, considers files symbol by symbol. A symbol is not necessarily a word in a natural language but rather a group of characters delimited in some way. In Chapter 6 we look at macroprocessors, in chapter 7 at the rudiments of text formatting and in chapter 8 at programs for producing concordances and reporting on collocations.

Because it may have some structure, a word is more than just a sequence of characters. In Part IV we consider word-based operations - hyphenation and spelling checking. In chapter 9 we look at hyphenation in formatters; word structure is important, generally a word may only be hyphenated between syllables. In chapter 10 we look at aspects of spelling checking and correction. Finally, in Part V we survey those techniques that treat the input as a file with meaning, at least as a stream of sentences. In chapter 11 we look at programs that assist writers in document evaluation, in chapter 12 we examine methods that have attempted to determine the authorship of a document. In chapter 13 we look at the process of generating an abstract from a document and, finally, in chapter 14 at ways in which computers can assist in document translation.

This text was developed from lecture notes for a course given to graduate and senior undergraduate students at California State University, Northridge. Students taking the course have a background in algorithms and data structures, have programmed in structured high-level languages, and are familiar with the Unix[†] operating system. It is assumed that readers have similar experience.

I would like to thank Hal Berghel and Alan Reed for constructive comments on parts of an early draft. Thanks are also due to E. J. Desautels, University of Wisconsin; Michael Lesk, Bellcore; and Robert F. Simmons, University of Texas at Austin, for many useful comments and suggestions.

---

† Unix is a registered trademark of AT&T.

I

Document Manipulation

1

Document Input and Assembly

In this chapter we look at some ways in which an initial document might be created in a text processing system. It might be input as a whole from some external source or it might be assembled from existing pieces.

1.1 Document input

There are two main ways to input a document into a computer-based text processing system. We can key in the text or we can capture an existing paper document. Recently, voice recognition systems have become a third option in some cases.

1.1.1 Keyboarding
In general, data entry from a keyboard is not very interesting except in considering alternatives to the conventional (QWERTY) keyboard. These include the devices used by court stenographers and the Dvorak keyboard layout.

The layout of the QWERTY keyboard was allegedly designed to minimize key jams on mechanical typewriters (though Gentner and Norman [1] cast some doubt on this theory). The aim was to make it difficult for characters that occur frequently next to each other to be typed in quick succession; in effect typists were deliberately slowed down. Because key jamming is not a problem in golf ball typewriters or in computer keyboards there has been some research into more efficient key layouts.

The Dvorak-Dealey keyboard [2, 3] was patented in 1936 and is probably the most widely studied alternative to QWERTY; Fig. 1.1 shows the positions of the letter keys in the two layouts. Dvorak options are available for some computer keyboards. The layout was designed to minimize finger movements though Gentner and Norman report improvements of only 5-10% in speed over QWERTY. This difference in performance is probably not high enough to cause a switch to the Dvorak layout.

Figure 1.1 Dvorak and QWERTY keyboard layouts


```
      P   Y   F   G   C   R   L
  A   O   E   U   I   D   H   T   N   S
      Q   J   K   X   B   M   W   V   Z
```

(a) Dvorak

```
  Q   W   E   R   T   Y   U   I   O   P
    A   S   D   F   G   H   J   K   L
      Z   X   C   V   B   N   M
```

(b) QWERTY

In some operating systems the command interpreter completes user-entered commands when enough of the command has been entered for it to be unambiguous. Similarly, some systems for disabled typists will present a menu of words after the first few characters have been typed. A word in the menu can be selected with a single key stroke. Such a system would probably be too distracting for most users if applied to every input word although Witten and Cleary [4] report that subjects using their "reactive keyboard" thought they were entering text faster. A word-completion system might be useful if restricted, for example, to proper nouns over a certain length; consider entering a chemistry text with the assistance of a program using a lexicon of chemical names.[1]

1.1.2 Document capture
If we capture an existing paper document we can either capture a facsimile image of the document, i.e. a bit map at a certain resolution, or we can go further and attempt to identify the characters comprising the text. Some products (for example TrueScan by Calera Recognition Systems) in conjunction with scanners, act as printers in reverse and, from an image of a page, produce a file that can be used directly by a word processor. Such systems can handle pages containing a mixture of graphics and text.

---

1. We refer to a word list as a *lexicon* and reserve *dictionary* for a structure containing words and definitions.

Facsimile image An advantage of capturing a facsimile image is that no distinction need be made between text and graphics. In the early days of facsimile transmissions there were compatibility problems. However, in the 1970s a UN standards organization (CCITT) worked with manufacturers to set standards (see McCullough [5]) and in November 1980 finalized recommendations. Documents were to be scanned from top to bottom and left to right. Horizontal lines were to be 215mm in length generating 1728 pixels.[2] Two vertical scanning standards were adopted, normal resolution was to be 3.85 pixels per mm with high resolution being 7.7 pixels per mm. High resolution vertical scanning is approximately 200 pixels to the inch, about the same as the horizontal scanning. The normal vertical resolution is adequate for most business documents.

A problem with the standard resolutions is that a page image requires close to 2 megabits of storage at normal resolution and twice that at high resolution. However, there are compression techniques that can reduce the storage required.

Horizontal compression Consider a single horizontal scan of a line. It is, in most cases, a series of white pixels followed by a sequence of black pixels followed by a sequence of white pixels and so on. Rather than store the pixels themselves we could store the lengths of the sequences. We can assume that the line starts with a white sequence (if in fact it starts black we assume an initial white sequence of length 0) and represent the line by a series of numbers.

One method used in facsimile systems is to represent a sequence of a certain length by a *make-up code* (for the appropriate multiple of 64 bits) followed by a *terminal code* (for the remaining bits). Thus, for example, a sequence of length 300 would be represented by the code for 256 followed by the code for 44. Run lengths are represented by Huffman codes (see 4.2.2) to minimize the average number of bits needed for an image. Because the distribution of white run lengths tends to be different from the distribution of black run lengths, two separate tables are used.

Vertical compression Run length encoding can only take advantage of horizontal redundancy. Vertical reference encoding takes advantage of the fact that, particularly at the higher vertical resolution, one line is usually very similar to the preceding one. We can thus represent a line compactly by the ways in which it differs from some reference line. Consider Fig. 1.2 in which a white pixel is represented by "." and a black pixel by "*". We can represent the current line by a list of positions of color changes expressing those positions relative to the position of the same change in the reference

---

2. European A4 paper is 210mm wide, US letter size is 216mm wide.

Figure 1.2 Vertical differences

```
Reference          .....**.....****.
Current            ..******....**...
```

line. Thus, in the example of Fig. 1.2, the first change from white to black is 3 pixels to the left of the same change in the reference line so we represent this by the code for "Left-3". The next change (from black to white) is one pixel to the right of the same change in the reference line so we represent this by the code for "Right-1".

As with horizontal encoding we can sample large amounts of text to get frequency distributions of the relative position values. We would expect positions with low integer values to occur frequently and this clustering to be more marked with the higher vertical resolution. It may be worth distinguishing between black-white and white-black changes. Given the frequencies we can devise minimal (e.g. Huffman) codes.

The similarity between the current line and the reference line is likely to decrease as the distance between them increases. Best compression is likely to be achieved by a combination of horizontal and vertical compression. For example, we could compress the first line horizontally, then the next N lines vertically using the first as reference, then compress the next line horizontally and so on. Such a strategy also limits the effects of errors in storing or transmitting an image file. The program that recreates the image can re-synchronize on the end-of-line character at the end of a horizontally encoded line.

An $8\frac{1}{2}$" by 11" page scanned at the CCITT high resolution standard generates about 3.7 million bits, half that if scanned at normal resolution. Compression techniques applied to a typical one page business letter can reduce the space needed to about 300,000 bits. Still further reduction is possible if the scanner can recognize common bit patterns, establish a "library" of these and replace an occurrence of a stored pattern by a pointer to the library. The library is prepended to the compressed document.

Taking this idea further we can have a system that both locates characters in a text image and identifies them. A character can now be represented by a standard character code.

ASCII stream The main advantage of capturing a document as a stream of character codes (including format information if appropriate) is that it is easier to perform certain text-oriented editing tasks (e.g. searching for and replacing all occurrences of a particular word). The document is also likely to take up much less space than a facsimile image. However, converting an image to a character stream requires location and identification of the characters.

Optical character recognition A typical optical character reader (OCR) looks like a photocopier. Material is placed face down on a glass surface, a scanning head moves along the lines of text and the reader transmits an appropriate stream of character codes. Advanced readers are capable of learning new fonts including non-Roman alphabets. Most normal paper can be handled, though glossy surfaces tend not to give good results and, if newsprint is scanned, the image on the other side of the paper is liable to confuse the device.

Data entry via OCR is up to 40 times faster than entry by a typist. It is cheaper too: scanning 1000 characters costs about $1 whereas keyboarding the same amount costs $1.75 [6]. As the cost of personnel increases and hardware costs decline, OCR is likely to become more important. An industry survey reports that sales of non-keyboard data entry equipment, primarily OCR, totalled $2.5b in 1987 and are projected to be $4.6b by 1995 [7].

There are typically three stages in the OCR processing of a character: isolation, normalization and recognition. The scanning hardware detects lines of text with more advanced models being able to deal with multi-column input. Within a line, characters are isolated by identifying surrounding white space; thus texts that have kerning and ligatures may cause problems. Kerning is the overlapping of adjacent characters such as AV. Devices that can process ligatures (such as ffi and ffl) typically treat them as a single character. A user can normally specify up to three characters to be transmitted from a single scanned character; this enables both ligatures and accented characters to be processed.

After the scanner produces a bit matrix image of a character, the image is normalized, i.e. standardized in some way, before recognition is attempted. For example, noise can be reduced by changing stray isolated bits to match their surroundings, the image can be rotated to compensate for a certain amount of skew in the input, and the image can be centered and possibly changed in size to fit guidelines.

Recognition strategies vary according to whether the reader is expected to recognize only a limited, predefined set of fonts or whether it is an omni-font device.

If the reader is designed to read only a fixed set of fonts then standard images of the recognizable characters can be held in read-only memory and compared with the input image. There are a number of ways in which two bit matrices may be compared. For example, the matching algorithm may simply count the number of positions at which stored and scanned image match. Alternatively, it could give more weight to two ones matching than to two zeros. There will typically be some threshold score which has to be exceeded for a match to be made.

The TOTEC TO-5000 is a limited-font reader; it scans at 300 cps, taking 15 to 20 seconds per page. List price at the time of writing is about $9000 plus $450 for each additional font (up to 8). Character, word, and line erase are transmitted as user-specified ASCII codes. The substitution error rate (erroneously identifying one character as another) is less than 1 in 300,000. The DEST Workless station costs under $1000 and takes about 15 seconds to read a page. It has a similar error rate to the TO-5000; unrecognizable characters are sent as "@". It has a limited set of fonts and gives up on page if there are too many unrecognizable characters. Given problems with print quality, paper quality, skew and so on, limited font OCR devices will tend to make 3 to 5 errors per page.

A reader designed to read any font must have a more general recognition method than matrix matching. A good strategy is for it to extract a list of features from the image and compare this list with lists of expected features for various characters. The description of a character should contain its essential features. For example, an "F" in most fonts might be expected to have a near-vertical line and two near horizontal lines. The horizontal lines are attached, close to their left ends, near the top and mid-point of the vertical line.

Feature extraction is non-trivial. The algorithm has to deal sensibly with small amounts of extra or missing ink that turn an open curve into a closed one and vice versa. At what point does a "Q" turn into an "O"? Currently, omnifont readers tend to make more errors per page than limited font readers but can read a greater variety of text.

The Kurzweil 4000 [8] is an example of an omnifont reader that uses feature extraction. When scanning a document it interacts with an operator in an initial training process, thereafter proceeding largely without operator intervention. It can recognize proportionally spaced type (in which different characters may have different widths), ligatures and mathematical symbols. Hockey [9] briefly describes experiences with the 4000 and has a longer discussion of the Kurzweil Data Entry Machine.

Recognition of hand-printed text If the source for printed text is originally keyed into some storage system then we could by-pass the optical character recognition device by capturing the original keystrokes. Such an option is not available if the text we are trying to read is hand-written or hand-printed.

In general, recognition of hand-written text (cursive script) is still a research problem. Though not as difficult a problem as recognition of connected speech, it has some features in common. Recognition of hand-printed text is more feasible because the character boundaries are usually clearer. However, it is more difficult than the recognition of machine-printed text because of the greater variation in instances of the same character even when printed by the same person. Recognition through matching bit matrices is not an option and feature analysis is more difficult because straight lines may appear to be curved and vice versa. Munson [10] reports the results of experiments in which people were asked to identify hand-printed characters shown out of context; typical error rates were about 4%. This error rate represents about 80 errors on a typical printed page.

Use of contextual information Recognition of hand-printed characters in isolation is difficult even for people; human readers use context to resolve ambiguities. To test this for yourself, try reading someone's writing in a language with which you are familiar and the same person writing in a foreign language. OCR software can use *a priori* information about the input to increase recognition rates.

We can modify the recognition logic so that it takes a wider view of the text. Initially, rather than making a definite decision as to the identity of each character in turn, it could make a "fuzzy" decision. A character image is assigned a vector of probabilities, one for each character in the alphabet of recognizable characters. A particular probability is based on the degree of similarity between the features of the scanned character and the particular predefined one. In most instances we would expect one of the probabilities in the vector to be close to 1.0 and the rest to be close to 0.0. Although, for example, when we scan a "Q", we might expect the vector entry for "O" to be comparatively high and vice versa.

The simplest use of *a priori* information would not use any context when identifying a particular character but would just take into account expected frequencies of individual characters. For each character in the alphabet, we would multiply the expected probability by the probability in the vector. If the highest product is greater than some threshold, we assume the corresponding character is the one seen.

Going beyond the character level, we could consider the expected frequencies of n-character groups. For each possible n-character combination we would multiply the appropriate product of probabilities from the vectors by the expected frequency of that combination.

The more information we use, the more storage we need, the slower the recognizer is likely to go and the less general it will be. For example, it is likely that English and FORTRAN have different single-character frequency distributions. In using expected character frequencies we would have to tell the recognizer in advance what type of text it is looking at in order that it uses the appropriate *a priori* data. The Kurzweil 5000 scanner [11] uses a 50,000 word lexicon; at the time of writing, lexicons are available for eight different languages.

1.1.3 Voice input

Ideally we would like a device that is the functional equivalent of a secretary taking dictation. However, recognition of continuous speech from each of a number of different speakers is a difficult problem. It is difficult to detect word boundaries and there is a lot of inter-speaker variation. While some good results have been obtained in cases where knowledge of the domain of discourse can be used to narrow down the possibilities, error rates are still comparatively high. For example, Young *et al.* [12] report a best error rate of 3.5%.

IBM announced in Summer 1987 an experimental 20,000 word PC-based system that appears to be oriented towards dictation of office correspondence (IBM claims that the vocabulary includes 97% of the words a speaker is likely to use in business). The system is speaker dependent and requires a 20-minute session per speaker during which a carefully designed training document is read and 200 sound patterns that characterize the reader are recorded. Brief pauses are required between words.

During normal (non-training) operation, the system uses the identity of the two preceding words to reduce the number of candidates for the current one. (It uses statistics based on 250 million words of office correspondence.) Succeeding utterances are also taken into account in making the final choice. Thus the designers hope to be able to process homophones.[3] Because of the use of context, there is a delay of a second or two between a word being spoken and its appearance on the screen. The PC has five special purpose signal processing chips.

1.2 Document assembly

Large documents typically comprise sections that can be developed separately. A text processing system needs a facility for managing such documents. A similar situation arises in the construction of large computer programs and here techniques for controlling source code are well developed [13]. Because source code is only a special case of text files, these same utilities can usually be employed in managing large documents.

1.2.1 File inclusion

A simple facility would allow a directive to be embedded in a file indicating that at that point the entire text of a named file should be read as if it appeared in the document. For example:

```
#include disclaimer
```

---

3. Homophones are distinct words that sound the same, examples are: (too, two, to), (here, hear), (there, their, they're).

should be equivalent to the complete text of the file *disclaimer*. Such directives should be nestable to an arbitrary level. Implementation could be at a low level in the system, for example at the point where records are read from disc, or it could be implemented in all utilities. In either case, the user should be able to suppress the expansion.

1.2.2 The make program

The Unix *make* program [14] is a useful utility for constructing up-to-date versions of documents; it uses a script file that indicates how to build certain target files. A simple *make* script is shown in Fig 1.3 (see 7.5 for a description of some of the utilities used).

Figure 1.3 Script for *make*

```
report.doc:    part1.doc part2.doc Appendix
        cat part1.doc part2.doc Appendix > report.doc

Appendix:      Appendix.nr
        nroff Appendix.nr > Appendix

part1.doc    part1.tbl table.1 table.2
        tbl part1.tbl table.1 table.2 | nroff -ms > part1.doc

part1.tbl    part1.nr macros biblio
        refer -e -p biblio macros part1.nr > part1.tbl

part2.doc    biblio part2.nr macros
        refer -e -p biblio macros part2.nr | nroff -ms > part2.doc
```

This script specifies, for example, that in order to make file part1.doc the files part1.tbl, table.1, and table.2 must be available. Given these files, the script shows how they must be processed by *tbl* and *nroff* to form the target file. If we issue the command:

make -f scriptfilename report.doc

the programs construct an up-to-date version of report.doc.

An important feature of *make* is that it will do the least amount of work necessary to create an up-to-date file. In general, the program builds a dependency tree having the given target file as its root. The dependency tree for report.doc is shown in Fig. 1.4. *Make* processes the dependency tree from the bottom up comparing the modification dates on component and target files. It only rebuilds those components that do not exist or are not current. For example, if we have an up-to-date version of report.doc then we modify table.1, rebuilding report.doc will only execute the following two commands:

    tbl part1.tbl table.1 table.2 | nroff -ms > part1.doc
    cat part1.doc part2.doc Appendix > report.doc

Figure 1.4 Dependency tree from the script of Fig. 1.3

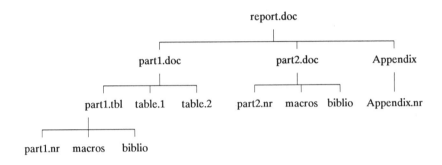

Make has a table of file suffixes and rules that it uses in the absence of user specified alternatives. This table is oriented towards the construction of programs. For example, it tells the program that in order to make file X.o, it should give file X.c to the C compiler and direct the object program to X.o. Given standardization of filename extensions, a similar set of default operations can be developed for text processing.

1.2.3 File differences

Documents are likely to be revised many times in the course of being developed. In addition, there may be periodic upgrades; for example, the rules of major league baseball or the catalog of a college may change slightly from year to year. It would be convenient to have a printed version of a file in which the changes with respect to another file were marked. In addition, it may be important to be able to process an earlier version of a file in some way. Rather than store many different versions of a document, some of which may only differ from each other in minor ways, we could minimize space requirements by storing a base version and the differences between it and other versions.

To support implement this strategy we need a means of identifying the differences between two arbitrary text files. The Unix *diff* program and the Document Compare facility of WordPerfect are two ways in which we might do this.

diff The *diff* program is line-oriented, it would find many differences between two files that differed only in the locations of the line breaks. Thus, it is better used for line-oriented text such as lists and source code. Advantages of *diff* are that it does try to identify the minimal set of differences between two files and that its output can be used by other utilities to create different versions of a document.

Writing a program to find the minimal set of differences between two files is non-trivial. Hunt and McIlroy [15] describe the algorithm that *diff* uses; Miller and Myers [16] describe and present an implementation of an algorithm that is superior to *diff* in some cases, though there are pathological cases where its behavior is much worse.

Document Compare The Document Compare feature of WordPerfect 5.0 [17] allows a user to compare the document on the screen with that in an arbitrary file. Documents are compared phrase by phrase; a variety of characters can delimit a phrase. A user can choose to cause codes to be inserted into the current document that identify new text, text that has been deleted and text that has been moved. Codes cause appropriate annotation when the document is printed but are not sufficient to recreate different version of a document. For example, the codes that delimit text that was moved do not show where it was moved from.

Example Figure 1.5 shows the contents of two files. A program which simply compared corresponding lines in the two files would produce a long list of differences; apart from the first line, no two corresponding lines are the same. However, if we look at the files as a whole, we see that the differences are cosmetic in the first paragraph, and in the second, a sentence has been moved from one end to the other and a single word has been inserted/deleted.

Fig. 1.6 shows the output from the Unix command

diff file.a file.b

The sequence listed in Fig 1.6 describes how to convert file.a into file.b. The single letter commands a, d and c represent append, delete and change respectively. The numbers before the commands refer to line numbers in file.a, those after the commands refer to line numbers in file.b. Output beginning with "<" shows an affected line in file.a; output beginning with ">" shows an affected line in file.b. Thus we can interpret the output in Fig. 1.6 as follows:

Change lines 4 through 6 to the following (lines 4 through 6 of file.b)
Append the following (lines 9 and 10 of file.b) after line 8
Change lines 12 through 13 to the following (lines 14 through 15 of file.b)

Figure 1.5 Two files for comparison

A small piece of text

Below is one of two versions of a short text paragraph. Changes
have been made in one of the versions to illustrate how software
reports on the differences between files.

Some software is line-oriented and reports on
changes in terms of lines that have to be modified in
one document to make it the same as another. Other
software is more flexible, ignores layout, and looks at
two files phrase by phrase. Both have their advantages
and disadvantages.
This should, I hope, be enough text to illustrate
the differences.

(a)

A small piece of text

Below is one of two versions of a short text paragraph.
Changes have been made in one of the versions to illustrate
how software reports on the differences between files.

This should, I hope, be enough text to illustrate the
differences.
Some software is line-oriented and reports on
changes in terms of lines that have to be modified in
one document to make it the same as another. Other
software is more flexible, ignores most layout, and looks
at two files phrase by phrase. Both have their advantages
and disadvantages.

(b)

Delete lines 15 through 17.

There is apparently redundant information in the output because it can
also be used to produce file.a given file.b.[4]

---

4. Reverse the sequence of commands and interchange "a" and "d" commands.

Figure 1.6 Output from *diff*

```
4,6c4,6
< Below is one of two versions of a short text paragraph. Changes
< have been made in one of the versions to illustrate how software
< reports on the differences between files.
---
> Below is one of two versions of a short text paragraph.
> Changes have been made in one of the versions to illustrate
> how software reports on the differences between files.
8a9,10
>     This should, I hope, be enough text to illustrate the
> differences.
12,13c14,15
< software is more flexible, ignores layout, and looks at
< two files phrase by phrase. Both have their advantages
---
> software is more flexible, ignores most layout, and looks
> at two files phrase by phrase. Both have their advantages
15,17d16
<     This should, I hope, be enough text to illustrate
< the differences.
<
```

Figure 1.7 shows the file of Fig 1.5(a) printed from WordPerfect after codes had been inserted to reflect the differences between it and the file of Fig 1.5(b). New text is highlighted, text not in Fig 1.5(a) is inserted in a struck through manner. Text that has been moved is identified.

Summary

A document can be input into a computer system in a variety of ways. Keyboarding is the predominant method for original material. State-of-the-art optical character readers can read virtually any printed material, possibly with user assistance during an initial training period. Voice input is still in its infancy.

If a document is at all large, it is often convenient to develop and process it in logical units, for example sections or chapters. Some of the tools that are used to maintain source code files can be used to manage text. They typically make it easy to maintain different versions of a document by storing a base version and differences between versions. A program to find the differences between two files of text is an important component of such a system.

Figure 1.7 Result of WordPerfect Document Compare

```
    A small piece of text

Below is one of two versions of a short text paragraph. Changes
have been made in one of the versions to illustrate how software
reports on the differences between files.


        Some software is line-oriented and reports on
changes in terms of lines that have to be modified in
one document to make it the same as another. Other
software is more flexible, ignores layout, ignores most
layout, and looks at two files phrase by phrase. Both
have their advantages and disadvantages.

  ‾
THE FOLLOWING TEXT WAS MOVED
        This should, I hope, be enough text to illustrate
the differences.

THE PRECEDING TEXT WAS MOVED
```

Exercises

(1) Implement and test a text entry program that completes words for the user. How does its usefulness depend on the size and type of its lexicon?

(2) A device that reads pre-printed text into a computer is an important component of a text processing system. Outline some of the difficulties there might be in constructing such a system. Distinguish, where appropriate, between hardware and software problems.

(3) The Unix *deroff* utility can output a version of a file with formatting directives removed and one word per line. How can this be used in conjunction with *diff* to produce output similar to that generated by WordPerfect?

References

1. D. R. Gentner and D. A. Norman, "The typist's touch," *Psychology Today*, pp. 66-72, March 1984.

2. A. Dvorak, N. L. Merrick, W. L. Dealey, and G. C. Ford, *Typewriting behavior,* American Book Company, New York, 1936.

3. D. W. Olson and L. E. Jasinski, "Keyboard efficiency," *Byte*, vol. 11, no. 2, pp. 241-244, February 1986.

4. I. H. Witten and J. G. Cleary, "Foretelling the future by adaptive modelling," *Abacus*, vol. 3, no. 3, pp. 16-36, 73, 1986.

5. T. L. McCullough, "CCITT standardization for digital facsimile," *Proceedings of the NCC*, vol. 49, pp. 409-413, AFIPS Press, May 1980.

6. *Panorama*, vol. 3, no. 1, pp. 6-7, April 1988. An Eastman Kodak publication.

7. K. Evans-Correia, "OCR future looking up," *Digital Review*, pp. 63-66, January 25th, 1988. Tech Report: Office Automation.

8. Kurzweil Computer Products, *Kurzweil 4000: intelligent scanning system*, Cambridge, MA, 1986.

9. S. Hockey, "OCR: The Kurzweil Data Entry Machine," *Literary and Linguistic Computing*, vol. 1, no. 2, pp. 63-67, 1986.

10. J. H. Munson, "Experiments in the recognition of hand-printed text: Part I - character recognition," *Proceedings of the AFIPS Fall Joint Computer Conference*, vol. 33, pp. 1125-1138, 1968.

11. Kurzweil Computer Products, *Kurzweil 5000: intelligent scanning system*, Cambridge, MA, 1989.

12. S. R. Young, A. G. Hauptmann, W. H. Ward, E. T. Smith, and P. Werner, "High level knowledge sources in usable speech recognition systems," *Communications of the ACM*, vol. 32, no. 2, pp. 183-194, February 1989.

13. M. J. Rochkind, "The source code control system," *IEEE Transactions on Software Engineering*, vol. SE-1, no. 4, pp. 364-370, December 1975.

14. S. I. Feldman, *Make--A program for maintaining computer programs,* Bell Laboratories, 1977. Unix Programmer's Manual: Supplementary Documents.

15. J. W. Hunt and M. D. McIlroy, "An Algorithm for Differential File Comparison," Comp. Sci. Tech. Rep. No. 41, Bell Laboratories, Murray Hill, New Jersey, June 1976.

16. W. Miller and E. W. Myers, "A file comparison program," *Software Practice and Experience*, vol. 15, no. 11, pp. 1025-1040, November 1985.

17. *WordPerfect Version 5.0 Reference manual,* WordPerfect Corporation, Orem, Utah, 1988.

Document Storage and Retrieval

Conceptually, one of the simplest things that can be done with a document is to store it for later retrieval. In this chapter we look at some aspects of document storage and retrieval; see Salton [1] for a good survey of some of the techniques. Although research in the area has been going on for 30 years, there is no obviously best method. Document storage and retrieval techniques are likely to become more and more important with the exponential growth in the sizes of document collections and the availability of high-density optical discs. In the first part of this chapter we look at ways in which index terms can be associated with a document to facilitate its retrieval. In the remainder of the chapter we look at some retrieval techniques.

2.1 Storage

Documents are usually stored in such a way as to facilitate subsequent retrieval. Typically, index terms or other tags that reflect the content of the text are associated with a document in order that those documents pertinent to a particular query can be retrieved. Tags might be associated with a document in one of two ways: they might be assigned by a human indexer or they might be derived in some way from the text of the document.

Assigned terms In some systems, the terms may have to be selected from a fixed list, in others, an indexer might be free to chose any terms to index a document. However, even in a "free" system, there may be constraints; in BIOSIS, for example, names of any species mentioned are always key terms. While a fixed-term system may constrain the indexer, it may be to the advantage of the retriever who otherwise has to guess what terms might have been used. Some fixed term lists are very large. For example, the MESH (Medical Subject Headings) list used in Index Medicus [2] contains over 12,000 terms divided into 15 categories each of which is a 7-level hierarchy. Table 2.1 contains examples from MESH: categories, subcategories and progressively more specific terms.

Table 2.1 Extracts from MESH

Categories	
Anatomy	A
Chemicals and Drugs	D
Psychiatry and Psychology	F
Subcategories	
Nervous system	A8
Sense organs	A9
Tissue types	A10
More specific terms	
Brain	A8.186.211
Brain Stem	A8.186.211.132
Mesencephalon	A8.186.211.132.659
Corpora Quadrigemina	A8.186.211.132.659.237
Inferior Collicus	A8.186.211.132.659.237.364

Hierarchical term structures are common; Table 2.2 shows an extract from the list used by Predicasts (economic and business forecasts).

Table 2.2 Extract from Predicasts index structure

366 2400	Electronic navigation systems
366 2450	Aircraft navigation systems
366 2454	Instrument landing systems

Automatic derivative indexing The problem in automatic derivative indexing is to extract or derive appropriate index terms from the text of a document. Automatic indexing is desirable because of the volume of new documents. While the author of a document could be asked to assign index terms as the document is developed, he or she may focus on a few aspects of current interest. In addition, using a program rather than a human indexer has the advantage of consistency. The same document run through the same program always produces the same set of index terms.

Early systems used the content-bearing words in the title of a document as its index terms. But while titles require little data entry, they may be too short to convey much meaning (e.g. "Textual bracketing") or not very indicative of the subject matter (e.g. "In the land of King Arthur" -actually about skin-diving in Wales) or meaningless out of context (e.g. "--And how to avoid them" - a reference to another publication).

Luhn was an early experimenter with full text. His method for extracting index terms was as follows:

(a)   Count the frequencies of the words in the document.

(b)   Discard the most frequent and least frequent words. The former are discarded because they occur too often to indicate the subject matter and the latter because they are too rare.

(c)   Use the remaining MFW (Middle Frequency Words) to give a score to each sentence. The score of a sentence is the number of MFW it contains.

(d)   The index terms of the document are the MFW in the sentences with the highest scores.

In determining the index terms of a document, it would be better to use relative rather than absolute frequencies. That is, to take into account frequencies across the complete document collection rather than just in the current document. For example, using Luhn's method, the term "algorithm" may be selected as a key term of a Computer Science paper. However, if our entire collection were composed of such papers, all having this term, it would not be a good discriminator.

Sparck Jones [3] proposes that the appropriate weight for a term in a document be

$$\frac{\textit{frequency in document}}{\textit{frequency in all documents}}$$

A weight close to 1 indicates that the almost all the occurrences of the term are in the particular document. Now we tag a document not with a simple list of terms but with a weighted list:

$$\{ (k_1, w_1), (k_2, w_2) ... (k_n, w_n) \}$$

where the k_i are the keywords and the w_i are the weights. This allows us to distinguish the more important terms from the less important ones.

Salton [1] outlines a 5-step process for arriving at a weighted list of terms from a document. His process is more sophisticated than Luhn's and operates as follows:

(a)   Make a list of the words occurring in the document and document supplements such as the title and extract.

(b)   Remove from the list words occurring in a *stop list* of non content-bearing words such as "the", "for" and "and".

(c)   Reduce each word to its stem form. Thus, for example, "computing", "computed", "computation", reduce to "compute".

(d)   Compute the weighting factor described above for each stem.

(e)   Represent the document by the weighted list of word stems.

The only non-trivial step is (c). A complete conflation process (one that reduces a word to its root form) would have to deal with irregular forms such as "knives", "phenomena", "matrices" and "criteria". Salton suggests that a small set of basic rules (as formulated by Lovins [4]) will give adequate results.

2.2 Retrieval

We have seen how index terms can be associated with a document. It is relatively simple to implement a document retrieval system that will identify those documents satisfying an arbitrary boolean expression of terms. Suppose we wish to find articles discussing the effect of stress on managers; a boolean formulation might be:

find ("manager" or "supervisor") and (("fatigue" or "stress") and not "metal")

Note that we broaden the search by using synonyms for managers and stress and try to exclude irrelevant articles dealing with metal fatigue.

Simple inverted indexes are sufficient to support this type of boolean expression. An inverted index for a term is a list of pointers to documents tagged with the term. Set operations (e.g. union, intersection and difference) are performed on the indexes for the terms in a query to get the set of documents that satisfy the query. If the document index terms have weights, we have a means for ranking the selected documents.

In the following sections we look at three systems that allow queries to be presented in other ways.

2.2.1 SMART
The SMART system (see for example Ref. 5), enables users to attach weights to query terms. Thus a query is of the form:

$$\{ (k_1, w_1), (k_2, w_2) ... (k_n, w_n): T \}$$

where T is some closeness threshold and k_i and w_i are keywords and weights as before. Weights in the query can be negative, corresponding to "not" terms in the boolean system. A document is retrieved if its distance from the query (measured in some way) is less than T. The SMART systems enables the weights in the query to be modified by "relevance feedback". That is, the user is asked to decide, for each document retrieved, whether or not it is relevant to the query. The query weights are adjusted according to the responses and in this way, the user is assisted formulating the best query.

2.2.2 STAIRS

STAIRS (STorage And Information Retrieval System) was developed by IBM Vienna and a modified version is now used in a commercial biblio-graphic retrieval system (BRS at SUNY). An unusual feature of STAIRS [6] is that it indexes every word in a document, not just a sub-set identified as index terms. In addition, the indexes not only identify the documents containing a particular word but the position of each its occurrences. Thus, for a particular word, the index is effectively a list of triples:

Document number, sentence number, position in sentence

A consequence of this indexing is that a user can retrieve documents containing an arbitrary phrase. Suppose, for example, a user requested documents containing

split pea soup

STAIRS merges the indexes for "split" and "pea" and "soup" and identifies those documents having sentences containing the three words (adjacent positions and in the specified order).

Because little information is discarded in indexing, STAIRS tends to give high precision retrievals. That is, much of what it retrieves is deemed relevant by the user.[1] However, Blair and Maron [7] report that because a STAIRS user has to guess at the words actually used in the document (instead of selecting from a controlled vocabulary) there may be low levels of recall in some applications. That is, a low proportion of the relevant documents may be retrieved.[2]

2.2.3 Message files

Disadvantages of STAIRS are the amount of space required by the index files and the work needed to update them when new documents arrive. The Message File system proposed by Tsichritzis and Christodoulakis [8] has neither of these problems.

In the Message File organization, documents ("messages") are assigned to one or more logical files (corresponding perhaps to file folders in a manual system) and a signature file is constructed from each document. The signature of a document is a concatenation of the hash values of the significant words in the text. A typical signature contains approximately 100 bytes per page of text and thus is about 5% the size of the document. Although hashing means that the representation of a document is not exact, Tsichritzis and Christodoulakis argue that this does not matter

---

1. Precision is the number of relevant documents retrieved divided by the total number of documents retrieved.
2. Recall is the number of relevant documents retrieved divided by the number of relevant documents in the collection.

because user formulation of queries leads to a certain percentage of irrelevant documents anyway and a few more added by coincidence of hash values is not likely to matter much.

To retrieve a document, a user specifies a logical file and a document type. The system displays a template for the fixed attributes of a document, for example, author, date and source. The user fills in the template as appropriate and also specifies a "pattern" of words. The eventual aim is to allow this pattern to be any regular expression of words.

The system performs a linear scan of the signature files of the documents in the specified logical file. If the document type or fixed attributes do not match then the signature file is skipped, otherwise the system compares the hashed pattern against the signature. Matching of regular expressions can be implemented efficiently in VLSI.

Current implementation

The current implementation [8] is Unix based with limited pattern capabilities. The four supported pattern types are:

w	single word
w1 w2 ...	sequence of (significant) words
all (w1 w2 ...)	satisfied if all are present
any (w1 w2 ...)	satisfied if any is present

A user cannot combine the four supported pattern types. Tsichritzis and Christodoulakis describe three configurations where message files would be useful:

(1)   A workstation with a 10MB disc and 10,000 "messages". Signatures would occupy about 1MB and could be searched quickly.

(2)   A document server in a local area network (LAN) supporting a group of 20 or so people, having a 300MB disc and 200,000 messages.

(3)   A LAN document server holding only the signatures with the documents themselves on microfiche. Millions of messages could be represented. A user would send a request over the network and the server would transmit a bit-map image of the document.

2.3 Large scale systems

There are many organizations offering on-line access to large bibliographic databases. Typically, the data in the databases are references to documents (title, author, journal, volume, etc.) rather than the documents themselves. In most cases the abstract of the document is also stored. Most of the databases are on-line versions of some printed index. The existence of these services is due to companies (e.g. Chemical Abstracts) compiling large bibliographic collections, the fact that long distance communications are reliable and that database management software has been developed. Henry *et al.* [9] have a good introduction to the topic.

Lockheed and SDC are pioneers of on-line bibliographic systems. Dialog, the Lockheed system, evolved from RECON that was developed for NASA. A 1979 survey showed Lockheed as the supplier having most online databases (about 100) and SDC having the second largest number (about 50). The National Library of Medicine had offered batch retrospective searches of Index Medicus as early as 1964; it began its on-line MEDLINE service in 1973. LEXIS, a service of Mead Data Central, allows access to the full text of Federal statutes and regulations as well as court decisions. It is used extensively by attorneys.

The strengths of an on-line service are the broadness of its scope. A particular database may contain references to dozens of different journals, far more than would be normally be held in a typical library. The major weakness of a service is limited retrospective coverage. Most of the queries will be for recent material so there is little incentive to enter older data just for completeness. In contrast, a library may have holdings of a journal dating back to the last century.

Table 2.3 contains information (based on data in Ref. 10) about some on-line databases. The number of entries is a January 1981 estimate, the start date refers to the earliest available on-line reference.

Table 2.3 Bibliographic databases

Name	Number of entries	Start date	Updates per year	New entries per update
ABI/Inform	130,000	1971	12	2,500
Biosis Previews	2,850,000	1969	12	25,000
CA Search	4,200,000	1967	24	20,000
FedReg	66,000	1977	52	360
Medline	860,000	1977	12	20,000
Psychological Abstracts	350,000	1967	12	2,000
SAE Abstracts	11,600	1965	4	200
World textiles	91,000	1970	12	6,500

Note that some individual databases are growing by hundreds of thousands of entries a year.

Typical on-line operation A user begins by selecting a database then uses the query language to create sets of references. The system typically reports the sizes of sets and allows a user to get rid of those no longer needed. The user can combine previously generated sets using set operations. The scope of a search can be narrowed in a number of ways, for example by requesting only material published between a pair of dates or only material published in a certain language. Printing of references is usually possible both locally and at some central site. Most systems have a variety of printing formats; the user can decide how much or how little of a reference is printed. It should be possible to print the references in a specified order, for example chronologically.

Term expansion It is usually possible for a user to specify an index term and to view the terms adjacent to it in the index-term lexicon. In this way, the user can find other words to try. In a free-term system this option is likely to show alphabetically adjacent terms. More usefully, the user may be able to see semantically adjacent terms. On systems using a hierarchical thesaurus, the user can ask to see more specific or more general terms.

Costs It is relatively expensive to use on-line bibliographic services. Charges range from $20 to $150 per hour of connect time, with the majority in the region of $50. There are additional charges for printing centrally. Part of the charge is to defray the cost of keeping the references on-line. BRS keeps charges down by storing only the two most recent years on-line and offering batch searches of older material. A BRS user can also buy time in advance at a discount. The European ESA-IRS system copes with a multitude of currencies by charging in "Accounting units" and periodically publishing a table of exchange rates.

One way that costs might be reduced and better use made of an on-line service is if the user used an intermediary - someone with knowledge of a particular retrieval system. Surveys (see, for example Ref. 11), have indicated that this can save a considerable amount of time (more than 50%), and hence money, and also produce better results (70% more references, 40% more useful references).

Some systems allow a user's search strategy to be saved so that it can be applied to more than one database without re-entry. An extension of this idea is SDI (Selective Dissemination of Information) whereby users' profiles of interests are stored and matched against new documents when they are added to the system. Thus a user maintains "current awareness". For example, a user interested in screen editing and formatters might set up the following profile

((screen and edit*) or format*) and Language=English and not CACM

excluding articles not in English and those in a journal already subscribed to. The cost to the user would be a function of the number of profiles set up and the number of notifications sent.

Summary

Storage and retrieval of complete documents are conceptually simple operations. We looked at ways in which index terms can be associated with a text. Manual indexing may not be feasible in some cases because of the large volume of documents that have to be processed. Some automatic techniques have been developed.

Given tagged documents, quite simple retrieval programs can be developed, for example, those based on inverted files. Variations, for example systems based on hashed lists, were examined. A retrieval system can assist a user in refining a query.

Exercises

(1)   Implement Luhn's technique for deriving index terms. How well does it work? Does using expected rather than absolute frequencies improve performance?

(2)   Compare the power of boolean and weighted-term queries. Is it possible for all weighted-term queries to be expressed as boolean queries? Is it possible for all boolean queries to be expressed as weighted-term queries?

(3)   Conflation is the process of reducing a word to its root form. Implement and test a conflation algorithm. (See Lovins [4] and Winograd [12, section 3.9] for ideas.)

(4)   Given your solution to Exercise 3, implement Salton' index derivation method. Compare the results of Salton's and Luhn's techniques applied to the same documents.

References

1.   G. Salton, "Another look at automatic text-retrieval systems," *Communications of the ACM*, vol. 29, no. 7, pp. 648-656, July 1986.

2.   "Medical Subject Headings 1988," *Index Medicus*, vol. 29, no. 1 Pt 2, National Library of Medicine, January 1988.

3.   K. Sparck Jones, "A statistical interpretation of term specificity and its application in retrieval," *Journal of Documentation*, vol. 28, no. 1, pp. 11-21, March 1972.

4.   J. B. Lovins, "Development of a stemming algorithm," *Mechanical Translation and Computational Linguistics*, vol. 11, no. 1-2, pp. 11-31, Mar-June 1968.

5.   G. Salton and M. J. McGill, *Introduction to Modern Information Retrieval*, McGraw-Hill, New York, 1983.

6.   IBM World Trade Corporation, *STAIRS, Storage and Information Retrieval System*, IBM World Trade Corporation, Stuttgart, Germany, 1973. General Information Manual No. GH 12.5107.

7.   D. C. Blair and M. E. Maron, "An evaluation of retrieval effectiveness for a full-text document-retrieval system," *Communications of the ACM*, vol. 28, no. 3, pp. 289-299, March 1985.

8.   D. Tsichritzis and S. Christodoulakis, "Message files," *ACM Transactions on Office Information Systems*, vol. 1, no. 1, pp. 88-98, January 1983.

9.   W. M. Henry, J. A. Leigh, L. A. Tedd, and P. W. Williams, *Online searching: an introduction*, Butterworths, London, 1980.

10. J. L. Hall and M. J. Brown, *Online bibliographic databases: an international directory*, Aslib, London, 1981. Second edition.

11. P. W. Williams and J. M. Curtis, "The use of online information retrieval services," *Program*, vol. 11, no. 1, pp. 1-9, 1977.

12. T. Winograd, "Understanding natural language," *Cognitive Psychology*, vol. 3, no. 1, pp. 1-191, January 1972. Also published in book form by Academic Press, 1972.

II

Character-by-Character Processing

3
Editors

An editor is probably the single most important component of a text processing system. Conceptually, it is one of the simplest: it is a program, typically interactive, that enables a user to change the contents of a file. Use of an editor when preparing a document means that correct text does not have to be re-entered; for this reason, the document preparation process is speeded up considerably.

We can identify desirable properties of an editor. With regard to its power, there should be no limit on the size of file that can be edited and it should be possible to do with an editor anything that can be done to a hard copy with scissors, copy machine and paste. Beyond this, an editor should take advantage of available processing capabilities and facilitate global changes, pattern matching and so on.

With regard to the user interface, the editor should provide the user with a simple, consistent, conceptual model of the editing environment. There should be as little as possible that the user has to remember and on-line help. If possible there should be a "training wheels" mode in which the user is protected from himself as much as possible. In addition, the user should be able to undo the effects of any command issued.

The user should be protected as much as possible against system crashes. The editor should write, to a keystroke file, every character the user enters so the whole of an editing session can be replayed if necessary. When saving a changed file, the editor should not overwrite the original file being edited but rather create a new generation of it. The number of old generations stored should be a matter for the user to decide.

Meyrowitz and van Dam [1] have a good survey of interactive editing systems. We follow their classification here and look at (1) line editors, (2) stream editors, (3) display editors, (4) graphic-based formatter/editors, (5) general purpose structure editors, and (6) syntax-directed editors.

3.1 Line editors

The conceptual model in a line editor has the user editing a file of lines. The "end-of-line" character thus has special significance as a line separator. Early editor programs were line editors; typically they modelled the operations that a user might perform in making changes to a deck of punched cards - the most common input medium at that time. The earliest editors of all were little more than merge routines that read a text file and performed updates according to the directives in a file of commands.

A typical line editor has a one-line editing buffer, that is, the editing command applies just to the current line. However, the user can normally arrange for the command to be applied to each of a range of lines. Because of the conceptual model, joining and splitting lines is difficult. Line editors have low overheads and are good for making quick changes to a file, for example changing all occurrences of a tab character to eight spaces. No special terminal screen capabilities are needed (they will even work on a teletype) so they tend to be very portable.

ed The Unix editor *ed* [2] is basically a line editor. A typical command is:

$$10,40s/cat/dog/g$$

The user is requesting that all occurrences of *cat* be replaced (s for substitute) by *dog* in each line in the range 10 to 40. If the final g (for global) were absent, only the first occurrence on each line would be changed. There is a conceptual line pointer; initially it points to the last line in the file. The command above would leaving it pointing to line 40.

Ed has useful pattern-matching facilities that can be used both in specifying line ranges and in operations within lines. For example, the first line affected by the command:

$$/^c/,/ing\$/s/.*/\& \&/$$

is the next line beginning with "c". The command applies to zero or more subsequent lines up to the line ending with "ing". The pattern ".*" matches any string and the character "&" represents the first parameter of the substitute command. Thus the effect of the command is to replace a line by two copies of itself separated by a space.

Ed is always in one of two modes: insert/append mode or command mode. The user gets into insert/append by issuing the appropriate command and exits by entering a line containing just ".". Some vanilla implementations of *ed* are poor in the feedback they give a user; it is easy to forget which mode one is in.

Ed has some disadvantages. A user has to memorize short commands that are not very mnemonic, there is no automatic feedback - the user has to give explicit display commands to see the result of an edit, and viewing a multi-line section of the file by applying a print command to a range of lines changes the line pointer to the last line displayed. On the other hand, it is easy to write an arbitrary set of lines to an arbitrary file at any time. In addition, *ed* enables a file encrypted by the *crypt* utility to be edited without it first having to be decrypted into a plaintext file.

Kernighan and Plauger [3, 4] describe the implementation of an *ed*-like editor. *Sed* [5] is a non-interactive version of *ed* that can be used as a filter; it passes its input to its output modified according to a file of editing directives.

3.2 Stream editors

A typical stream editor regards the file to be edited as a linear sequence of characters (possibly divided into "pages"). For the most part, in the character stream end-of-line characters have no special significance. Like line editors, stream editors require no special terminal screen capabilities.

TECO TECO (Text Editor and COrrector) [6] is probably one of the most powerful stream editors. It has the properties of a programming language interpreter and has been used to implement more user-friendly editors (such as EDMACS [7]). TECO's raw command language is low-level and obscure, though high-level commands can be created. An example command sequence is:

5lfsfrogESCbatESC6d3vjESC

where ESC represents the escape character. This sequence moves forward 5 lines in the file, finds the first occurrence of *frog* and replaces it with *bat*. It then deletes the next six characters, displays 7 lines of the buffer (3 before and 3 after the current line) then moves the pointer to the beginning of the buffer. Command sequences can be repeated by enclosing them in angle brackets. Newline characters can appear both in strings being searched for and in text being inserted into the buffer.

TECO reads from the file until the buffer limit is reached or until an end-of-page mark is encountered. After the user has made changes to the buffer, it is appended to the output file before the next section is read in. Within these limits on the order of editing actions, files of unlimited length can be modified. TECO's conceptual pointer is character-oriented and is positioned either before the first character in the buffer, after the last character or between two characters. Thus the insert command, for example, is defined to insert at the current pointer position.

Like *ed* there is no automatic feedback of actions. In the sequence above we had to request a display of part of the buffer. Though very powerful, TECO's main disadvantage is the low-level nature of the raw command language. In the study of Moran and Roberts [8] (see 3.8), TECO had a significantly longer learning time than the other eight editors.

3.3 Display editors

We categorize as display editors those general purpose editors that enable a user to make changes to a document and see the effects of changes immediately, without having to issue additional commands. Such editors typically require a display with at least cursor addressing capabilities (rather than a "glass teletype"). Usually a large portion of the display is dedicated to providing a window into the file buffer.

The commonest conceptual model (due to Irons and Djorup [9]) maps the text onto an infinitely extensible quarter plane. Imagine the file on a two-dimensional plane with the first character of the first line at the origin. The user is free to write on the plane to the right and down from the origin. That is, there is no limit on the length of lines or on the number of lines. The editor enables a user to move around the quarter plane and to make changes to the display; using normal cursor control commands, the cursor cannot be moved above the first line of the file or to the left of the first character position on a line.

While to the user it may appear that commands are directly changing the display, in fact the commands issued modify the file buffer and the display is then modified to represent the new buffer contents (see Fig. 3.1). Particular editors may implement extensions to the basic conceptual model. For example, there may be multiple windows into the file buffer and there may be multiple buffers.

Figure 3.1 Block diagram of typical display editor

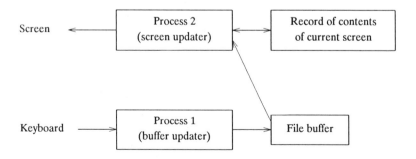

In Fig. 3.1 Process 1 accepts commands from the keyboard and makes the appropriate changes to the file buffer. Process 2 looks at both the file buffer and at a data structure that represents the current screen. It writes characters to the display depending on what the screen currently looks like and what it should look like. A typical alphanumeric screen is 24 by 80 characters so the current screen image would occupy about 2K bytes.

Display editors vary in the relative priorities that they give to the two processes of Fig. 3.1. It is a little annoying, for example, if the editor persists in redrawing part of the screen that is already out of date. Figure 3.2 shows a two overall strategies. In 3.2(a) the screen is completely updated after one command before the next command is processed. In 3.2(b) repainting may be interrupted to process a command.

Figure 3.2 Command interpretation and screen updating strategies

```
repeat if command to be interpreted
        then Update file buffer
             if screen out of date
             then Update screen
until exit
```

(a)

```
repeat  while there is a command to be interpreted
           Update file buffer
        while (screen is out of date) and no command to be interpreted
           Update screen a little (more)
until exit
```

(b)

Terminals vary in the control characters that they use to direct cursor movement, perform scrolling, clear sections of the screen and so on. There will typically be some mechanism, such as virtual screens or an editor-accessible file of terminal capabilities, that allows an editor to be used on a variety of terminals.

e The *e* editor developed by the Rand Computation Center [10] uses control characters for control functions, such as cursor movement and initiating string searches. Non-control characters are either inserted at the current cursor position or overwrite the character at that position. Insert/Overwrite mode is toggled with a simple command, an indicator on the screen indicates the current mode. The user can have multiple windows (possibly into different files); a "change window" command moves to the next window in a circular list. A keystroke history file is generated as the user types and, in the event of an uncontrolled exit, the history can be replayed. A variety of commands can be issued in "command" mode including some oriented towards document preparation such as filling and justification of paragraphs.

The editor does unexpected things to tabs and spaces on lines that it modifies. Trailing tabs and spaces are deleted, groups of leading spaces are converted to tabs and embedded tabs are converted to spaces.

EMACS EMACS [11, 12] is probably the most widely available full-screen editor. Implementations of it, and clones, are available on a large variety of systems from super-computers to micros. There is even a USENET newsgroup (comp.emacs) devoted to "EMACS editors of different flavors". One reason for its popularity is that its design enables it to be customized to suit particular users and applications; if necessary it can also be made to behave like a particular non-EMACS editor.

EMACS interprets user keystrokes using one or more tables, each of which has an entry for each ASCII character. The table entry for a character may specify a function to be carried out or may point to another table. If a function is specified then that function is performed, if the pointer points to another table then that table is used to interpret the next keystroke. In this way, multi-character commands are implemented. For example, while control-L causes EMACS to redraw the screen, the effect of control-X depends on what follows it:

control-X control-O	delete blank lines
control-X control-S	save current file
control-X control-W	resize window

There are sensible defaults, for example the graphic characters are bound to "self insert" - a function that causes them to be inserted into the file buffer at the current cursor position.

A user can create a set of key-bindings and cause it to be loaded into the table(s). For example, the space character could be bound to a function that checks the location of the right margin and, if necessary, backs up and inserts a newline, thus providing auto-wrap. Similarly, a period could initiate the look-up of the preceding symbol in a list of abbreviations. Closing brackets of various kinds could start a check for previously occurring opening ones. In particular, EMACS can be customized with routines knowing about the syntax and user-preferred format of certain programming languages, e.g. C and LISP.

Disadvantages of EMACS are that it may be complex for a beginner to use, (but it can be made simple using the key-bindings) and that it requires more memory and CPU time than simpler editors. Many concurrent EMACS users on a system can cause a noticeable performance degradation.

The categories of editor we have looked at so far require progressively more sophisticated terminals. Line and stream editors work on dumb terminals and display editors require addressable screens. Editors in the next category typically require bit-mapped displays.

3.4 Graphic-based editor/formatters

A typical editor/formatter displays the text on the screen as it would appear when printed. Such systems can be categorized as WYSIWYG (What You See Is What You Get) editors. Because such software normally supports more than one font, typically proportionally spaced, and the terminal must be capable of showing them, the editor/formatter requires a high-resolution, pixel-addressable display. The two examples below are top-of-the-line workstation systems; examples of more common microcomputer systems are given in 7.1.

Xerox BRAVO The Xerox Bravo editor was developed in the mid-1970s. It introduced features that are now commonplace, such as a mouse-controlled pointer. The mouse could control positioning in a document, both locally and, by moving a "thumbnail" on a scale, over longer distances. Mouse buttons enabled the user to define the scope of a command.

Bravo recognized that text objects, such as titles and paragraphs, have properties that affect the way in which they are displayed. The user can edit the properties of an object, such as the size of the characters in a title and the margin alignment of a paragraph, as easily as editing the text.

Xerox STAR The Xerox STAR [13, 14] dates from about 1981. Its screen has desktop icons now familiar in many user interfaces. The display is large enough to include both icons and an $8\frac{1}{2}$" by 11" page. Non-Roman alphabets are implemented by means of virtual keyboards; a user can direct the pointer to a key on the display of the virtual keyboard or press the corresponding actual key.

Disadvantages of editor/formatters are the relatively expensive hardware that they require and the fact that they require the document author to pay attention to both the content and appearance of a document at the same time. A case can be made for having the author simply identify the logical components of the text and defer the formatting to a separate process. The formatting program could incorporate a facility that allows a user to preview the printed pages.

3.5 General purpose structure editors

Most texts being edited have some kind of structure. Many large documents, for example, have a hierarchical structure. Fig. 3.3 represents a typical document structure. In addition to providing commands for operating on the text, a structure editor provides commands for operating on the structure of a document. The two examples given here are, in their own ways, much more than simple structure editors.

Figure 3.3 Typical document structure

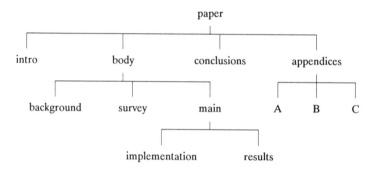

NLS NLS (oN-Line System) was developed at SRI around 1970 and is the forerunner of more recent hypertext systems [15]. All NLS information is stored in hierarchical form, even the paper by Engelbart and English [16] describing their system is presented with hierarchical labelling. A user can create, and move around, a network of links that connect various points in a document; in general, the end points of a link can be in different documents on different systems. For example, a table might be linked to all text passages that refer to it. The structure commands include those that allow a user to locate the next or previous node in the tree, to move/copy nodes (with appropriate renumbering), and to rearrange neighboring nodes. NLS implemented "chalk passing" protocols that allowed multiperson editing of a document.

s An editor is a program that updates a data structure in response to user commands. Much other software does the same, for example debuggers, games, and file system utilities. Fraser's *s* [17] provides a common frontend display editor shell and translates user commands into calls on user-supplied back-end routines. Consider file system utilities. To make changes to the files in a directory, a user invokes *s* which displays a listing of the directory showing file names, protection codes, owners, last access times and so on. User commands to edit this listing (for example, changing the name of a file or deleting a line) cause appropriate routines to be executed (renaming a file, deleting a file). In a particular application there are likely to be commands that are invalid or have to be constrained. For example, the user should not be allowed to create a non-empty file simply by inserting information into the directory display. Field protection should prevent a user from changing a field such as time of last access or file size.

3.6 Syntax-directed editors

In some ways, syntax-directed editors are the logical extension of structure editors. A syntax-directed editor ensures that the structure being edited conforms at all times to a given set of syntax rules. Until the development of a grammar that covers a large subset of a natural language, the principal application of syntax-directed editors is in the preparation of computer programs. Reps and Teitelbaum [18] describe a synthesizer generator: a program that can generate a language-specific display editor given information about the language.[1]

Cornell program synthesizer The Cornell Program Synthesizer [18, 19] uses three types of high-level entities: templates, placeholders and phrases. Templates are program constructs with holes to be filled in. An example is:

if < condition >
then < statement >
else < statement >

Placeholders are tags in a template that describe acceptable substitutions for a hole. In our example < condition > and < statement > are placeholders. Phrases are pieces of text that the user types to replace a placeholder. The user thus enters a program in a top-down manner selecting from menus of options to replace placeholders in the current text. Invalid phrases are highlighted as soon as a user enters them. For efficiency, something like < identifier > might be a terminal symbol in the grammar requiring the editor to be able to distinguish between a valid one and an invalid one.

Actions on the file buffer are typically constrained. For example, it is normally not possible to delete part of a structure or to edit the fixed parts of a template or even to move character-by-character through the file.

---

1. The information needed is: abstract syntax, context-sensitive relationships, display format, concrete input syntax and transformation rules for restructuring programs.

The Cornell program synthesizer knows about the syntax of PL/C and Pascal.

In the preceding six sections we have looked at a variety of editor types. In the next section we look at some implementation problems that are likely to be common to many editors.

3.7 Some implementation considerations

In this section we look at details of how particular aspects of an editor's operation might be handled. Specifically, we will examine:

(1) Representation of the text to be edited
(2) Updating the screen display
(3) Recovering from user or system errors
(4) Searching for strings.

Finseth [20] has a useful guide to many aspects of editor implementation.

3.7.1 Representation of text

If we have a large main memory (real or virtual) then possible data structures for the file buffer (which may hold the whole file or possibly just a page of it) include a doubly-linked list of line records and a linear buffer. If space is at a premium, or we wish to allow the editor random access to files of virtually any size, we could represent the text by a list of piece descriptors.

(a) Doubly-linked list of line records In the case of line editors, structuring the file buffer as a doubly-linked list of records appears to be the natural choice. The minimal contents of a each line record are shown in Fig. 3.4. Such a structure enables lines to be inserted and deleted easily.

Figure 3.4 Line record

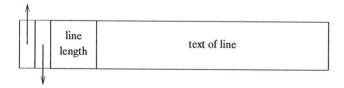

How much space should be allocated for the text of the line? If it is fixed, then there are problems when the user wants a longer line and also wasted space when a line is shorter then the maximum. Instead, we could hold the text in a linked list of segments each perhaps 8 or 16 bytes long. Now, in addition to the field containing the actual length of the line (in bytes) we need a field containing the allocated length (in bytes or segments).

Recall from Fig. 3.1 that a display editor typically has a process that updates the user's screen from time to time. We could assist this process if our line record also had a flag indicating whether or not the line had been changed since the last screen update. This leads us to the line record shown in Fig. 3.5.

Figure 3.5 A more sophisticated line record

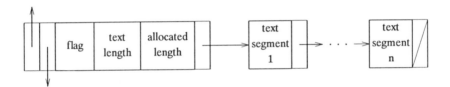

(b) Linear buffer The linked line record structure is not optimal for stream editors because in such editors we need to be able to manipulate strings that span lines. A better buffer structure might be a simple linear array of characters.

We need free space in the buffer for insertions and for changes where the new text is larger than the old. One solution is to read text from the file and leave the free space at the end of the buffer; this arrangement is shown in Fig. 3.6.

Figure 3.6 Simple buffer

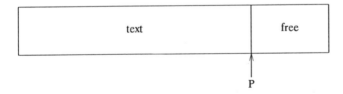

Note that with this configuration, moving the conceptual pointer requires no movement of text but both insertions and deletions require, on average, half the file to be shuffled along the buffer. P changes whenever the amount of text in the buffer changes.

A "split sequential" buffer is an alternative arrangement to that of Fig. 3.6. Many editors (TECO, for example) regard the conceptual file pointer as being positioned before the first character in the buffer, after the last character in the buffer, or between two characters in the buffer rather than pointing to a particular character. We could reflect this by organizing the buffer as shown in Fig. 3.7.

Figure 3.7 Split sequential buffer

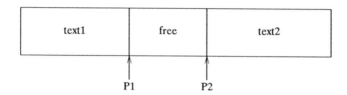

Text1 is the (possibly null) text before the conceptual pointer position and text2 is the (possibly null) text after the conceptual pointer position. Thus initially, with the conceptual pointer before the first character in the buffer, the buffer is the reverse of Fig. 3.6 in that all the free space is at the beginning.

Note that when the conceptual pointer moves, text has to be copied from one side of the free space to the other and pointers P1 and P2 change. In contrast when text is inserted at the conceptual pointer position it is written to the beginning of the free space and pointer P1 advances with it. When text is deleted at the conceptual pointer position, pointer P2 advances past it.

An alternative strategy is to keep the gap at the last insert/delete point, even when the conceptual pointer moves, and to have the buffer configuration lagging behind pointer movement. Movement of the pointer is faster and the gap need only be realigned if an insertion or deletion is done at the new location.

(c) List of pieces The technique of representing a file by a list of descriptors, each of which describes a section (piece) of the text, is used by both the Lara text editor [21] and the Rand Corporation e editor.[2] No part of the file being edited need be in main memory. At the end of an editing session, a new version of the file is created by traversing the piece list and appending appropriate text to an output file.

Implementations vary but typically each piece descriptor identifies: (1) the file it is a piece of, (2) the starting position of the piece in the file, and (3) the length of the piece. In an editor with line-oriented commands

---

2. Gutknecht [21] credits the designers of Bravo with the idea, whereas Yost [22] attributes it to Bilofsky who used it in the original Rand editor in 1974.

there may also be information about the lines in a piece.

Initially, we have a configuration such as that shown in Fig. 3.8 (in our examples the length of a piece is in bytes counting one for a newline character).

Figure 3.8 Initial list and file

File descriptor list: ⬚ X ⎹ 1 ⎹ 101 ⎹/

File described   File X

Mary had a very little lamb   Mary had a very little lamb
And everywhere that Mary went   And everywhere that Mary went
Its fleece as snow   Its fleece as snow
The lamb was sure to go.   The lamb was sure to go.

If we delete "very " from the first line, the new descriptor list is as shown in Fig. 3.9.[3] Note both that file X has not changed and also the way in which we can maintain a list of descriptors for deleted text, thus enabling a user to undo a deletion.

Figure 3.9 Descriptor list after deletion

File descriptor list: ⬚ X ⎹ 1 ⎹ 11 ⎹ → ⬚ X ⎹ 17 ⎹ 85 ⎹/

Deleted text list: ⬚ X ⎹ 12 ⎹ 5 ⎹/

File described   File X

Mary had a little lamb   Mary had a very little lamb
And everywhere that Mary went   And everywhere that Mary went
Its fleece as snow   Its fleece as snow
The lamb was sure to go.   The lamb was sure to go.

Suppose we now insert text, for example, " was white" after "fleece". New text can be appended to a workfile and can be referenced in the same way as the file being edited. The new configuration, with the workfile denoted

---

3. In practice, the descriptor list may be doubly-linked with a root record pointing to the first and last descriptors.

*, is shown in Fig. 3.10.

Figure 3.10 Descriptor list after insertion

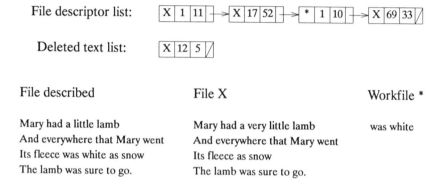

File descriptor list:

Deleted text list:

File described	File X	Workfile *
Mary had a little lamb	Mary had a very little lamb	was white
And everywhere that Mary went	And everywhere that Mary went	
Its fleece was white as snow	Its fleece as snow	
The lamb was sure to go.	The lamb was sure to go.	

The piece descriptor technique makes it easy to move and copy sections of text. To complete our correction of the nursery rhyme we need to exchange the second and third lines; Fig 3.11 shows the result.

Figure 3.11 Descriptor list after line swap

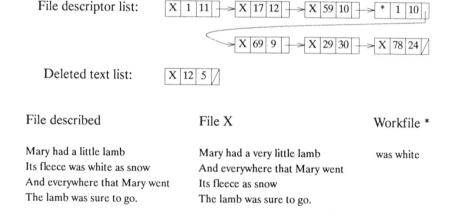

File descriptor list:

Deleted text list:

File described	File X	Workfile *
Mary had a little lamb	Mary had a very little lamb	was white
Its fleece was white as snow	And everywhere that Mary went	
And everywhere that Mary went	Its fleece as snow	
The lamb was sure to go.	The lamb was sure to go.	

An advantage of the piece descriptor approach is that a copy of the file being edited need not be in main memory and thus we can edit files larger than can be represented using linked line records or a linear buffer. As can be seen from our examples, the space required for the descriptor list grows with the number of changes made to the file. If many changes are to be made, a user may have to accomplish them in a series of editing sessions.

3.7.2 Redisplay
Earlier, in Fig. 3.1, we presented a two-process model of a display editor. Process 1 modifies the file buffer according to commands from the keyboard; Process 2 updates the screen as the file buffer changes. In this section we look as some aspects of the operation of the display updating process.

There are likely to be trade-offs according to the speed at which characters can be sent to the display. The slower the speed, the more worthwhile it will be to do computation to reduce the number of characters needed to repaint the image. We assume we have a slow display.

Assume also that we use the split sequential buffer technique described in 3.7.1. Fig. 3.12 represents the version of the file currently displayed on the screen; T points to the character that is the first on the first line of the display.

Figure 3.12 Old split sequential buffer

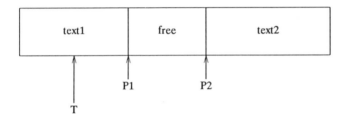

After Process 1 responds to a user command, there would appear to be two cases of interest:

(1)   the conceptual pointer/cursor/free space is at T or no more than RowsInDisplay lines beyond T

(2)   the conceptual pointer is either more than RowsInDisplay lines beyond T or is before T.

In the first case, we can leave T where it is; in the second case, we have to find a new position for T. The preferred new position for the cursor in the new display is probably close to the middle, so we count back RowsInDisplay/2 lines from P1 to get T. Having decided where the new top of screen will be, we now need to cause the display to reflect the buffer contents.

When it comes to repainting the screen, there are basic and advanced techniques. The basic technique described first requires only that cursor addressing, Clear-End-Of-Line and Clear-End-Of-Screen control sequences can be sent to the display. The more advanced algorithm assumes that we can send sequences to the terminal that cause it to insert and delete lines. In either case we can implement a user "redraw" command by clearing the display and the record of current screen contents and calling the redisplay algorithm.

Basic redisplay algorithm The basic redisplay algorithm is shown in Fig. 3.13. It is largely self-explanatory. We assume that the "Record of contents of current screen" shown in Fig. 3.1 is a two-dimensional array (CCS). The algorithm starts at position T in the buffer and the first column and row in CCS. It iterates simultaneously through the two structures and, if it finds the screen (as represented by CCS) to be out of date, it updates the screen and CCS. If a line is longer than the number of display columns, the extra portion is not displayed.

Figure 3.13 Simple screen updating algorithm

```
{ In the algorithm
    R : current row in CCS
    C : current column in CCS
    T2 : pointer to file buffer
}
    R ← 1
    C ← 1
    T2 ← T

    repeat if C ≤ ColsInDisplay
        then if Buffer[T2] ≠ CCS[R,C]
            then position cursor at screen(R,C)
            if Buffer[T2] = end-of-line
              then Send Clear-End-Of-Line to display
                  Set to spaces rest of row R in CCS
                  C ← 0
                  R ← R + 1
              else Write Buffer[T2] to display
                  CCS [R,C] ← Buffer[T2]
        T2 ← T2 + 1
        C ← C + 1
    until R > RowsInDisplay or T2 = End-of-Buffer

    if T2 = End-of-Buffer
    then Send Clear-End-Of-Screen to display
```

Advanced redisplay algorithm The basic algorithm wastes a lot of time looking at lines that have not been changed by the last user command. A more advanced algorithm employs tags to determine whether a line needs to be redrawn.

A possible technique assigns unique identification numbers to each line in CCS and to each line in the buffer. We can imagine an index to the file buffer with an entry for each line. An index entry would contain the identification number and a pointer to the position of the line in the file buffer. After a redisplay operation, corresponding screen and buffer lines have the same identification numbers. When a buffer line is modified by a user command it is given a new (unique) number.[4] The advanced redisplay algorithm that takes advantage of this extra information is shown in Fig. 3.14. Given the operations we assume are possible on the terminal, CCS should probably be a linked list of line records rather than an array.

Figure 3.14 Advanced screen updating algorithm

```
{ In the algorithm
    R : current row in CCS
}
    R ← 1

    repeat  If CCS[R].id ≠ File buffer line id
              then Determine type of mismatch.
                   Update screen and screen array.
            R ← R + 1
            Advance file buffer pointer
    until R > RowsInDisplay
```

The types of mismatch referred to in Fig. 3.14 are shown in Fig. 3.15 where single characters represent lines of text or the corresponding identification numbers.

In 3.15(a), the user has inserted a new line into the buffer. This is detected when the algorithm makes the connection between the two occurrences of Q. A control sequence is issued to open up a screen line and the new line is written. A copy of the new line is inserted into CCS with the identification number of the line in the file buffer.

In 3.15(b), the user has deleted a line. This is detected when a match is made between the two instances of R. A control sequence is issued to close (delete) a line on the screen. Line Q is deleted from CCS.

---

4. Every time we need a unique number we could increment an integer having a large range.

Figure 3.15 Three types of buffer/CCS mismatch

CCS	Buffer		CCS	Buffer		CCS	Buffer
P	P		P	P		P	P
Q	X		Q	R		Q	Q′
	Q		R			R	R
	(a)			(b)			(c)

In 3.15(c), the user has made a change to a line. This is detected when the two instances of R are matched. One approach to changing the line is to find the longest common prefix for Q and Q′ and also the longest common suffix. If the lengths of the lines are the same then the part of Q′ between prefix and suffix is written to the appropriate part of the screen and CCS. If the lines differ in length then as much overwriting as possible is done and the remaining changes are performed with character insert/delete operations. Myers and Miller [23] describe two algorithms for line updating that are optimal in the number of bytes sent to the display given certain assumptions about the display and display-update sequences.

3.7.3 Error recovery
It is certainly possible to arrange matters so that a user can reverse the effect of an ill-judged command. For example, the editor can write a keystroke file to disc that captures every user keystroke. A user can be allowed to exit the editor in a manner that preserves this file. Subsequently, the keystroke file can be used as input when the editor is applied to a backup version of the file being edited. The user can stop the replay before the unintended action is performed.

While this shows that recovery is possible, it is not very convenient. For example if the user wished to reverse the effect of the 200th command in an editing session, it would be very tedious to replay the preceding 199. Ideally, we would like an undo command that would immediately undo as many of the preceding commands as we wish.

If the editor maintains a record of changes to the file buffer in the form of insertions and deletions, it should be possible to return the file buffer to an arbitrary prior state by replaying the sequence of insertion and deletion operations backwards substituting "insert" for "delete" and vice versa. A record of an insertion or deletion would have to consist of both the text involved and the address in the buffer where the change was made.

Some commands, such as "write" and "save", affect the file system as well as the file buffer. Because of this, some editors may not permit the undoing of commands issued before the most recent save/write.

Because the editor buffer is in main memory, its contents are normally lost if there is a system crash. The user can write the buffer to disc periodically or, more reliably, the editor can do this at some pre-determined intervals. For example, the editor can save the buffer in a work area on disc after every N keystrokes. WordPerfect [24] allows the user to specify that the buffer be saved every k minutes. If there has been any activity in that interval the buffer is written to save files that are erased on normal exit from the system.

3.7.4 String matching

When editing a file, a common requirement is to have the conceptual pointer move to the next occurrence of a particular string. This may be just a positioning action or part of a find-and-replace command. We would like the string to be located as quickly as possible in the buffer. In this section we look at the problem of finding a *pattern* of M characters $P_1 ... P_M$ in a *string* (buffer) containing N characters $S_1 ... S_N$. For simplicity, we will assume that the search is in the forward direction, that it begins at the beginning of the buffer and that the pattern contains no special characters such as "wild cards". We look at four ways of carrying out the search: a simple algorithm, the Knuth-Morris-Pratt algorithm, the Boyer-Moore algorithm and Harrison's signature method.

Simple search algorithm A simple search compares P_1 with S_1, P_2 with S_2 and so on until there is a mismatch or there is a successful match of the complete pattern. If there is a mismatch then conceptually we slide the pattern one place to the right and begin again at the left end of the pattern comparing P_1 with S_2, P_2 with S_3 and so on. Figure 3.16 gives a simple search algorithm.

In the worst case this algorithm can be very slow. Consider the case where the pattern is "aaa ... aab", that is, a series of "a"s terminated by a "b" and the string is composed entirely of "a"s. In each possible matching position we would go right to the end of the pattern before finding a mismatch. The number of character-character comparisons is O(m×n), that is, proportional to the product of the length of the pattern and the length of the string. In practice, we would expect most potential matches to be rejected early so the number of comparisons will be O(n).

A disadvantage of the simple search is that we may have to back-track in the string. If a match fails at P_i, S_j (i>1) and the pattern is slid to the right one place, matching recommences with P_1, S_k (k<j). The Knuth-Morris-Pratt algorithm eliminates this backtracking.

Figure 3.16 Simple string matching

```
{ In the algorithm
    i : string pointer
    j : string pointer
    k : pattern pointer
}
  i ← 0
  while ( i < N-M+1 )
  |   i ← i + 1
  |   j ← i
  |   k ← 1
  |   while Pk = Sj
  |   |    if k = M
  |   |    then exit (pattern found starting at i in string)
  |   |    else j ← j+1
  |__|___      k ← k+1
```

exit (pattern not found)

Knuth-Morris-Pratt The Knuth-Morris-Pratt (KMP) algorithm [25] also starts with the pattern and string aligned at their left ends and also compares characters from left to right. However, the action taken when a mismatch occurs is different from that in the simple algorithm. The string pointer remains where it is and the pattern is slid forward, possibly by more than one position. (The problem of course is determining how far forward we can slide the pattern without missing any possible matches.) In addition, in cases where there is repetition of sub-patterns within the pattern, the algorithm avoids repeating comparisons that we know (by examination of the pattern) must succeed.

In general, if the mismatch involves P_j and S_k, i.e.

```
          P1 ... Pj ... PM
    S1    ...    Sk     ...    SN
```

the next match we try will be P_i and S_k where i = MISMATCH(j). P_i is the mismatch successor character of P_j. MISMATCH is a function of the pattern that can be computed as soon as the search pattern is known; typically it will be represented by a table. In the special case where MISMATCH returns 0, the pattern is slid right past S_k and the next comparison is between P_1 and S_{k+1}. Fig. 3.17 shows the KMP algorithm assuming that the MISMATCH table has been established.

The MISMATCH function is a reflection of how much the pattern repeats itself. If the first mismatch at a particular alignment is when $P_j \neq$

Figure 3.17 Knuth-Morris-Pratt algorithm

{ In the algorithm
  j : pointer to pattern
  k : pointer to string
}
    $j \leftarrow 1$
    $k \leftarrow 1$
    while $k \leq N$
    | while (j > 0 and $S_k \neq P_j$)
    | $j \leftarrow$ MISMATCH (j)
    | if j = M
    | then exit (pattern found starting at k-M in string)
    | else $k \leftarrow k + 1$
    |_____ $j \leftarrow j + 1$

    exit (pattern not found)

S_k then we know that $P_1 \ldots P_{j-1}$ matches $S_{k-j+1} \ldots S_{k-1}$. We want the value of MISMATCH (j) to be the largest integer i such that

$$i < j \text{ and } P_1 \ldots P_{i-1} \text{ matches } S_{k-i+1} \ldots S_{k-1}$$

That is, $P_1 \ldots P_{i-1}$ matches $P_{j-i+1} \ldots P_{j-1}$. Recall that MISMATCH(j) gives us the index of the next character in the pattern to be aligned with S_k. It should be the largest (rightmost) i satisfying the conditions so that we do not miss potential matches.

Note that MISMATCH is defined entirely in terms of the pattern. Figure 3.18 gives an algorithm for computing a table representing the MISMATCH function for pattern P.

Figure 3.18 MISMATCH function

MISMATCH[1] $\leftarrow 0$
$j \leftarrow 2$
while $(j \leq M)$
| $i \leftarrow$ MISMATCH[j-1]
| while (i > 0 and $P_i \neq P_{j-1}$)
| $i \leftarrow$ MISMATCH[i]
| MISMATCH[j] $\leftarrow i+1$
|__ $j \leftarrow j+1$

The examples in Table 3.1 show the values in the MISMATCH table for three 10-character patterns: a typical search string, a string chosen to show the effect of repetition in the pattern and the worst case example from the simple search.

Table 3.1 Examples of MISMATCH[i]

		Pattern	
i	Procedures	abcabcabcd	aaaaaaaaab
1	0	0	0
2	1	1	1
3	1	1	2
4	1	1	3
5	1	2	4
6	1	3	5
7	1	4	6
8	1	5	7
9	1	6	8
10	1	7	9

Note that the smaller the value returned by MISMATCH, the more we slide the pattern down the string. In the case of the string "Procedures", the further we have gone into the pattern before mismatching, the more we can slide. In the case of "aaaaaaaaab", we slide pretty much as we did in the simple algorithm (one place at a time) but we avoid repeating comparisons that we know succeed. However, observe how the KMP algorithm behaves in an example using pattern "abcabcabcd":

```
String                          abcabcxxabcabc
Pattern (initial)               abcabcabcd
Pattern (next alignment)           abcabcabcd
```

Intuitively we might feel that we can do better than this. It may seem obvious to us that the second alignment is bound to fail also because the string character that caused the mismatch (x) is not in the pattern at all. It is this kind of information that is used in the third technique we examine - the Boyer-Moore algorithm.

Boyer-Moore The Boyer-Moore algorithm [26] improves over both the simple search and, in many cases, over the Knuth-Morris-Pratt algorithm as well. It begins in the same way as these two methods, with the pattern aligned at the left end of the string, but differs from them in that character comparisons are done right-to-left rather than left-to-right. If a mismatch is detected, like KMP it uses information derived from the pattern to determine how far the pattern can be shifted without missing a possible match.

Again, suppose that in general the first mismatch occurs when $P_j \neq S_k$. It may be, as in the following example, that S_k is not in the pattern at all. In this case we can slide the pattern right past S_k.

```
String    ... and this also uses only a small ...
Pattern       bakes
Pattern           bakes
```

More generally, S_k may appear somewhere in the pattern. If its rightmost occurrence is to the left of the mismatch position P_j then we slide the pattern forward to align this occurrence with S_k. If its rightmost occurrence is to the right of P_j then such an alignment would actually cause the pattern to move backwards, in this case we just slide the pattern one place forward as in the simple search. Applying these rules to our example yields the next two alignments:

```
String    ... and this also uses only a small ...
Pattern           bakes
Pattern             bakes
Pattern                 bakes
Pattern                 bakes
```

We can do better than this in some cases. If $j \neq M$ then we have matched some portion of the pattern when the mismatch occurs. If the sub-pattern $P_{j+1} \ldots P_M$ occurs again to the left of the mismatch point we can slide the pattern to align the sub-pattern and that part of the string known to match with it. This is shown in the following example:

```
String    ... of nuclear fusion on the power ...
Pattern            ionization
Pattern                  ionization
```

Boyer and Moore encapsulated the shift quantities into two functions: DELTA1 for the character alignment, DELTA2 for the subpattern alignment. DELTA1 takes S_k as parameter, DELTA2 takes j as parameter. Clearly we want to shift by the larger of these two quantities. Figure 3.19 shows the Boyer-Moore algorithm.

Figure 3.19 Boyer-Moore Algorithm

```
{ In the algorithm
    j : pointer to pattern
    k : pointer to string
}
    k ← M
    while (k ≤ N)
    |   j ← M
    |   while (j > 0 and S_k = P_j)
    |       j ← j-1
    |       k ← k-1
    |   if j = 0
    |       then exit (pattern found starting at k+1 in string)
    |___    else k ← k + max (DELTA1(S_k), DELTA2(j))

    exit (pattern not found)
```

The DELTA1 function takes a character parameter. If the character is not in the pattern, it returns M (the pattern length); if the character is in the pattern, it returns M-j where j is the index of the rightmost occurrence of the character. Typically DELTA1 will be implemented as a table; Fig 3.20 shows how table entries are computed. Note that the size of the table depends on the size of the alphabet of characters that can appear in patterns.

Figure 3.20 Computation of DELTA1

```
for each character (c) in the pattern alphabet
    DELTA1[c] ← M

for j ← 1 to M
    DELTA1[P_j] ← M-j
```

The DELTA2 function is a little more involved. It takes as parameter the index of the mismatch character in the pattern and returns the amount we can shift the pattern to align the matched sub-pattern in the string and its "rightmost plausible reoccurrence" in the pattern. DELTA2 can also be represented as a table; the number of entries is equal to the length of the pattern. The value of DELTA2 is always at least 1 so this takes care of the backward sliding problem. Figure 3.21 shows an algorithm to compute DELTA2 (slightly modified from [27]) and Table 3.2 shows some example patterns and tables.

Figure 3.21 Computation of DELTA2

```
for j ← 1 to M
    DELTA2[j] ← 2 × M - j
j ← M
t ← M + 1
while j > 0
 |   f[j] ← t
 |   while (t ≤ M) and (P_j ≠ P_t)
 |    |   DELTA2[t] ← min (DELTA2[t],M-j)
 |    |__ t ← f[t]
 |   j ← j-1
 |__ t ← t-1

for k ← 1 to t
    DELTA2[k] ← min (DELTA2[k], M+t-k)

tp ← f[t]
while t ≤ M
 |   while t ≤ tp
 |       DELTA2[t] ← min (DELTA2[t],tp-t+M)
 |       t ← t + 1
 |__ tp ← f[tp]
```

Table 3.2 Examples of DELTA2[j]

		Pattern	
j	Procedures	dcbacbacba	abcdeabcde
1	19	19	14
2	18	18	13
3	17	17	12
4	16	9	11
5	15	15	10
6	14	14	14
7	13	9	13
8	12	12	12
9	11	11	11
10	1	1	1

Horspool [28] compared implementations of Boyer-Moore and simpler algorithms. He concluded that in practice it was not worthwhile setting up the DELTA2 table because the repetitive patterns that would otherwise behave badly rarely occur.[5] Implementations with and without the table had very similar performance figures. Horspool suggested that if pattern length were shorter than some system-dependent threshold (5 on his system) then a modified version of the simple search should be used rather than Boyer-Moore. The modified simple search algorithm scans the string for occurrences of that character in the pattern having the lowest expected frequency in the string.

Harrison's signature method Each of the three searching techniques above treats the string as a uniform sequence of characters. Harrison's method [30] on the other hand, divides the string into segments (typically at newline characters) and computes a "signature" for each segment. When we search for a pattern, a signature is similarly computed for the pattern. By comparing a segment's signature with the pattern's signature we can determine if the pattern can be in the segment. Signature comparison provides a necessary but not sufficient test for the pattern to be in a segment.

A signature of a text segment S is a vector of N bits. We initialize all the bits in the vector to 0 and then set certain bits to 1 as follows. We take overlapping substrings of length k from S (i.e. $S_1 ... S_k$, $S_2 ... S_{k+1}$, and so on) and apply to each substring a hash function that maps substrings to the integers 1..N. We set to 1 the bits addressed by the hash values. The resulting vector is termed the "hashed k-signature of S", denoted $H^k(S)$.

Suppose, for example, that our string segment is "A SMALL LINE", that N is 16 and k is 2. We need a hash function that maps 2-character strings to the integers 1..16. Let our hash function interpret the string as a base 27 number (A=1, B=2,...,Z=26, space=27) and return this value modulo 16 plus 1.[6]

```
substring   A_ _S SM MA AL LL L_  _L LI IN NE
hashes to    7 13 15  1  8  9 16   6 14  2 16
```

and H^2(A SMALL LINE) is 1100011110001111.

How exactly do signatures help? Observe that if pattern P is in segment S then wherever there is a 1 bit in $H^k(P)$ the corresponding bit in $H^k(S)$ will also be 1. Conversely, if there is any bit position where there is a 1 in

---

5. Galil [29] shows how the Boyer-Moore algorithm can be modified so that the worst case behavior is linear rather than O(m×n).
6. For example, S = 19, M = 13, so SM = 19 * 27 + 13 = 526 (decimal). Hash (SM) = 526 mod 16 + 1 = 15.

$H^k(P)$ and a 0 in $H^k(S)$ then P cannot be in S. Using bitwise operations, the necessary condition for P to be in S is:

$$\text{logicaland}(H^k(S1), \text{inverse}(H^k(S2))) = 0$$

Note that this condition being met does not guarantee that P is in S. Consider the following examples:

H^2 (ALL) = 0000000110000000
H^2 (ABC) = 0000000001000100
H^2 (MAT) = 1000000000000001

Comparing the signatures with the one in the earlier example we determine that whereas "ABC" could not be in "A SMALL LINE" (see bit position 10) the other two strings might be. A character-by-character comparison would reveal that "MAT" was not in fact in the string either.

Harrison's technique is most suitable for line editors; in a stream editor an occurrence of a pattern may straddle segments. The signature of a line (usually an integral number of bytes) could be stored as part of the line in the file. Signatures would be computed as the file is created and modified as necessary as the file is edited. Alternatively, the signatures could only exist when the file is being edited and be computed as lines are read into the file buffer - see Exercise 6.

The value of k and the hash function need to be carefully chosen so that not too many and not too few bits are set to 1 in the signature. We want to minimize the number of "false drops" that is, unsuccessful character-by-character searches of a segment, as in the case of "MAT" above.

Tharp and Tai [31] present a hash function designed to map character pairs (i.e. k=2) evenly onto bit positions in signatures of length 64 and 128. They used the function in experiments involving a document file and a file containing a source program. In one set of experiments, search strings were generated randomly, in a second set, search strings were extracted from the files. Tharp and Tai measured the number of lines that were searched character by character and the number of times the pattern was actually found.

Increasing the signature length reduced the number of lines searched exhaustively. This is to be expected because we are holding more information about the line in the signature. As the pattern length increases the number of lines searched falls rapidly. They suggest that while increasing k would reduce the number of false drops there would be a problem in computing the signature of a string of fewer than k characters.

Tharp and Tai conclude that the signature method is an important technique in fast string searching if the extra storage cost is acceptable.

Comparison of string matching methods De Smit [27] compared the simple search strategy with the algorithms of Knuth-Morris-Pratt and Boyer-Moore. Search patterns of lengths 1 through 14 were extracted from a 5000-character string and additional search patterns not in the string were generated. Measurements were taken of the performance of each algorithm in searching for each pattern both with and without the pre-processing costs of Knuth-Morris-Pratt and Boyer-Moore.

De Smit computed the ratio of character-character comparisons to number of characters passed. For all pattern lengths tested, the average performances of the simple algorithm and Knuth-Morris-Pratt were very similar (ratios of about 1.1). However, as we have seen, the worst case of the simple algorithm is much worse than that of Knuth-Morris-Pratt.

For patterns longer than 4 characters, Boyer-Moore was superior to the other two methods. The ratio declined as pattern length increased and levelled off at around .3 when pre-processing costs were included and around .2 when they were excluded. De Smit suggests that since its worst case situation rarely occurs, the simple algorithm be used in cases where Boyer-Moore performs comparatively badly, that is, when the pattern is shorter than 4 characters.

Davies and Bowsher [32] compared four string-finding techniques including the simple search algorithm, Knuth-Morris-Pratt and Boyer-Moore.[7] They concluded that both pattern length and alphabet size were important in performance. They recommended that an editor use Knuth-Morris-Pratt if the alphabet is small (e.g. binary) or the pattern is short. In other cases Boyer-Moore should be used although, because of initial overheads, it will not be better if the pattern occurs soon in the string.

Incremental string searching We can regard the pattern to be searched for as a parameter of the search command. Some editors have the user give a command then its parameters, other editors require the parameters first. In the former case it is possible that we could have an incremental search, i.e. begin the search before the user has completely specified the pattern and refine it as more pattern characters become available.

Of the four searching techniques described above, all except the simple search require the whole pattern to be available before the search can begin. This is because of the search-speeding information that they calculate from the pattern. An incremental search therefore is typically a variation on the simple search.

---

7. The fourth technique, due to R. M. Karp and M. O. Rubin is described in Sedgewick [33 pp. 252-253]. It applies a hash function to overlapping M-character substrings of the string and compares the results with the hash value of the pattern. It is $O(M+N)$.

Consider, for example, a search for "Mouse". As soon as the "M" is entered we start a search for the first "M". When the "o" is entered, we check to see if "o" is the first character following the "M" we found. If not, then we search forward for "Mo". Thus, by the time the "e" is entered we have already eliminated many possible partial matches.

A complete incremental search system should allow for the user erasing characters in the pattern after they have been entered. We can maintain a stack of pointers into the file buffer, so that if the kth pattern character is erased, we can return to the point where the first k-1 characters matched.

3.8 Evaluation of editors

It is difficult to say that editor X is better than editor Y in any meaningful sense. Roberts and Moran [8] propose an evaluation methodology for text editors and present results of applying it to 9 different editors.[8] Their evaluation is based on the performance of different users (representing a range of experience) performing a benchmark set of 53 editing operations on four documents. Roberts and Moran considered four dimensions: time, error cost, learning and functionality and concluded that their methodology appears to be an effective tool for evaluation along those dimensions. However, it is difficult to arrange meaningful experiments of this kind because the performance of a particular user depends to a certain extent on familiarity with the editing environment - screen size, response time, predictability of response time and so on.

Summary

An editor is probably the single most useful tool in a text-processing system. Apart from providing a simple, consistent conceptual model of the editing process, and allowing a user to do anything that can be done with scissors, paste and a copy machine, a good editor should protect a user from the consequences of his/her mistakes and allow infinite undoing of actions. The user should not feel that he or she is walking a tightrope.

Simple editors can be little more than merge programs that operate in batch mode on a text file and a file of amendments. More satisfactory are display editors that are interactive, immediately show the changes made and allow a user to see a portion of one or more files. Given appropriate displays, an editor/formatter can show a file as it would appear when printed.

---

8. TECO, WYLBUR, EMACS, NLS, BRAVOX, BRAVO, a WANG word processor, STAR and GYPSY.

Editor response to user commands should be as fast as possible. When editing a large file, it is important that searching for an arbitrary string be as fast as possible. We saw that there are techniques that can be much better than a simple search.

The last of the string searching techniques that we examined uses signatures derived from text segments. In some ways a signature can be regarded as a compressed version of the segment in which some information is thrown away. In the next chapter we look at more useful text compression methods in which there is no information loss.

Exercises

(1)   Assume that you are designing a text editor specifically for students unfamiliar with interactive computer systems. Describe four desirable features of such an editor. For each of the features you describe, outline briefly how it might be implemented.

(2)   How could the Boyer-Moore algorithm be changed to enable searching to begin at an arbitrary point in the file?

(3)   What happens if the Boyer-Moore algorithm is used to search for the null pattern $(m=0)$?

(4)   How could the Boyer-Moore search technique be changed to allow searching backwards as well as forwards from an arbitrary point in the file?

(5)   A certain editor uses the Boyer-Moore algorithm for finding occurrences of strings in a test buffer. The designers of the editor wish to add a "wild- card" capability to the editor as follows:

      ? in a pattern represents any character
      [] in a pattern represents a set of characters,
         e.g. [aeiou] represents the set of vowels.

What changes would be necessary to the Boyer-Moore algorithm to support the new features?

(6)   Use of Harrison's string signatures can save time when editing a file. What are the advantages and disadvantages of storing the signatures as part of the file when it is not being edited?

(7)   In each directory where it has been used to edit a file, the Rand editor (e) writes that contains information about the last editing position: what file was being edited, the position in the file, windows, mode, and so on. How would you extend this idea so that such information could be remembered for each edited file?

References

1. N. Meyrowitz and A. van Dam, "Interactive Editing Systems (Parts i and ii)," *ACM Computing Surveys*, vol. 14, no. 3, pp. 321-415, September 1982.

2. B. W. Kernighan, *A tutorial introduction to the UNIX text editor*, Bell Laboratories, 1977. Unix Programmer's Manual, Seventh Edition.

3. B. W. Kernighan and P. J. Plauger, *Software Tools*, Addison-Wesley, Reading, Mass., 1976.

4. B. W. Kernighan and P. J. Plauger, *Software Tools in Pascal*, Addison-Wesley, Reading, Mass., 1981.

5. L. E. McMahon, *SED--A non-interactive editor*, Bell Laboratories, 1977. Unix Programmer's Manual, Seventh Edition.

6. Digital Equipment Corporation, *Standard TECO: Text editor and corrector for the VAX-11, PDP-11, PDP-10 and PDP-8*, February 1980. User's guide and language reference manual.

7. M. A. Bloom, *EDMACS: Interactive screen-oriented editor for RSTS/E*, 1981. On-line documentation, California State University, Northridge.

8. T. L. Roberts and T. P. Moran, "The evaluation of text editors: methodology and empirical results," *Communications of the ACM*, vol. 26, no. 4, pp. 265-283, April 1983.

9. E. T. Irons and F. M. Djorup, "A CRT editing system," *Communications of the ACM*, vol. 15, no. 1, pp. 16-20, January 1972.

10. *The Rand Editor, e*, Computer Services Department, The Rand Corporation, April 1984.

11. R. M. Stallman, "EMACS: The extensible, customizable, self-documenting, display editor," AI Memo #519, Artificial Intelligence Laboratory, Massachusetts Institute of Technology, June 1979.

12. R. M. Stallman, "EMACS: the extensible, customizable, self-documenting, display editor," *ACM SIGPLAN Notices*, vol. 16, no. 6, pp. 147-156, June 1981. Proceedings of the ACM SIGPLAN/SIGOA Symposium on text manipulation, Portland, Oregon, June 8-10, 1981.

13. J. Seybold, "Xerox's 'Star'," *Seybold Report*, vol. 10, no. 16, April 27, 1981.

14. D. C. Smith, C. Irby, R. Kimball, B. Verblank, and E. Harslem, "Designing the Star user interface," *Byte*, vol. 7, no. 4, pp. 242-282, April 1982.

15. J. Conklin, "Hypertext: an introduction and survey," *IEEE Computer*, vol. 20, no. 9, pp. 17-41, September 1987.

16.   D. C. Engelbart and W. K. English, "A research center for augmenting human intellect," *Proceedings of the AFIPS Fall Joint Computer Conference*, vol. 33, pp. 395-410, 1968.

17.   C. W. Fraser, "A generalized text editor," *Communications of the ACM*, vol. 23, no. 3, pp. 154-162, March 1980.

18.   T. Reps and T. Teitelbaum, "Language processing in program editors," *IEEE Computer*, vol. 20, no. 11, pp. 29-40, November 1987.

19.   T. Teitelbaum, T. Reps, and S. Horwitz, "The why and wherefore of the Cornell Program Synthesizer," *ACM SIGPLAN Notices*, vol. 16, no. 6, pp. 8-16, June 1981. Proceedings of the ACM SIGPLAN/SIGOA Symposium on text manipulation, Portland, Oregon, June 8-10, 1981.

20.   C. A. Finseth, "Theory and practice of text editors or a cookbook for an EMACS," MIT/LCS/TM-165, Laboratory for Computer Science, Massachusetts Institute of Technology, May 1980.

21.   J. Gutknecht, "Concepts of the text editor Lara," *Communications of the ACM*, vol. 28, no. 9, pp. 942-960, September 1985.

22.   D. Yost, "LA, a line-access file I/O package," (On-line document distributed with the Rand editor), Rand Corporation, Santa Monica, CA, July 1980.

23.   E. W. Myers and W. Miller, "Row replacement algorithms for screen editors," *ACM Transactions on Programming Languages and Systems*, vol. 11, no. 1, pp. 33-56, January 1989.

24.   *WordPerfect Version 5.0 Reference manual*, WordPerfect Corporation, Orem, Utah, 1988.

25.   D. E. Knuth, J. H. Morris, Jr, and V. B. Pratt, "Fast pattern matching in strings," *SIAM Journal of Computing*, vol. 6, no. 2, pp. 323-350, June 1977.

26.   R. S. Boyer and J. S. Moore, "A fast string search algorithm," *Communications of the ACM*, vol. 20, no. 10, pp. 762-772, October 1977.

27.   G. De V. Smit, "A comparison of three string matching algorithms," *Software Practice and Experience*, vol. 12, no. 1, pp. 57-66, January 1982.

28.   R. N. Horspool, "Practical fast searching in strings," *Software Practice and Experience*, vol. 10, no. 6, pp. 501-506, June 1980.

29.   Z. Galil, "On improving the worst case running time of the Boyer-Moore string matching algorithm," *Communications of the ACM*, vol. 22, no. 9, pp. 505-508, September 1979.

30.   M. C. Harrison, "Implementation of the substring test by hashing," *Communications of the ACM*, vol. 14, no. 12, pp. 777-779, December 1971.

31. A. L. Tharp and K-C Tai, "The practicality of text signatures for accelerating string searching," *Software Practice and Experience*, vol. 12, no. 1, pp. 35-44, 1982.

32. G. Davies and S. Bowsher, "Algorithms for pattern matching," *Software Practice and Experience*, vol. 16, no. 6, pp. 575-601, June 1986.

33. R. Sedgewick, *Algorithms,* Addison-Wesley, Reading, Mass., 1983.

Compression

Although the cost of a byte of storage has declined rapidly, and is still declining, use of data compression techniques can almost always reduce the effective cost still further by squeezing more data into the same space. Consider a text archive or collection of documents. It may be advantageous to hold it in compressed form to save space if access to a particular document is infrequent (therefore expansion of it is performed rarely) but the document may be required quickly (thus it needs to be on-line). Compression can save also save time (and money) when data is transmitted; for example, compression of source code might reduce the number of diskettes needed to distribute software. In this chapter we examine some methods for compressing text. Lelewer and Hirschberg [1] cover most of them, and others, in their survey.

Data compression relies on there being redundancy in the input. Random strings of characters are not compressible to any great degree, neither are object files. Natural language text is redundant in that not all text units (characters, character pairs, words) occur with equal frequency. Compression tends to remove the redundancy, thus compression of a compressed file is normally not worthwhile. Usually compression without loss of information is required, that is, the input file should be exactly recoverable by application of some corresponding expansion technique. In some cases, an inexact reversal may be acceptable. For example, when expanded, a source program in a free format language may not need to have exactly the same layout as the original.

There are many ways of measuring the degree of compression achieved, the following is a useful one:

$$\frac{length\,(input) - length\,(output) - size\,(X)}{length\,(input)}$$

X is any information that we need in addition to the compressed text in order to be able to recreate the original. For example, if the original file is 2000 bytes long and is compressed to 1000 bytes, and a 100-byte table is required to expand the file back again, then the degree of compression is 45%. Because of overheads, the "compressed" version of a short file might be larger then the original.

In general, compression techniques operate by mapping sections of the input file onto (smaller) sections of the output file. We can classify techniques by the type of the input object replaced (fixed or variable length) and the type of output object (fixed or variable length). In the following sections we look at the four categories of methods this leads to. Additional characteristics of a compression method are whether the mapping is adaptive (varies as the input is processed) or static and whether the compression requires one pass or more than one pass over the input file.

Compression is not without disadvantages: reduced redundancy makes a file more vulnerable to storage and transmission errors. Lelewer and Hirschberg discuss the susceptibility to error of the output of various algorithms. They note, for example, that the output from adaptive algorithms is more vulnerable than the output from static algorithms but even when a static algorithm is used, an error can propagate through an entire file.

4.1 Fixed-length onto fixed-length mapping

Our first category of methods compresses by mapping fixed-length portions of the input file onto fixed-length codes. Clearly, for space to be saved, the number of bits per character in the output file must be less than in the input file.

A typical computer system uses an 8-bit byte for each character in a text file. In theory this permits a 256-character alphabet. However, for some types of file, for example program source files or inter-office memos, a much smaller alphabet may be adequate. Thus we might compress simply by allocating smaller fixed-length codes to fixed size units of the input file.

Suppose our input file has a 30-character alphabet; perhaps we are compressing mailgrams with only a few symbols in addition to the upper case letters. We can allocate each character a 5-bit code, pack three characters into a 16-bit word that normally only holds two and compress a file to two-thirds its size.

In general, the compressed units can be N-character segments of the input file. Suppose, for example, that our input file uses a 40-character alphabet. Compressing a character at a time means that each requires 6 bits and we can still hold only two in a 16-bit word. However, we can treat a 3-character section of the file as a base 40 number and represent it by the corresponding binary value. There are $40 \times 40 \times 40 = 64,000$ combinations of three characters; this value is just small enough to fit into a 16-bit word (0..65,535). Thus a file with a 40-character alphabet can also be compressed to two-thirds its normal size.

Standard FORTRAN-77 requires only 49 characters (digits, upper case letters, and 13 special characters $= + -*/(),.\$':$ and space) [2]. Using either of the techniques above we can pack five characters into a 32-bit word. Using an 8-bit code we could only pack four characters, thus we can compress a FORTRAN-77 text to 80% of normal size.

In most text, input sections occur with different frequencies, for example, in English, "e" is more common than "x". We may achieve a greater degree of compression by having shorter output codes for commoner sections and longer codes for those that occur less often. In the next section we look at methods that use variable-length output codes.

4.2 Fixed-length onto variable-length mapping

Our second category of methods also divides the input into fixed length sections, typically one character sections, but the number of bits allocated to each section in the output file may vary. When determining the set of output codes, we must be careful that the coding scheme is unambiguous. That is, given a particular compressed file, there must be a unique expansion. Preferably, the codes should be instantaneous, that is, the expansion program does not need to look ahead. Table 4.1 shows three sets of codes for A, B, C and D.[1]

Table 4.1 Various coding schemes

	Ambiguous	Unambiguous not instantaneous	Instantaneous
A	1	1	0
B	10	10	10
C	11	100	110
D	100	1000	111

In this section we look at shift codes and Huffman codes. With shift codes a character is represented by its position within a character set. If it belongs to a different set than the previous character then its coding is prefixed by set identification information. In Huffman coding, codes are devised in such a way that shorter codes are assigned to more common characters; Huffman coding is either one-pass or two-pass.

---

1. Consider the encoded string 11100111. Decodings using the first code include CDCA and AADAC. Using the second code, the string decodes uniquely to AACAAA but, for example, we do not know that we have a C rather than a D until we read the first bit of the next character. Using the third code, the string decodes to DAAD without such look-ahead.

4.2.1 Shift codes

The interpretation of an ASCII code does not depend on any preceding code; in that sense it is a context-free system. To illustrate how a context-sensitive code might work, let us assume three things. First, that we have eliminated the shift key on the keyboard and can only change case by means of the CAPS LOCK key. Second, that whenever we depress the CAPS LOCK key, a shift character code is transmitted and whenever we release it a second (different) shift character code is transmitted. Finally, we assume that a normal key sends the same code regardless of the current position of the CAPS LOCK key. Thus, for example, whether or not a particular code represents an upper case or a lower case letter depends on the most recent shift character. Denoting a depression of CAPS LOCK by ↓ and a release of the CAPS LOCK by ↑, the sentence

   This is John McKay reporting

is transmitted as

   ↓t↑his is ↓j↑ohn ↓m↑c↓k↑ay reporting

Normally, a 5-bit code allows us to represent 32 different characters. If we reserve two of the 32 codes to represent the two shift characters, each of the remaining 30 codes can have two different meanings depending on which of the two shifts we are in. Thus we have a 60-character set. To represent the same number of characters using a context-free coding requires 6-bit codes. We can take the idea further and reserve more and more of our 32 codes for shift characters. The maximum return is achieved when we have 16 shifts and can give 16 interpretations to each of the remaining 16 codes. This allows us to represent 256 characters, a set that requires an 8-bit context-free code.

How many bits per character does our context-sensitive code require? This depends on the number of shift characters we have to include. If the current character is in the same shift group as the previous one then we only need 5 bits. If it is in a different group then we need 10 bits: 5 for the shift change and 5 for the character. Suppose, for example, that we have to have 1 change of shift every 12 characters. The average number of bits per character is

$$(1*10 + 11*5) / 12 = 5.42$$

In general, if we have an N-bit code and 1 in P characters requires a shift change then the average number of bits per character is

$$N \times (P + 1) / P$$

To minimize the number of bits transmitted, we need to minimize the number of shift changes. This suggests an analysis of the type of text that we wish to represent and an optimal clustering of characters into sets. For example, we can count the frequency of occurrence of (overlapping) character-pairs in text samples. The pair with the highest relative frequency should be put in the same group. We can now consider them a single character, adjust the frequency distribution, look for the next highest pair, and so on.

A disadvantage of context-sensitive codes is that if a shift character is mis-transmitted or otherwise garbled, the text up to the next shift character may be mis-interpreted.

4.2.2 Huffman codes

Huffman codes are devised so that shorter codes are allocated to more frequently occurring input sections. Thus, we save over fixed length codes if there is a non-rectangular frequency distribution. A Huffman code is instantaneous, because of the way that codes are constructed, thus the expansion algorithm does not need to look ahead. Huffman codes can be assigned in a static manner so that the same mapping is used throughout the file or the codes can vary and adapt to changing frequency distributions in the input.

Static compression The static Huffman method [3] begins by reading the file to be compressed and tabulating the frequencies of the different input sections. A binary tree is then constructed with the sections as leaves and the relative frequencies determining the internal structure of the tree (see below). The two branches from a node are labelled "1" and "0". The code assigned to a section is the reverse of the bit string obtained by walking up the tree from the appropriate leaf to the root. The expansion algorithm uses an identical tree, typically supplied as part of the compressed file. The bits in the compressed file are used to traverse the tree from the root downwards; when a leaf is reached, the appropriate section is output and the program returns to the root.

Suppose we are compressing character by character and that a scan of the input file produces the relative frequency distribution shown in Table 4.2. We construct a tree in an iterative manner. At each iteration we create a new node having as children the two parent-less nodes with the smallest values. The value assigned to the new node is the sum of the values associated with its children. Figure 4.1 shows a tree that results from applying this technique to the data of Table 4.2. Note that in this case, at certain iterations, there are parent-less nodes with the same values and thus choices as to which nodes to combine. In general, a frequency table will not produce a unique tree structure. The labelling on the branches is also arbitrary. From the tree of Fig. 4.1 we get the codes

Table 4.2 Example frequency distribution

Char	Rel. Freq.
A	.35
B	.10
C	.16
D	.12
E	.12
F	.05
space	.10

Figure 4.1 Huffman tree from the data of Table 4.2.

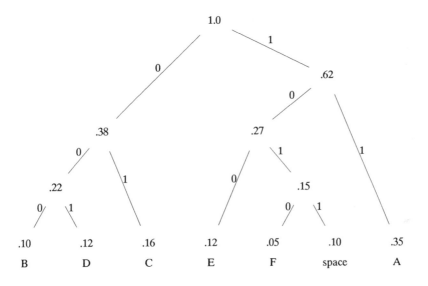

shown in Table 4.3. Using these codes the text "A BAD FEED" compresses to:

$$1110110001100110111010100100001$$

The average weighted code length for the example of Table 4.3 is 2.64.[2]

___
2. Sum the products of the code lengths and the relative frequency for each character. The same result is obtained by summing the weights on the interior nodes of the tree because the number of times each frequency contributes to this sum depends on the code length.

Table 4.3 Codes from tree of Fig. 4.1.

Char	Code
A	11
B	000
C	01
D	001
E	100
F	1010
space	1011

Huffman coding is optimal in that there is no other assignment of codes to sections that will have a shorter average weighted code length. The theoretical minimum average weighted code length for a set of sections with relative frequencies $p_1, p_2, ... p_N$ is:

$$- \sum_{i=1}^{N} p_i \times \log(p_i)$$

Taking a character at a time, non-technical English requires about 4.5 bits per character. Alteratively, we can say that, on average, a character represents 4.5 bits of information when characters are examined in isolation. Assuming that the original text is represented in 8 bit ASCII codes, we would expect static Huffman coding to compress a file to about 56% of its original size (excluding the space needed for the code tree).[3]

Adaptive Huffman compression For the static Huffman compression to be optimal, we must know the frequencies of the characters before we begin compression. However, there may be applications where this is not possible. For example, we may have to begin transmitting a data stream before we have read all of it. In addition, we may wish to have a compressing filter (in the Unix sense) that we can insert in a stream of processes. Gallagher [4] devised an adaptive Huffman coding method that is close to optimal for the part of the input file read to date. Knuth [5] gives an improved version of Gallagher's algorithm and Vitter [6, 7] improves on Knuth.

Assuming we are compressing character by character, adaptive Huffman coding works as follows. During compression the tree has leaves representing the characters seen so far in the source together with information about their frequency. There is also a leaf node (termed the 0-node) that represents the possible characters not yet encountered; the initial tree consists solely of the 0-node. The tree structure is optimal for the

---

3. Looking ahead at Table 4.11, we can see that 56% is a pretty good estimate.

current frequencies.

An input character falls into one of two classes. If it has been seen before, the corresponding code is transmitted and the appropriate frequency is updated. The new value may require the tree to be restructured. If the character is a new one, a leaf is created for it as a sibling to the 0-node, the tree is restructured, and the code for the 0-node is sent together with information identifying the new character. In this way the tree gradually adapts to the actual distribution of characters.

The expansion program begins with the same initial tree as the compression program and changes it in a parallel manner. After a code has generated a character, the count for the character is increased and, if necessary, changes are made to the tree structure.

Comparison of static and adaptive encoding Adaptive Huffman compression may not compress a file as much as static Huffman compression if we just compare the space occupied by compressed characters. However, the savings due to not having to prepend a code tree to the output file may outweigh this, particularly if the input file is small.

In addition, it is not difficult to conceive of a file that might be compressed more by the adaptive method. Consider a large FORTRAN program that has a DATA statement in the middle of it containing several hundred numbers. When frequencies of characters in the whole file are computed, digits may be as frequent as any other characters. However, in the DATA statement they predominate. The static Huffman method will assign to the digits codes that are approximately as long as those for other characters. The adaptive method, as it reads the DATA statement, will assign shorter and shorter codes to the digits. The net result may be greater overall compression.

Vitter [6] shows that his adaptive Huffman algorithm compresses a file to between $S - n + 1$ and $S + t - 2n + 1$ bits, where S is the number of bits required by the static Huffman method, t is the number of characters in the input and n is the number of different characters in the input. Thus it is never worse than one bit per character worse than the static algorithm.

Variations on Adaptive compression Benson [8] compared the adaptive Huffman compression algorithm described above with an algorithm that took into account the previous character in the input file. Instead of a single tree, his method used a tree for each character in the input alphabet. The structure of the tree for a particular character represents the distribution of characters that follow it in the text. There is greater redundancy in digrams (character pairs) than in single characters. That is, the distribution for characters following a particular character is more skewed than the distribution for characters in general. As an extreme example consider the "Q-tree" for characters following Q; practically every occurrence of Q is followed by "U".

When compressing, the tree used depends on the previous character. For example, if the text were "CAT", we would use a general tree to compress "C", then the "C-tree" to compress "A" and the "A-tree" to compress "T". Although more space is needed during compression than if only a single tree were used, recall that in adaptive compression the tree(s) do not become part of the compressed file.

Benson compared the performance of four algorithms: static and adaptive single-character Huffman compression and static and adaptive digram Huffman compression. Test files included English text (about 4.2 Megabytes) and source programs in COBOL, Pascal and FORTRAN. In general, using digrams rather than single characters saved about 1.5 bits per character. Using adaptive rather than static compression saved between .1 and .3 bits per character. Results for English and non-English texts were similar; non-English was a little more compressible.

4.3 Variable-length onto fixed-length mapping

In the third category of compression techniques, varying length sections of the input file are mapped to fixed length portions of the output file. Cooper and Lynch [9] point out that, typically, compression/expansion is slower when the variable length units are in the input rather than the output. If the input units are fixed size and the method is a static one then the operation can proceed largely by table look-up. In an information retrieval system holding compressed files, expansion is typically much more common than compression so it may be more efficient overall to use a variable-to-fixed rather than a fixed-to-variable compression.

4.3.1 Run-length encoding
In run-length encoding, a sequence of N instances of a character (e.g. "X") in the input file is compressed to a 3-byte sequence:

$$\text{warning byte, count byte (N), X}$$

where the warning byte is some character that does not otherwise appear in the input. Clearly no space is saved unless N is greater than 3. This technique is easily implemented; an algorithm is shown in Fig. 4.2. It is useful for compressing indented source files (where runs of spaces are common) and sometimes for large data files (runs of zeros). However, the degree of compression may not be great; Table 4.4 shows the results of compressing a set of C source files using this method.[4]

---

4. On our system, the files are in /usr/src/sun/suntool/*.c and are actually stored using the *unexpand* program that replaces runs of spaces by tabs wherever

Figure 4.2 Run-length encoding algorithm

```
{ In the algorithm
      getnextc : function returning the next character from the input
      outbytes : outputs appropriate 3 bytes for a sequence of "count"
            instances of "oldc".
      count : count of characters in current sequence
      oldc : current sequence character
}
      oldc ← getnextc
      count ← 1
      repeat
          if not eof
            then c ← getnextc
                while (c = oldc) and not eof
                    count ← count + 1
                    if not eof then c ← getnextc
                outbytes(oldc,count)
                oldc ← c
                count ← 1
      until eof
      outbytes(oldc,count)
```

4.3.2 Symbol sets

The method of Cooper and Lynch [9] is an iterative one. It begins by assigning codes (e.g. from a set of 256 8-bit codes) to characters in the input alphabet. The file (or a sample of text) is compressed using these codes. Next, if there are any spare codes, character pairs that occur more often than some threshold frequency are assigned codes. For example, in compressing English, the pair "th" might be allocated its own code at this stage. The input is compressed again, this time using the enhanced symbol set. The process is repeated until the set of output symbols is exhausted.

A feature that distinguishes this method from some similar ones is its facility for dropping a multi-character symbol from the set if it occurs too infrequently. Typically the usefulness of such a symbol will have been lessened by the generation of longer strings. For example, if the string "from " has its own code, we would expect the symbol "fro" to be dropped. Reference 9 gives an example of a set of 256 symbols generated after six passes through a sample of English. Common words may appear in the symbol set as a by-product of the aggregation process.

---

possible. The original sizes shown in Table 4.4 are the *expanded* versions of the files.

Table 4.4 Run-length encoding on C source files

File	Original size	Compressed size	(% original)
1	3355	2207	(65.78)
2	15150	13073	(86.29)
3	19405	14493	(74.69)
4	4503	3918	(87.01)
5	5138	5138	(100.00)
6	8052	6285	(78.06)
7	19220	12538	(65.23)
8	6368	4677	(73.45)
9	7304	4810	(65.85)
10	5467	4435	(81.12)
11	7233	5587	(77.24)
12	10091	7577	(75.09)
13	21858	17934	(82.05)
14	29206	21115	(72.30)
15	667	615	(92.20)
16	11644	8780	(75.40)
17	5733	4564	(79.61)
18	44912	33244	(74.02)
19	7166	5599	(78.13)
20	12018	8529	(70.97)
21	19639	13655	(69.53)
22	2276	1872	(82.25)
23	27695	20399	(73.66)
24	2563	2286	(89.19)
25	20396	17947	(87.99)
26	2769	2348	(84.80)

Using the symbol set, encoding is done using a "greedy" algorithm in a left-to-right, longest-match manner. Cooper and Lynch report that methods that find the optimal compression typically take three times longer and have little effect (perhaps 0.5%) on the degree of compression. They claim 50% compression based on 8-bit codes.

4.3.3 Lempel-Ziv

Lempel-Ziv compression [10, 11] is a one-pass method that uses a table of strings. The index of a string in the table is used as its representation in the output file; typically the table size is a power of 2. Actual index values have no significance so strings can be hashed into the table for fast retrieval.

Initially, the table contains one entry for each of the single characters in the input alphabet. As the input file is read, strings are added to the table

and appropriate codes are output. Figure 4.3 contains an algorithm for
Welch's LZW compression [12], a variation on Lempel-Ziv.

Figure 4.3 Welch's LZW compression

```
{ In the algorithm
        c : a character
        S : a string
        getnextc : function returning the next character from the input
}


Initialize table with single characters
S ← getnextc

while not eof
  |  c ← getnextc
  |  if S + c is in the table
  |    then Append c to S
  |    else Output code(S)
  |        Add S + c to the table
  |_____   S ← c

Output code(S)
```

Each string added to the table is an existing string plus one character. It
can therefore be represented by a fixed-length pair of items: the index of
the prefix string and the character. This avoids the problem of storing a
table of strings of various lengths.

Table 4.5 contains a trace of the algorithm of Fig. 4.3 applied to the
example string ("ababcbababaaaaaaa") used by Welch.[5] For each iteration
of the loop, Table 4.5 shows the character read, any code output and any
string added to the table. Note that the final code is output outside the
loop. Table 4.6 shows the final string table assuming, for simplicity, that
strings are added in a linear manner. We follow Welch and assume a 3-
character alphabet; thus the first three entries are put in as part of table
initialization and the remainder are added during processing of the input.

Expansion The expansion algorithm corresponding to the LZW compression algorithm of Fig. 4.3 is shown in Fig. 4.4. It is a simplified version of
the one given by Welch. Expansion is a little more complex than compression because of a special case that may arise: the expansion algorithm may
not have a table entry for a code it has just read. In this case, however, the

_____
5. Welch's trace of the same example contains minor errors.

Table 4.5 Trace of LZW compression of ababcbababaaaaaaa

Iteration	Input	Output	Added to table
1	b	1	ab
2	a	2	ba
3	b		
4	c	4	abc
5	b	3	cb
6	a		
7	b	5	bab
8	a		
9	b		
10	a	8	baba
11	a	1	aa
12	a		
13	a	10	aaa
14	a		
15	a		
16	a	11	aaaa
		1	

Table 4.6 Final string table for the example of Table 4.5

Symbol	Code
a	1
b	2
c	3
ab	4
ba	5
abc	6
cb	7
bab	8
baba	9
aa	10
aaa	11
aaaa	12

appropriate string can be derived from the previously output string. Table 4.7 shows a trace of the LZW expansion algorithm using the output of Table 4.5 as the input; note that the first code is read outside the loop.

Figure 4.4 Simplified version of Welch's LZW expansion

```
{ In the algorithm
        code, oldcode, incode : codes for strings
}
    Initialize table with single characters
    Read code  { first string code }
    oldcode ← code
    output table(code)       { a one-character string }

    while not eof
    |   Read code
    |   incode ← code
    |   if table(code) = ""
    |     then { put in appropriate string }
    |         Add table(oldcode) + firstchar(table(oldcode)) to the table
    |         Output table(code)
    |     else Output table(code)
    |         Add table(oldcode) + firstchar(table(code)) to the table
    |__ oldcode ← incode
```

Table 4.7 Trace of LZW expansion algorithm

Iteration	Input	Output	Added to table		
	1	a			
1	2	b	ab	at	4
2	4	ab	ba	at	5
3	3	c	abc	at	6
4	5	ba	cb	at	7
5	8	bab	bab	at	8
6	1	a	baba	at	9
7	10	aa	aa	at	10
8	11	aaa	aaa	at	11
9	1	a	aaaa	at	12

Limitations A limitation of LZW compression is that it is not adaptive once the table is full. It could perform badly if characteristics of the input change after this occurs, for example, if the text changes from a natural to a programming language.

4.3.4 Rubin's method

Rubin's technique for compressing a text file [13] involves choosing a set of substrings from the input file and replacing each occurrence of one of the substrings by an "output representation". The correspondence between substrings and output representations is stored as part of the compressed file. A representation of the algorithm is shown in Fig. 4.5. There appear to be three problem areas: (a) determining the best substrings to use, (b) determining output representations and (c) replacing substrings.

Figure 4.5 Rubin's compression algorithm

Let input groups be single characters.
Encode the file.
repeat
    Count frequencies of all substrings
    Choose "best" set of substrings
    Select output representations
    Replace substrings with output representations
    Prepend correspondence between substrings and
      output representations to the file
until file not shortened by this process

Determining the best substrings If there is an upper bound on the length of substring we wish to consider then we can use a technique due to J. P. McCarthy. Suppose that the upper limit is L. We take all overlapping substrings of length L in the input file and sort them alphabetically. Apart from inaccuracies due to the final L-1 characters in the file being under-represented, we can easily get the frequency of every substring of length L or less from the sorted list.

For example, suppose we have an upper limit of 4 and process the following string:

abcdbcefbcdefabcdbabcffbcefab

Table 4.8 shows the substrings extracted before and after sorting. Given the inaccuracies, we can see from the sorted list, for example, that "b" occurs seven times, that "cd" occurs three times, and that "efa" occurs twice.

We can get the frequency (f) of any substring from the sorted substring list and thus compute the total savings if it is replaced. For example, if the output representations are single characters:

Table 4.8 Substrings derived and sorted

Substrings	Sorted substrings
abcd	abcd
bcdb	abcd
cdbc	abcf
dbce	babc
bcef	bcdb
cefb	bcdb
efbc	bcde
fbcd	bcef
bcde	bcef
cdef	bcff
defa	cdba
efab	cdbc
fabc	cdef
abcd	cefa
bcdb	cefb
cdba	cffb
dbab	dbab
babc	dbce
abcf	defa
bcff	efab
cffb	efab
ffbc	efbc
fbce	fabc
bcef	fbcd
cefa	fbce
efab	ffbc

Substring	f	Savings per occurrence	Total Savings
bc	6	1	6
cd	3	1	3
efa	2	2	4
efab	2	3	6

Determining output representation A method similar to that of Cooper and Lynch would work. Keep a list of unused codes and allocate from it until the list is exhausted.

Replacing substrings Even if we have selected the substrings and chosen the output representations, the replacement may not be straightforward. Rubin offers the following example: suppose that the substrings and codes are as follows

Substring	ar	arg	gu	um	me	en	ment	t
Output rep.	1	2	3	4	5	6	7	8

and "argument" is the text to be replaced. The left-to-right "greedy" approach (replace the longest possible substring) yields "2468". Whereas the optimal replacement gives "137". An algorithm to produce the optimal encoding would have to consider several alternatives at once.

4.4 Variable-length onto variable-length mapping

Our final category of compression techniques consists of those in which both the sections of the input file and the sections of the output file may vary in length. Note that this category includes algorithms such as Lempel-Ziv modified to output variable-length codes.

4.4.1 Syntax trees
The algorithm of Katajainen *et al.* [14] is worth noting although it has limited application. Because it operates on text definable by a context-free grammar it can be applied to programs in many high-level programming languages but not to natural language text. The source text is compressed to a parse tree and a symbol table. Because a lexical analyzer discards layout information, the source typically cannot be recreated exactly.[6] Results of compressing small Pascal programs (fewer than 10K characters) show the compressed file to be about 40% the size of the original.

4.4.2 BSTW
Bentley, Sleator, Tarjan and Wei (BSTW) [15] describe a method that exploits clusters of symbol occurrences in the input. A symbol that has occurred recently is given a shorter code than one with a more distant previous occurrence. Because such locality is likely to be found at the word rather than the character level we include the technique in this section rather than in section 4.2.

Using the BSTW algorithm the compression program maintains a list of symbols encountered in the input. If the symbol to be compressed is in the list, its current position is output, then the symbol is moved to the front of

---

6. If the source were the output from a "pretty-printer" program, the result of expansion could be run through the same tool.

the list. If the symbol is a new one, the value of listlength+1 is output, followed by the symbol in full. The new symbol is added at the front of the list. Because of the move-to-front strategy, the integer output for a symbol is one more than the number of different symbols that appeared since its last occurrence. The expansion algorithm maintains an identical list.

How can we output integers to the compressed file in such a way that we can uniquely expand it? One technique for outputting variable length integers prefixes the binary representation of i with $\lfloor \log_2 i \rfloor$ zeros. Thus, for example, 14 is output as 0001110, 15 as 0001111 and 16 as 000010000. Using this method the number of bits required to encode a text is never more than 2S+1 where S is the number of bits required using static (2-pass) Huffman encoding. On typical input, BSTW compresses to about the same degree as static Huffman encoding. It can be much better, given favorable input.

4.5 Implementations and comparisons

Many systems have expansion and compression programs; in addition, some have utilities to display compressed files. Table 4.9 lists programs available on the local Sun Unix system.[7] In this section we compare the performance of these programs on some typical text files.

Table 4.9 Compression/expansion programs

Compression	Expansion	Algorithm
compress	uncompress	Lempel-Ziv
compact	uncompact	Adaptive Huffman
pack	unpack	Huffman

Compress/uncompress (Lempel-Ziv) A user can select the upper bound on the length of codes for common substrings (that is, they can determine the size of the table). The local limits are 9 to 16 bits with 16 as the default. The length of codes and a magic number that prevents compression of compressed or random files are written to the beginning of the compressed file.

---

7. Sun Unix 4.2 Version 3.5.

Compact/uncompact (Adaptive Huffman) An advantage of the adaptive Huffman method is that only one pass over the input is required; *compact* can thus be used as a filter. In addition, no tree need be included in the compressed file. The *compact* program prepends a two-byte code (177437_8) to the output file to identify it as a compacted file. The *uncompact* program expects this code; *compact* will not recompact a file.

Pack/unpack (Huffman) *Pack* will not compress "trivial" files, those where the compressed file is larger than the original. This generally means small files because, unless the character distribution is very skewed, there will be no net space saving because of the presence of the decode tree in the compressed file.

Comparisons

Several files were created each containing only N repetitions of a single character. The results of compressing these files with *compress* and *compact* are shown in Table 4.10; sizes of compressed files include marker bytes. This test shows how rapidly the coding tree used by *compact* adapts and allocates a single-bit code to the repeated character and also how *compress* gives better results for longer files.

Table 4.10 Compression of N instances of the same character.

N	Compaction (Adaptive Huffman)		Compression (Lempel-Ziv)	
	Bytes	Bits/char	Bytes	Bits/char
8	5	5.00	8	8.00
16	6	3.00	10	5.00
32	8	2.00	12	3.00
64	12	1.5	16	2.00
128	20	1.25	21	1.31
256	36	1.13	29	0.91
512	68	1.06	39	0.61
1024	132	1.03	54	0.42

Table 4.11 shows the results of running the three Unix compression programs on book chapters (the text of Ref. 16). For each of the files, the table shows the file size after compression both in bytes and as a percentage of the original file. Note the similarity of compression over all chapters, the similarity between the adaptive and static Huffman compression, and the superior performance of Lempel-Ziv. In the case of Lempel-Ziv the default upper limit of 16 bits for an output code was used. For comparison, Fig. 4.12 shows the results when only the first 100 lines of each of the chapters file were processed. Even here the Lempel-Ziv algorithm was superior.

Table 4.11 Comparison of compression programs

File	Original Size	Compact (Adaptive Huffman) Size	%	Compress (Lempel-Ziv) Size	%	Pack (Huffman) Size	%
1	34703	20117	(57.97)	14533	(41.88)	20100	(57.92)
2	84777	49191	(58.02)	35619	(42.01)	49148	(57.97)
3	54196	30140	(55.61)	21948	(40.50)	30109	(55.56)
4	50221	29023	(57.79)	20863	(41.54)	28992	(57.73)
5	83998	49984	(59.51)	35362	(42.10)	49935	(59.45)
6	91137	52868	(58.01)	35713	(39.19)	52816	(57.95)
7	52894	30710	(58.06)	22671	(42.86)	30678	(58.00)
8	40619	23842	(58.70)	17949	(44.19)	23812	(58.62)
9	68926	41239	(59.83)	26861	(38.97)	41209	(59.79)
10	35430	20234	(57.11)	14888	(42.02)	20219	(57.07)
11	48335	28583	(59.14)	20151	(41.69)	28548	(59.06)
12	46234	28253	(61.11)	20026	(43.31)	28218	(61.03)
13	33653	20254	(60.18)	15874	(47.17)	20230	(60.11)
14	36136	21488	(59.46)	17177	(47.53)	21465	(59.40)

According to the manual pages, Huffman-type methods compress English text to about 60-75% of its original size, Pascal to about 50-60%, C about the same as English and binary by only about 10%. It is claimed that Lempel-Ziv reduces English to 40-50% of its original size and does it faster.

Compact vs Pack Adaptive Huffman (as implemented in *compact*) performs about the same as static Huffman (as implemented in *pack*) even in cases that would seem to favor it. For example, two files were compressed, each was 3906 bytes long and consisted of a 62 by 62 matrix of characters. In file A each line contained the lower case alphabet followed by the upper case alphabet followed by the digits. File B was the transpose of file A, that is, each line consisted of 62 repetitions of a single character. As might be expected, *pack* compressed both files to the same extent (3007 bytes). *Compact* might have been expected to perform better on file B where repetitions of a character followed each other. In fact file B was not compressed as much (3004 bytes) as file A (2996 bytes) and both were not significantly smaller than the output from *pack* that also contained a decode tree.

Table 4.12 Comparison of compression programs on smaller files

	Original	*Compact* (Adaptive Huffman)		*Compress* (Lempel-Ziv)		*Pack* (Huffman)	
File	Size	Size	%	Size	%	Size	%
1	5120	2975	(58.11)	2782	(54.34)	2983	(58.26)
2	3615	2171	(60.06)	1964	(54.33)	2183	(60.39)
3	4509	2626	(58.24)	2458	(54.51)	2635	(58.44)
4	4039	2380	(58.93)	2322	(57.49)	2389	(59.15)
5	4563	2627	(57.57)	2456	(53.82)	2638	(57.81)
6	5168	2967	(57.41)	2731	(52.84)	2970	(57.47)
7	4009	2368	(59.07)	2236	(55.77)	2375	(59.24)
8	4858	2848	(58.62)	2560	(52.70)	2853	(58.73)
9	4530	2600	(57.40)	2387	(52.69)	2610	(57.62)
10	5684	3317	(58.36)	3005	(52.87)	3320	(58.41)
11	4705	2764	(58.75)	2471	(52.52)	2773	(58.94)
12	3227	1999	(61.95)	1899	(58.85)	2009	(62.26)
13	4657	2786	(59.82)	2662	(57.16)	2792	(59.95)
14	4146	2586	(62.37)	2455	(59.21)	2599	(62.69)

Code length for compress The *compress* program can use from 9 to 16 bits for substring codes. Table 4.13 shows, for each of three files, the original file size and the size of the compressed file using different upper bounds (N) on the size of output codes. The value of N at which compressibility levels off depends on the number of strings the algorithm needs to store. Recall that the value of N affects the size of the table required during compression and expansion.

Table 4.13 *Compress* with different maximum code lengths

	File 1	File 2	File 3
Original size	468	26153	173211
N = 9	368	20524	135708
10	361	15524	110947
11	361	14113	98368
12	361	12472	90848
13	361	12011	85612
14	361	12011	81875
15	361	12011	80571
16	361	12011	78499

Summary

Compression of text is useful way of saving space and, when the text is transmitted, of saving time and money too. Compression relies on there being redundancy in the input file; this is normally true in the case of text in a natural or programming language.

Compression methods in general map sections of the input file onto sections of the output file. Techniques can be classified according to whether the input sections are fixed- or variable-length and whether the output sections are fixed- or variable-length. In addition, some methods are one pass, others require more than one pass over the input. An advantage of one pass methods is that they can be used as a filter, they can begin to output compressed text before the input is completely read. However, multiple-pass methods may achieve greater compression.

Redundancy of languages is important for compression; it is also a factor in encryption techniques. We look at encryption in the next chapter.

Exercises

(1)   Implement a clustering algorithm for finding the best allocation of characters to shift groups.

(2)   Implement a translator from ASCII to a context-sensitive code for different numbers of shifts.

(3)   Construct a Huffman tree from the data of Table 4.2 that is different from that of Fig. 4.1.

(4)   Expand 0111000101111101110001001001010 using Table 4.2.

(5)   The adaptive Huffman method encodes the character using the current tree then changes the tree. Could we change the tree then encode the character? If so, why. If not why not?

(6)   Under what circumstances does adaptive Huffman coding perform poorly?

(7)   How would you modify the Lempel-Ziv algorithm so that shorter codes are output for the more frequent sub-strings?

(8)   Devise a robust Huffman expansion algorithm. It should be able to deal with codes that do not correspond to any character and thus attempt to expand a file in which a few bits have been corrupted.

References

1.   D. A. Lelewer and D. S. Hirschberg, "Data compression," *ACM Computing Surveys*, vol. 19, no. 3, pp. 261-296, September 1987.

2. E. B. Koffman and F. L. Friedman, *Problem solving and structured programming in FORTRAN 77*, Addison-Wesley, Reading, MA, 1987. Third edition.

3. D. A. Huffman, "A method for the construction of minimum-redundancy codes," *Proceedings I.R.E*, vol. 40, pp. 1098-1101, September 1952.

4. R. G. Gallagher, "Variations on a theme by Huffman," *IEEE Transactions on Information Theory*, vol. IT-24, no. 6, pp. 668-674, November 1978.

5. D. E. Knuth, "Dynamic Huffman coding," *Journal of Algorithms*, vol. 6, no. 2, pp. 163-180, June 1985.

6. J. S. Vitter, "Design and analysis of dynamic Huffman codes," *Journal of the ACM*, vol. 34, no. 4, pp. 825-845, October 1987.

7. J. S. Vitter, "Algorithm 673: Dynamic Huffman coding," *ACM Transactions on Mathematical Software*, vol. 15, no. 2, pp. 158-167, June 1989.

8. C. E. Benson, Jr., *An adaptive digram huffman encoding algorithm*, Computer Science Department, CSUN, Northridge, CA, 1986. MS Thesis.

9. D. Cooper and M. F. Lynch, "Text compression using variable- to fixed-length encodings," *Journal of the American Society for Information Science*, vol. 33, no. 1, pp. 18-31, January 1982.

10. J. Ziv and A. Lempel, "Compression of individual sequences via variable-rate coding," *IEEE Transactions on Information Theory*, vol. IT-24, no. 5, pp. 530-536, September 1978.

11. J. Ziv and A. Lempel, "A universal algorithm for sequential data compression," *IEEE Transactions on Information Theory*, vol. IT-23, no. 3, pp. 337-343, May 1977.

12. T. A. Welch, "A technique for high-performance data compression," *Computer*, vol. 17, no. 6, pp. 8-19, June 1984.

13. F. Rubin, "Experiments in text file compression," *Communications of the ACM*, vol. 19, no. 11, pp. 617-623, November 1976.

14. J. Katajainen, M. Penttonen, and J. Teuhola, "Syntax-directed compression of program files," *Software Practice and Experience*, vol. 16, no. 3, pp. 269-276, March 1986.

15. J. Bentley, D. D. Sleator, R. E. Tarjan, and V. K. Wei, "A locally adaptive data compression scheme," *Communications of the ACM*, vol. 29, no. 4, pp. 320-330, April 1986.

16. P. D. Smith and G. M. Barnes, *Files and databases: an introduction*, Addison-Wesley, Reading, Mass., 1987.

5

Encryption

Documents are a valuable resource and in any collection there are likely to be some to which access is restricted. Examples are medical records, tax records, personnel files and planning documents. Any operating system should implement measures that limit access to a file containing sensitive material. In addition, the physical media on which documents are stored may be secured. A third line of defense is to encrypt documents, making them unintelligible to someone without the appropriate decryption capabilities. An advantage of electronic documents over documents which exist only on paper is the ease with which they can be encrypted and decrypted. The commonest encryption methods operate character by character which is why we include encryption in this section of the text.

Because of the applications of encryption techniques in protecting classified documents, there is likely to be a wide disparity between the state-of-the-art as represented in published papers and books and the actual state-of-the-art as represented by the capabilities of agencies such as NSA. In this chapter we look at a few techniques that are fairly simple to implement and provide a degree of protection for documents. With one exception (see 5.2.4), documents encrypted by the techniques we describe could not be considered completely secure. Many books list programs that implement encryption algorithms, Patterson [1] contains Pascal programs for most of the techniques discussed in this chapter.

Terminology The human readable text that we wish to protect is called the **plaintext**. A **key** is some information used in conjunction with an encryption algorithm to produce an encrypted form of the plaintext. We term this encrypted form the **ciphertext**. The same key (or information related to it) is used with a decryption algorithm to recover the plaintext from the ciphertext. Thus we have the configuration shown in Fig. 5.1.

We can also conceive of an **attacker** or **opponent** being someone who is trying to decipher the ciphertext without some of the information available

Figure 5.1 Encryption and decryption

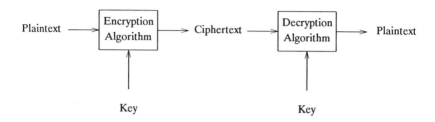

to legitimate decrypters.

The effort worth expending on encrypting a document depends on the perceived threats to it and the value of the encrypted material. That value may change over time; consider, for example, a company's financial report due to be made public in 48 hours. The encryption method used to protect it need only resist attack for that time.

Some of the inconvenience of having documents only in encrypted form can be alleviated if users can edit ciphertexts without having to decrypt them first. The Unix editors *ed*, *vi*, and *ex* allow documents encrypted with *crypt* to be edited in such a manner. The user sees plaintext but that decrypted text exists only in the editor buffer. Wordperfect [2] allows users to protect a file with a password that is used to encrypt it. On receipt of the correct password, WordPerfect decrypts the file as it is read from disc.

Encryption techniques can be classified broadly according to how much of the encryption process need be kept secret in order not to compromise encrypted texts. Clearly it is best to have to protect as little as possible of the encryption process. In sections 5.1 through 5.3 of this chapter we consider three categories of methods that require protection for respectively:

(1) The encryption algorithm
(2) The key
(3) Parameters of the method by which the key was produced.

5.1 Private algorithm

Our first category of methods requires that the encryption algorithm itself be kept secret (private) because knowledge of the encryption algorithm is sufficient to produce a decryption algorithm. Note that such an algorithm typically does not use a key as described above. For example, encryption may consist of a sequence of reversible steps. If the steps were known, the inverse operations could simply be applied in the reverse order to decrypt a ciphertext. An example of a four-step algorithm is shown in Fig. 5.2.

Figure 5.2 Four-step encryption algorithm

1. Translate the text from English to Navajo.

2. Write the input row-by-row in a matrix of a certain size, output the matrix column-by-column.

3. Compress the file using Huffman coding.

4. Swap disjoint pairs of bytes.

5.2 Public algorithm, private key

Our second category of methods does not require that the encryption algorithm be kept secret. Knowledge of the algorithm may allow a more focussed attack on a ciphertext but is not by itself sufficient. An arbitrary ciphertext file is protected by keeping secret the key needed to decrypt it. The size of the key space, that is the number of possible keys, is important in any encryption technique that uses keys. It should not be feasible for an attacker to decrypt a ciphertext via a direct search of the key space. In the case of each of the algorithms discussed in this section, the key to encrypt a file is also used to decrypt it.

5.2.1 Caesar code
To encrypt a file, replace each character by the character K further on in the (wrap-around) alphabet. Figure 5.3 shows an alphabet and the alphabet shifted 9 places.

Figure 5.3 Caesar code - alphabet shifting

```
ABCDEFGHIJKLMNOPQRSTUVWXYZ abcdefghijklmnopqrsᴸuvwxyz
rstuvwxyzABCDEFGHIJKLMNOPQRSTUVWXYZ abcdefghijklmnopq
```

To encrypt, find the character on the top row and replace it by the corresponding character on the bottom row. To decrypt, reverse the process. Thus, for example,

plaintext: This is a secret message
ciphertext: KZ jR jRSRjWUiWkRdWjjSYW

This method is easily attacked because of the small set of keys; the number of effective keys is the same as the size of the alphabet.

5.2.2 Simple substitution code

Suppose we write out the alphabet, as in the top row of Fig. 5.3, and make the bottom row a permutation of it. Figure 5.4 shows an example.

Figure 5.4 Simple substitution code

```
ABCDEFGHIJKLMNOPQRSTUVWXYZ abcdefghijklmnopqrstuvwxyz
PEteIsOSTICYpg xBrWNfkjFuoRJXcmUwAZaMGzvKndbLVDQhHyqi
```

The same encryption and decryption techniques are used and now we get

plaintext: `This is a secret message`
ciphertext: `NZaVRaVRJRVUcLUDRvUVVJAU`

The number of possible keys is now larger (N! rather than N, where N is the size of the alphabet). However, the method is easily attacked because every occurrence of a particular character in the plaintext is mapped onto a particular character in the encrypted text. We saw in the previous chapter that natural language is redundant - letters and letter groups do not occur with equal frequencies. In English, the rank ordering of the most frequent half-dozen or so letters is fairly constant from text to text.[1] If the text is large enough, the frequency distribution of the characters in the ciphertext gives clues as to their identity in the plaintext. Even in the short example above we might deduce that a space is represented by R because of the frequency and spacing of that character. It is an interesting project to write an interactive program that helps discover the key (see Exercises 1 and 2).

---

1. Frequencies of letters in the first four chapters of this text were counted. Mapping lower onto upper case letters, the ranks were:

Chapter 1 E T A I O R N S
Chapter 2 E T A S O I N R
Chapter 3 E T A I R N S O
Chapter 4 E T A O S I N R

For comparison, the ranking in the million word Brown Corpus [3] is

E T A O I N S R

Because it is frequently used at the beginning of a sentence, T is typically the most common upper case letter in a text.

5.2.3 Repeated keywords

We can avoid the one-to-one correspondence between characters in the plaintext and characters in the encrypted text by merging the plaintext in some way with (repetitions of) a keyword. See Kernighan and Plauger [4 sec. 2.6] for a discussion of this method.

For example, suppose we choose "Pascal" as our keyword and we use the same plaintext as in our previous examples.

```
we merge        This is a secret message
with            PascalPascalPascalPascal
```

The kth character of the ciphertext is some function (such as exclusive or) of the kth character in the plaintext and the kth character in the repeating keyword string. The decryption algorithm applies the repeating keyword to the ciphertext and reverses the letter function to recover the plaintext. If we map our alphabet onto the integers 0 to 52 and perform modulo 52 addition on a pair of characters, the ciphertext resulting from our example can be represented:

hIaVAUHATCTQrSXWAYtTkDHQ

Note that if we further encrypt the result with a (repeating) keyword of, for example, length 7, we get something of the same effect as if we encrypted once with a keyword of length 42 (LCM(6,7)). However, repeating patterns make the ciphertext more vulnerable than if an arbitrary 42-character keyword had been used.

5.2.4 One-time pad

The repetitious nature of the string with which we merged the plaintext in our previous example leaves it vulnerable to attack. We can avoid this if we merge the plaintext with a file of the same length containing a genuinely random sequence of characters. In this technique, the key is the complete file of random characters. The method is theoretically unbreakable because without the key, any alleged decryption of the appropriate length is no more or less valid than any other.

Note that to be theoretically unbreakable, the random key must be truly random and not the product of some pseudo-random generator. The latter would have subtle patterns. In addition, a particular key must never be used more than once (thus we have a "one-time pad") otherwise analysis of two or more files encrypted using the same key would assist an attacker.

While the requirements for the key make the method unwieldy for spontaneous use, there is no reason why secure keys could not be established in advance of their use. Now the encrypter and decrypter need only know which key is to be used with which file.

5.2.5 Data Encryption Standard

The National Bureau of Standards Data Encryption Standard (DES) [5]
was developed from work done at IBM. Figure 5.5 shows a black box
representation of the operation of DES. Of the 64 bits in a key, 56 are
significant (the other 8 are parity bits) thus the size of the key space is 2^{56}
(approximately 7×10^{16}). The key is used to both encrypt and decrypt
blocks of 64 bits.

Figure 5.5 DES encryption: overview

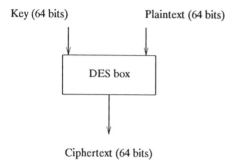

Key (64 bits)   Plaintext (64 bits)

DES box

Ciphertext (64 bits)

A DES box can be used in a variety of ways. In Electronic Code Book
(ECB) mode, the plaintext is taken 64 bits at a time and encrypted using a
constant key. In Cipher Block Chaining mode (CBC), the first 64-bit block
of the plaintext is exclusive-ored with an Initialize Vector before going into
DES. The 64-bit output both forms part of the ciphertext and is used as
the vector in the processing of the next block of the plaintext. DES can
also be used to generate a pseudo-random sequence of bits: start with a
plaintext and key (thus in effect two keys) and feed the output back in as
the next "plaintext". The resulting string can be merged with a plaintext
message (see 5.2.4).

The DES algorithm Figure 5.6 shows the operation of DES encryption in
more detail. DES encryption starts with an initial permutation of the 64-
bit plaintext block and ends with the inverse permutation. In between are
16 repetitions of a (non-linear) substitution and a permutation. Every bit
of the output is dependent in some way on every bit of the key and every
bit of the input block.[2]

---

2. Meyer [6] shows that this dependency is achieved after only five rounds.

Figure 5.6 DES encryption: more details

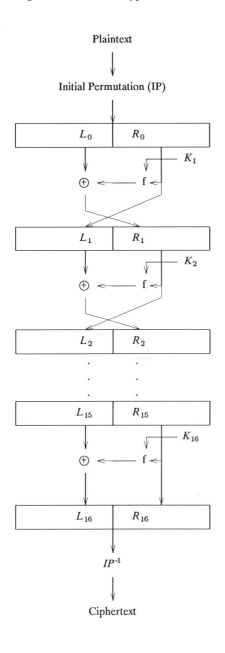

The 64 bits being processed are divided into left (L) and right (R) 32-bit sections as shown in Fig. 5.6. The transformations are defined as follows (where $\oplus$ is the exclusive-or operation):

$$R_i = L_{i-1} \oplus f(R_{i-1}, K_i) \quad 0 < i < 16$$

$$L_i = R_{i-1} \qquad 0 < i < 16$$

$$R_{16} = R_{15}$$

$$L_{16} = L_{15} \oplus f(R_{15}, K_{16})$$

Questions that remain are: what is function f and how is K_i derived from the key?

The operation of function f is shown in Figure 5.7.

Figure 5.7 Schematic of function f

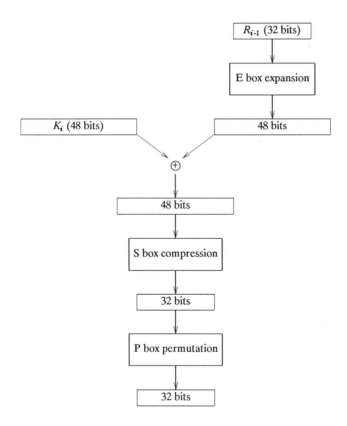

The 32-bit R input is expanded via an "E-box" to 48 bits.[3] Next, the 48-bit string is exclusive-ored with the 48-bit K_i. The result is compressed to 32-bits using the "S-boxes". Finally, the 32-bit string is permuted with the "P-box".

The way in which the K_i are derived from the key is shown in Figure 5.8.

Figure 5.8 Derivation of K_i

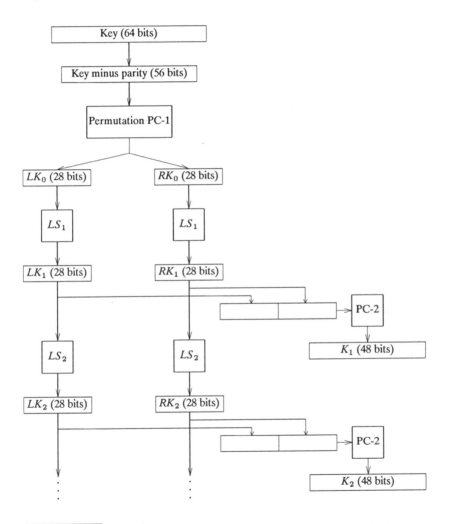

---

3. The various boxes mentioned in the text and shown in the figures are simply tables that indicate how an output bit, or group of output bits, is obtained from the input.

The parity bits (bits 8, 16, 24, etc) of the 64 bit key are discarded. The remaining 56 bits are permuted by PC-1 then split into two 28-bit sections. At each iteration the two halves are shifted left cyclically 1 or 2 places.[4] K_i is derived by combining the two halves and passing it through PC-2 which selects 48 of the 56 bits.

Given the tables, DES can be implemented in a high-level language by a reasonably proficient programmer (see Exercise 5). Some Unix systems have a *des* program that can encrypt/decrypt a file in either ECB mode or CBC mode. Because of the relatively simple nature of the DES bit manipulations, efficient VLSI implementations are possible. Chips in the 20 Megabit/second class facilitate high speed secure data transmission.

DES Decryption To decrypt a ciphertext block, apply the transformations shown in Fig. 5.6 except that the keys K_1, K_2, ... K_{16} are used in the reverse order.

As far as is known, DES has to date resisted analytical attack. It is a matter of controversy as to whether government agencies such as NSA are able to break DES [7]. It may be significant that while DES has been used in electronic funds transfers, including such transfers by the Department of Commerce, it has not been adopted by the Department of Defense. Diffie and Hellman [8] showed that an attack on a ciphertext where the plaintext was known could be accomplished feasibly using 1977 hardware. They indicated that a direct attack on the key space using a highly parallel architecture (10^6 keys tried concurrently) could be expected to determine the key in about 12 hours. As the cost of hardware declines, it is apparent that the security of DES is weakening. A solution is to increase the key size to perhaps 128 or 256 bits while retaining the properties of the algorithm.

5.3 Public algorithm, public key

In the methods described in the previous sections, at least some of the details of the encryption process (the key or the algorithm) has to be protected. In the final class of methods, the encryption and decryption algorithms are public, as are the keys used to encrypt texts. Thus anyone may encrypt a document. The corresponding decryption keys are kept private.

No key has to be passed from the encrypter to the decrypter because the key needed to decrypt a document is different from the key used to encrypt it. Although the two keys are related, it is required that they be created in such a way that it is computationally infeasible to derive the private decryption key given the corresponding public encryption key. Diffie and

---

4. The number of places to shift depends on the iteration and is held in (another) table. The total number of shifts for the 16 iterations is 28.

Hellman [9] describe the properties of public key encryption. One additional advantage of this technique is that a user can "sign" a document with an unforgable signature.

Each user of the system has two keys. The encryption key is public and can therefore be used by anyone in conjunction with a public encryption algorithm to encrypt documents intended to be read by the user. The second key is private and is used in conjunction with a public decryption algorithm to decrypt documents. The two keys are generated from a common (secret) source but given the public key it is not feasible to derive the private one. The public key technique is thus based on "trap door" functions - functions that are easily computed but for which it is computationally infeasible to determine the inverse function without information about the construction of the function.

Normal encryption and decryption is straightforward. Figure 5.9 represents a document for user B being encrypted using B's (public) encryption key and decrypted using B's (private) decryption key.

Figure 5.9 Public key encryption

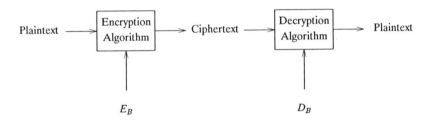

In addition, the public key method provides a means of storing signed documents. Consider the process shown in Fig. 5.10 representing user A creating a signed document to be read by user B.

Figure 5.10 Protocol for signed documents

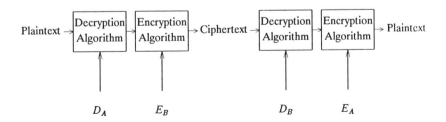

The document is first *decrypted* using the private key of the A.[5] To the result is prepended some text identifying A as the author. The whole is then encrypted using the public key of the recipient. When reading the document, B decrypts it, like all other documents intended for him, using his private key. This reverses the encryption phase of Fig. 5.10. The output is unintelligible except for plaintext identifying A as the author. To verify that the document was indeed written by A, user B *encrypts* the message using the encryption algorithm and the public key of A. If the result is successful, B knows that the document was written by someone with access to the private (decryption) key of A - presumably A himself.

Trap-door function A possible trap-door function was proposed by Rivest, Shamir and Adelman [10]. The RSA technique is based on the fact that currently it is comparatively simple to determine whether or not a number is prime but, by comparison, finding the factors of a composite number is extremely slow (but algorithms are getting faster!).

To create an encryption key and the corresponding decryption key, a user first finds two large (> 60 digit) prime numbers P and Q.[6] Typically this will not consume a great deal of processor time. The user's encryption key is a pair of integers (R,S) where

$R = P * Q$
S = a number relatively prime to both P-1 and Q-1

The decryption key is also a pair of integers. It is of the form (R,T) where

$R = P * Q$
T = the multiplicative inverse of S, i.e. an integer with the property that

$$TS \text{ modulo } ((P\text{-}1)(Q\text{-}1)) \equiv 1$$

T can only feasibly be calculated by someone who knows P and Q. Deriving T from knowledge of only R and S is essentially the same problem as factoring R, so the decryption key can be made arbitrarily secure from someone knowing only the encryption key.

---

5. We assume that both the encryption and decryption algorithms will accept any file of bytes and produce a file of bytes as output.
6. The 60 may not be appropriate for certain levels of security. As algorithms and technology improve, the number of digits can be made arbitrarily large.

RSA encryption The plaintext is mapped to a sequence of integers, $P_1, P_2,$ $P_3, ... P_N$. We could map strings to integers or simply use the bytes of the text, singly or in groups. To encrypt, each number P_i in the representation of the plaintext is converted to a corresponding integer C_N in the cipher-text in the following manner:

$$C_i = P_i^S \ modulo \ R$$

The following example is from Simmons [11]. The numbers are unrealisti-cally small but serve for illustrative purposes.

Let P = 421 and Q = 577
and S = 101 (a number having no factors in common with 420 or 576).

The public key is therefore the pair (242917, 101).

If P_i is 153190

then $C_i = 153190^{101}$ modulo 242917 = 203272

RSA decryption The decryption algorithm is similar to encryption except that this time the private key is used. Thus

P = 421 and Q = 577
S = 101 => (101 * T) modulo 241920 = 1
T = 9581

The private key is therefore the pair (242917, 9581).

If C_i is 203272

then $P_i = 203272^{9581}$ modulo 242917 = 153190

There are fast algorithms for modulo arithmetic: we can raise a number to a power by squaring and use the modulo result at each stage without affecting the final result (see Exercise 3).

To generate keys, we can imagine a hardware device generating P and Q and emitting a public key and the corresponding private key. The values of P and Q themselves are never revealed.

5.4 Compression and encryption

A measure of goodness of an encryption method is the uniformity of the output file. If the frequency distributions of bits, bytes, and higher-order groupings are largely flat, an attacker has few clues as to the method of encryption or the plain text. Not surprisingly, ciphertext files do not compress much. Chapter 7 of these notes was encrypted using the Unix *des* and *crypt* utilities. None of the three compression programs discussed in the previous chapter (*pack*, *compact* and *compress*) was able to compress the resulting ciphertext files at all.

Compressing a text before encrypting it makes an attack on the ciphertext more difficult, particularly if, as with dynamic Huffman encoding, the bit pattern associated with a particular character may vary throughout the text.

Summary

Encryption is a reversible process that produces a version of a document that requires application of a corresponding decryption process in order to be intelligible. Encrypting a document provides a measure of security against unauthorized access to the contents. The amount of effort expended in encryption typically depends on the value of the documents. A variety of encryption techniques are available each having a certain resistance to various forms of attack. Some of the more resilient require little to be kept secret other than a relatively short key.

This chapter marks the end of the section of the text in which we have been concerned with treating a file as a character stream. In the next three chapters we look at techniques that operate at a slightly higher level by grouping characters into symbols in some way.

Exercises

(1)   Write an interactive, display-oriented program that assists a user in deciphering a text encrypted using a simple substitution code. Your program should be capable of showing, perhaps in separate windows, statistics derived from the ciphertext and plaintexts of various kinds (e.g. natural and programming languages). A user should be able to make and remove associations between plaintext and ciphertext characters and see the results on the screen.

(2)   Assume that the ciphertext is the result of simple substitution coding. Write a program that decrypts the text with interactive user assistance. Your program should use language statistics and could

assume that every word in the plain text is in a certain lexicon, for example that used by your local spelling checker.

(3)   Write an efficient routine for computing A^B for integer A,B. Devise a method of mapping text into integers such that the text can be recovered. Use your solutions to verify RSA encryption/decryption using the keys of 5.3 (or others of your own devising).

(4)   Write a program to decipher a text that was encrypted using the Caesar code algorithm with an unknown key. An attack is to form the frequency distribution of the ciphertext and determine which key value would best change it into that of English (the presumed source language). Alternatively your program could decrypt the text, or a sample of it, with alternative keys and check to see if the result contains commonly expected words.

(5)   Implement the DES encryption/decryption algorithm in a high-level language of your choice. (Patterson [1] is a good source for the contents of the various tables.) Verify that the original plaintext can be recovered from the ciphertext.

(6)   Devise tests for measuring the uniformity of a file, that is, measure the flatness of the distributions of various n-bit groups. Enhance your solution to Exercise 4 so that it will perform only the first k of the 16 principal transformations. For a variety of plaintexts and keys, encrypt the plaintext using your algorithm with k = 1, 2, ... 16. Compute the uniformity of the ciphertexts and plot against k.

References

1.   W. Patterson, *Mathematical cryptology for Computer Scientists and Mathematicians,* Rowman and Littlefield, Totowa, NJ, 1987.

2.   *WordPerfect Version 5.0 Reference manual,* WordPerfect Corporation, Orem, Utah, 1988.

3.   C. K. Kucera and W. N. Francis, *Computational analysis of present-day American English,* Brown University Press, Providence, RI, 1967.

4.   B. W. Kernighan and P. J. Plauger, *Software Tools,* Addison-Wesley, Reading, Mass., 1976.

5.   *Data Encryption Standard,* National Bureau of Standards, U. S. Department of Commerce, 1977. Federal Information Processing Standard (FIPS) Publication 46.

6.   C. H. Meyer, "Ciphertext/plaintext and cyphertext/key dependence vs number of rounds for the data encryption standard," *Proceedings of the NCC,* vol. 47, pp. 1119-1126, AFIPS Press, June 1978.

7.   "Foiling computer crime," *IEEE Spectrum,* vol. 16, no. 7, pp. 31-41, July 1979.

8.   W. Diffie and M. E. Hellman, "Exhaustive cryptanalysis of the NBS Data Encryption Standard," *Computer*, vol. 10, no. 6, pp. 74-84, June 1977.

9.   W. Diffie and M. E. Hellman, "New directions in cryptography," *IEEE Transactions on Information Theory*, vol. IT-22, no. 6, pp. 644-654, November 1976.

10.   R. L. Rivest, A. Shamir, and L. Adelman, "A method for obtaining digital signatures and public-key cryptosystems," *Communications of the ACM*, vol. 21, no. 2, pp. 120-126, February 1978.

11.   G. J. Simmons, "Symmetric and asymmetric encryption," *ACM Computing Surveys*, vol. 11, no. 4, pp. 305-330, December 1979.

III

Symbol-by-Symbol Processing

Macroprocessors

In chapter 4 we looked at text compression and expansion. The operation of a macroprocessor is similar in some ways to a text expansion algorithm: text is read and output and short strings are replaced by longer strings.

Terminology The term **macro** is used in a variety of ways in a variety of software from spreadsheet programs to command line interpreters to word processors. In what follows we define a macro to be a pair of character strings: a **macro name** and a **replacement text**. A **macroprocessor** is a program that accepts input that may contain both **macro definitions** (associations of names with replacement texts) and normal text. The basic operation of a macroprocessor is to copy its input to its output. If a macro definition is encountered, it is stored in a table. If a macro name is encountered, a **macro call** may result (though detection of calls can be suppressed - see later.) Typically this will cause the macroprocessor to replace the name by the appropriate replacement text. Fig. 6.1 depicts the operation of a macroprocessor; the table stores macro definitions encountered in the input. In this chapter we assume that macroprocessing proceeds symbol by symbol; some macroprocessors (for example GPM [1] and TRAC [2, 3]) operate character by character.

Figure 6.1 Operation of a macroprocessor

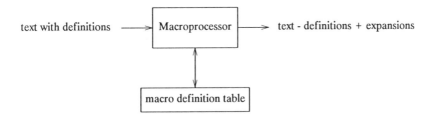

The reader is probably familiar with the macro capabilities found in a typical assembler: a user is able to associate a mnemonic with a sequence of instructions and have that sequence replace occurrences of the mnemonic. Stand-alone macroprocessors are more general in that the input does not need to be in a particular language or format. Most such macroprocessors were developed as programming tools, for translating one language into another. Cole [4] surveys some systems and applications, Campbell-Kelly [5] looks at macros in low and high-level programming languages and Brown [6] looks at their use in software portability. In this chapter we will look at more general uses and illustrate some possibilities with examples from M4 [7] and ML/I [6]. For the most part we ignore details of how the macroprocessor is implemented. Kernighan and Plauger [8, 9] describe in detail the implementation of a macroprocessor similar to M4.

6.1 Basic features: M4

In this section we look at some of the simpler features of macro processing, such as parameter passing and conditional text expansion, and use M4 to illustrate them. M4 is a tool distributed with the Unix operating system. In section 6.2 we examine more advanced features.

Normally, the replacement text of a macro is longer than the macro name so a macro can be regarded as a kind of shorthand. In a word-processing environment, macros could be defined that associate simple mnemonics with standard paragraphs and clauses. These pieces of text could then be generated in the appropriate places in a document by inclusion of the appropriate mnemonic. For example, it is usually relatively easy to use a macroprocessor to generate the kind of form letters sent out by magazine publishers and sweepstakes organizers.

Macro definitions The general form of an M4 macro definition is:

define(name, replacement text)

Define is a built-in function taking two parameters: the macro name and its replacement text. Fig. 6.2 shows an example macro definition. A macroprocessor will usually have a facility for switching off detection of macro names in the input stream. In this chapter we use the skip characters [and] to switch name detection off and on.[1] One level of skip characters is stripped off when the macro replacement text is read and stored. This is why we have skips round the replacement text. We need to "skip

---

1. The M4 default skip characters are ' and '. They can be changed to the slightly more readable square brackets by a call of the built-in function changequote, thus: changequote([,]).

Figure 6.2 Simple M4 macro definition

define(letter,[Dear Sir[,]
            Thank you for your [letter] of enquiry.
            We are pleased to be able to supply goods
            as ordered.

            Yours sincerely[,]

    ])

out" the comma after "Sir" and the comma after "sincerely" otherwise they would be taken as marking the end of the second parameter of define (the replacement text).

Macro calls When a macroprocessor encounters a macro call, it can do one of two things with the replacement text. It can pass it through to the output or it can push it back onto the input stream. Generally, the latter is more useful, it means that we can have macro calls within a replacement text, that is, nested macro calls. It does mean, however, that we have to be careful not to have unintended macro calls. In our definition of *letter* we have to skip out the word "letter" in the replacement text otherwise a call of *letter* would lead to a call of *letter* and a call of *letter* and so on.

Fig. 6.3 shows how we can use nested macro calls. The first and last parts of a letter are defined as separate macros that are then called from within the letter macro.

Figure 6.3 Nested macro calls

define(signoff,[We remain, yours sincerely[,]

                    XYZ Department Store
        ])
define(hithere,[Dear Sir[,]
            Thank you for your [letter] of enquiry.])
define(letter,[hithere
            We are pleased to be able to supply goods
            as ordered.
            signoff
    ])
letter

The output when Fig. 6.3 is input to M4 is shown in Fig. 6.4.

Figure 6.4 Output from the input of Fig. 6.3

Dear Sir,
            Thank you for your letter of enquiry.
            We are pleased to be able to supply goods
            as ordered.
            We remain, yours sincerely,

                    XYZ Department Store

    The replacement text can also contain macro definitions. These will take effect when the replacement text is scanned. This will either be when the macro definition containing the replacement text is stored (if not skipped out) or when it is called. Consider the definitions and calls in Fig. 6.5. The two macro definitions each contain a macro definition in the replacement text; in the latter it is enclosed in skip characters, in the former it is not. Figure 6.6 shows the output when the text of Fig 6.5 is input to M4.

Figure 6.5 Macros containing macro definitions

```
c
define(b,define(c,cat))
c
d
define(d,[define(e,elk)])
e
d
e
```

Figure 6.6 Output from Fig. 6.5

```
c

cat
d

e

elk
```

Note that the macro definition of c takes effect as soon as macro b is defined implying that the definition of macro c is stored when the definition of b is scanned. In contrast, the macro definition of e does not take effect until macro d is called and the replacement text (definition of e) pushed back on the input. The difference is due to the skip characters.[2]

Macro processors may vary in the "binding time" between a calling macro and a called macro. Consider the definitions and call shown in Fig. 6.7.

Figure 6.7 Macros redefined

define(B,cat)
define(A,B)
define(B,dog)
A

The output when this is input to M4 is "dog". This is because the replacement text is not scanned for macro calls when a macro definition is stored. Hence the replacement text of A is the character B. When A is called, it pushes the replacement text (B) back on the input where it triggers a second call and is replaced by "dog".

Macros with parameters The letter in Fig. 6.4 looks as though it has been generated by a computer. It is fairly simple to arrange for macros to take parameters; this will enable us to generate customized letters. Macros in M4 use parameters in a very informal way; unlike most programming languages there is no checking on type or number of actual parameters. Within a replacement text, $0 refers to the macro name and $1, $2 ... $9 refer to parameters 1, 2, ... 9. If, in a call of the macro, an actual parameter is omitted, it is treated as the empty string. Consider the personalized version of our earlier letter, shown in Fig. 6.8. Fig. 6.9 contains the output from the following calls:

    letter(Joe, Friday, saws and hammers)
    letter(Mr Brown, May 17th, bolt cutters, irons, car stereos)

Note that actual parameters are delimited by commas and that both our calls have multi-word parameters. The fourth and fifth actual parameters in the second call are not used.

---

2. Recall that text other than macro definitions and calls, in particular newline characters, is passed directly from the input to the output. This explains some of the extra vertical spacing in Fig. 6.6. M4 provides a mechanism for diverting this text, see Ref. 7.

Figure 6.8 Macro with parameters

define(letter,[Dear $1[,]
            Thank you for your [letter][,] dated $2[,] concerning
            $3. We are pleased to be able
            to supply goods as ordered.

            Yours sincerely[,]

    ])

Figure 6.9 Results of parameterized calls

Dear Joe,
            Thank you for your letter, dated Friday, concerning
            saws and hammers. We are pleased to be able
            to supply goods as ordered.

            Yours sincerely,

Dear Mr Brown,
            Thank you for your letter, dated May 17th, concerning
            bolt cutters. We are pleased to be able
            to supply goods as ordered.

            Yours sincerely,

    The replacement text of a macro can be null, we could use this to define
a comment capability. For example, defining

    define(comment,)

means that

    comment(this is a comment)

generates no output.[3]

_____
3. It may be better to define comment in terms of the built-in function dnl thus:

    define(comment,[dnl])

Conditional text Although our parameterized letter is an improvement over the earlier one, it is still basically a template into which parameters are fitted. All letters will be of the same form. It is desirable to be able to vary the form of the replacement text, for example including or excluding text according to the results of tests performed at macro expansion time. M4 supports this to a limited extent with a built in macro called *ifelse*.

The most common invocation of *ifelse* is *ifelse(a,b,c,d)*. If string *a* is equivalent to string *b* then the result of the macro expansion is string *c* otherwise it is string *d*. Usually, for the call of *ifelse* to be useful, one or both of *a* and *b* will be a parameter of the calling macro or a macro call itself. We have seen that M4 treats missing parameters as empty strings so the following forms of ifelse are commonly used too.

```
ifelse(a,b,c)
ifelse(a,b,,c)
```

In the first case, no text is generated if a and b are different, in the second case no text is generated if a and b are the same. Fig. 6.10 shows an improved version of our letter macro using *ifelse*.

Figure 6.10 Macro with conditional text

```
define(letter,[Dear $1[,]
        Thank you for your [letter][,] dated $2.
        ifelse($3,late, We apologize for the delay in replying.)
        ifelse($4,ok,
            The items you need are in stock.,
            Unfortunately we are currently out of:
            $5
            $6
            )

        Yours sincerely[,]
])
```

Fig. 6.11 shows the output from the following calls:

```
letter(Joe, Jan 29th, late, ok)
letter(Mr Brown, May 17th,,notok, bolt cutters)
letter(Mrs Green, Friday,, ok).
```

Our final example, in Fig. 6.12, includes various features we have looked at

---

Dnl consumes text up to and including the next newline character.

Figure 6.11 Conditional output

Dear Joe,
> Thank you for your letter, dated Jan 29th.
> We apologize for the delay in replying.
> The items you need are in stock.

> Yours sincerely,

Dear Mr Brown,
> Thank you for your letter, dated May 17th.

> Unfortunately we are currently out of:
>> bolt cutters

> Yours sincerely,

Dear Mrs Green,
> Thank you for your letter, dated Friday.

> The items you need are in stock.

> Yours sincerely,

and provides concise, if cryptic, macros for generating form letters to students. The macro *cop* (change of program) generates a letter notifying a student that he/she has been added to a class or that he/she has been dropped from a class. *Cop* calls macro *more* if its first parameter is "add" and calls macro *remove* if its first parameter is "drop". (If the first parameter is neither of these strings then no text is generated - maybe some newlines.) The macro *more* is a straightforward template-type macro. Macro *remove* is similar to our letter macro of Fig. 6.10. However, by testing for empty parameters $4 and $5 it generates a nicer list of items (in this case up to three prerequisite classes the student is missing). The output from the following calls is shown in Fig. 6.13:

    cop(drop,Bill Bones,COMP 461,COMP 332)
    cop(drop,Richard Roe,COMP 461,COMP 332,COMP 322,COMP 380)
    cop(add,Joan Doe,COMP 122,51234).

The first letter shows a single element list of missing prerequisites, the second letter shows a list of three. The final letter is an example of the

Figure 6.12 Student letter macros

```
define(remove, [Dear $1[,]
        This letter is to inform you that you are being
disenrolled from $2 because you have not taken the following
ifelse($4,,prerequisite:,prerequisites:)

    $3ifelse($4,,,[ifelse($5,,[ and $4.],[[,] $4, and $5.])])

                Yours sincerely,
])
define(more, [Dear $1[,]
    I am happy to inform you that there is now a place
in $2 (ticket number $3).

                Yours sincerely,
])
define(cop,[ifelse($1,add,[more($2,$3,$4)])
ifelse($1,drop,[remove($2,$3,$4,$5,$6)])
    ]
)
```

letter adding a student to a class.

Limitations of M4 While adequate for simple processing, M4 has deficiencies which make it less useful than some other macroprocessors for more sophisticated applications. First, the syntax of macro calls is unnatural and rigid. The macro name must be followed immediately by a comma-separated list of actual parameters enclosed in parentheses. The user cannot change this. Second, there is a limit on the number of actual parameters. Although there are ways to extend it beyond nine, they are messy. Third, no loops are possible in the replacement text, only choice structures. Finally, no indexing of parameters is supported; for example, $8 is legal, $i is not.

The ML/I macro-processor [6] has none of these deficiencies. In the next section we use it to illustrate some advanced macroprocessing features.

6.2 Advanced features: ML/I

ML/I was developed primarily as software portability aid. A piece of software would be coded in a "descriptive language" (a language designed specifically for that particular software) and versions of it in other

Figure 6.13 Generated letters to students

Dear Bill Bones,
         This letter is to inform you that you are being
disenrolled from COMP 461 because you have not taken the following
prerequisite:

COMP 332.

                    Yours sincerely,

Dear Richard Roe,
         This letter is to inform you that you are being
disenrolled from COMP 461 because you have not taken the following
prerequisites:

COMP 332, COMP 322, and COMP 380.

                    Yours sincerely,

Dear Joan Doe,
         I am happy to inform you that there is now a place
in COMP 122 (ticket number 51234).

                    Yours sincerely,

languages generated by passing the descriptive language code, and
appropriate macro definitions, through a macroprocessor such as ML/I. A
macro would be devised for each statement type in the descriptive
language. Clearly, in order to deal with a variety of statement types, the
macroprocessor would have to be flexible in the type of input it could
accept.

Macro definitions An M4 macro call consists of the macro name followed
by a comma-separated list of actual parameters enclosed in parentheses.
In ML/1 the user is free to choose the symbols that will delimit the actual
parameters. However, as a consequence, these delimiters must be
specified when the macro is defined. Figure 6.14 contains an ML/I macro
to generate letters similar to those of Fig. 6.9. The reserved word

Figure 6.14 ML/I macro definition

MCDEF letter , ; .
AS <Dear %A1.,
      Thank you for your <letter> dated %A2.
      concerning %A3.. We are pleased to be able
      to supply goods as ordered.

      Yours sincerely,

>

MCDEF introduces the macro definition. The next symbol is the name of the macro and this is followed, if appropriate, by information about parameter delimiters.[4] In the example of Fig. 6.14, the first line of the definition indicates that there will be three actual parameters. The first will be delimited by a comma, the second by a semi-colon and the last by a period. A typical call of the macro is:

   letter Mr. Johnson, Wednesday, 3rd April; electric drills.

Note that the first parameter is everything between the macro name and the first delimiter. Similarly, the second parameter is everything between the first and second delimiters. (The macro name can be considered delimiter 0.) An actual parameter can span many lines of text.

Returning to the definition in Fig. 6.14, the angled brackets are the skip characters, equivalent in function to the square brackets in our M4 examples. The characters "%" and "." delimit a parameter substitution indicator which, in this example, consists of "A" (for argument) followed by an integer.

Alternative delimiters The delimiter structure of our first example can be represented by a very simple directed graph thus:

ML/I enables users to set up very much more complex graphs. Suppose we wish our delimiter structure to be:

---

4. There is a way to have multi-symbol macro names and parameter delimiters.

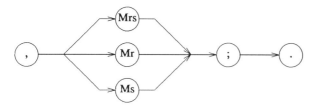

That is, the first delimiter will be always be a comma, the third always a semi-colon, and the fourth always a period, but the second may be any of the three symbols "Mrs", "Mr" and "Ms". We can specify this structure in the macro definition as shown in the first line of Fig. 6.15.

Figure 6.15 Alternative delimiters in ML/I

MCDEF letter2 , OPT Mrs OR Mr OR Ms ALL ; .
AS <   Department of English
                    %A1.
     Dear %D2. %A2.,

                    Your score on the recent %A3.
          was %A4..

                    Yours,

     >

Alternative delimiters are listed between OPT and ALL and are separated by OR. In the replacement text note how we can include actual delimiters as well as actual parameters. We use D rather than A as the indicator character. An example call of *letter2* is shown in Fig. 6.16 with the parameters and delimiters marked. The letter generated is shown in Fig. 6.17.

Figure 6.16 Macro call showing arguments and delimiters

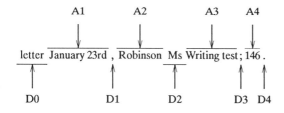

Figure 6.17 Letter generated

Department of English
January 23rd
Dear Ms Robinson,

Your score on the recent Writing test
was 146.

Yours,

Unlimited parameter lists So far we have seen just series and choice
forms in the delimiter list. ML/I also has a facility that permits iteration
in this list. Using this facility we can define a macro that takes an indefinite
number of arguments.

Let us write a letter-generating macro that allows us to inform a student
that he or she is being added to one or more courses. We do not wish there
to be an upper limit on the number of courses. The following are examples of macro calls we would like to make:

enroll John Doe in CS122, CS132, CS242, CS194.
enroll Billy Bob Roe in CS222, CS325 and Lab.
enroll Mary Jo Doe in CS222.
enroll Jean-Paul Roe in CS325 and Lab, CS232.

Note we are using the word "in" as the name delimiter; it helps make the
macro calls a little more readable. Following that delimiter is a comma
separated list of one or more course names. The list is terminated with a
period.

The delimiter structure we need is

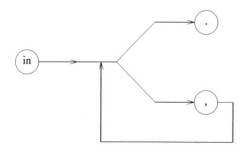

That is, having found "in", ML/I should next look for a comma or a period.

If it finds a period it has found the last delimiter. On the other hand, if it finds a comma it continues to scan for a comma or a period, and so on. This delimiter structure is reflected in the fragment of the macro definition shown in Fig. 6.18.

Figure 6.18 Macro heading: indefinite argument list

MCDEF enroll in N1 OPT , N1 OR . ALL
AS < ...

What we have done is label (with N1) the point in the delimiter structure to which we wish to return if we find a comma. This label then follows the comma in the list of alternate delimiters to indicate to ML/I the point to which to move in the parameter list.

Now the problem we have is how to process the argument list in the replacement text. ML/I has three features which make this relatively straightforward. The first is the existence of macro-time variables and arithmetic. Macros can make use of both local and global variables at macro expansion time. The second feature is the fact that we can index both the actual parameters and the delimiters. The item following A or D in the indicator need not be a constant. Finally there are gotos (conditional and unconditional) which allow us to set up loops in the replacement text.

Let us jump in at the deep end and see how all these features are used in completing the macro of Fig. 6.18. The complete definition is shown in Fig. 6.19.

Figure 6.19 Processing of indefinite argument list

MCDEF enroll in N1 OPT , N1 OR . ALL
AS <   Computer Science Department
    Dear %A1.,
        We are pleased to inform you that you
have been added to the following class(es):

MCSET T1=1
%L1. MCSET T1 = %T1.+1
    %A%T1..
    MCGO L1 UNLESS %D%T1.. = .

        Yours,

>

T1 is a macro-time local variable. It is initialized to 1 by the first MCSET statement and incremented by 1 by the second. The lines beginning MCSET do not generate any output text, instead they carry out macro-time arithmetic (i.e. performed at macro expansion time). %T1. expands to the current value of variable T1.

In M4, we could only use constants to index actual parameters (we had $6, $2 and so on). In ML/I both parameter and delimiter lists can be indexed with variables. Suppose that during the expansion of the first of our example calls above, T1 contains the number 3. Now %A%T1.. expands to %A3. which in turn expands to CS132.

The MCGO statement allows us to jump to a labelled location in the replacement text. Like the MCSET statement, a MCGO statement generates no text. Labels are of the form Ln. In a MCGO we can index labels in the same way that we index parameters and delimiters. After the label there can be a condition on the jump (as in Fig. 6.19). In our example we use T1 to index both the parameter and delimiter list and return to process another parameter if the current delimiter is not a period. All we do with the second and subsequent parameters (the first is the student name) is include them in the replacement text, one to a line. Figure 6.20 shows the output from the last of our proposed calls.

Figure 6.20 Generated letter to student

       Computer Science Department
Dear Jean-Paul Roe,
       We are pleased to inform you that you have been added to the following class(es):

CS325 and Lab
CS232

       Yours,

Our final example will show how powerful, yet compact, ML/I macros can be. We will define a memo-generating macro called *memoall*. *Memoall* will take three parameters. The first parameter, delimited by the word "on", is the name of a macro which generates a single copy of the macro. (We assume that the single-copy macro takes two arguments: a date, delimited by a semi-colon, and a name, delimited by an asterisk. Fig. 6.21 shows a typical example.) The second parameter to *memoall* is the date. This will be delimited by the word "to". The final parameter is a list of recipients of the memo. The names will be comma separated and the list terminated by a period. *Memoall* will generate an individual copy of the memo for each recipient.

A possible definition of *memoall* is shown in Fig. 6.22.

Figure 6.21 Single-copy memo macro

```
MCDEF budget3Q ; *
AS < XYZ Corp. Internal Memorandum
    Date: %A1.
    To: %A2.
    From: B. B. Roe, VP Finance

        Please see my secretary to arrange a meeting
        about the 3rd quarter budget for your department.
    >
```

Figure 6.22 Memo generating macro

```
MCDEF memoall on to N1 OPT , N1 OR . ALL
AS <    MCSET T1=2
    %L1 MCSET T1 = %T1.+1
    %A1. %A2.; %A%T1..*
    MCGO L1 UNLESS %D%T1..=.
    >
```

Note that the third line in the replacement text of *memoall* is the only one that generates any output. In this case it expands to a call of the macro that generates a single memo. The name of this macro is the first parameter of *memoall* (thus %A1.). This macro is given as parameters the date (second argument of *memoall* - %A2.) and the name of one of the recipients of the memo (indexed parameter of *memoall* - %A%T1..). Given the definition of Fig. 6.21 we can call:

memoall budget3Q on January 23rd to J. Jones, P.E. Bones, D. Stones.

and generate three memos.

We can go further than this. The fact that parameters are expanded before being substituted allows more abbreviation. If the following are put in a "standard prelude" file.

```
MCDEF JJ AS <J. Jones>
MCDEF PEB AS <P. E. Bones>
MCDEF DS AS <D. Stones>
```

then our call can be abbreviated to

memoall budget3Q on January 23rd to JJ, PEB, DS.

Because any macro expansion is pushed back onto the input, we can go further still and define mailing lists. For example, the following could also be in the standard prelude.

MCDEF Personnel AS <JJ, MPT, RTD, TLA, KLS>
MCDEF R&D AS <DS, AJTC, MKF, SEW, JDW, SYS>
MCDEF Heads AS <JJ, PEB, DS>

Now we can send a memo to the department heads as follows:

memoall budget3Q on January 23rd to Heads.

Summary

A macroprocessor accepts input consisting of text and macro definitions (pairs of strings). It stores the definitions and carries out string replacement; if the first of a pair occurs in the input it is replaced by the second. Typically the replacement text will be pushed back onto the input allowing it in turn to be scanned. Thus we may have nested macro calls. Macroprocessors vary in the format of definitions and calls. Some, for example ML/I, allow the user to specify the format of a macro call in sophisticated ways. While some macroprocessors operate character by character, those we examined in this chapter operate symbol by symbol.

In the simplest case, the replacement text can be a constant string. It is more useful, however, if the macroprocessor supports parameter substitution. Parameters and other strings can be used in tests performed at macro expansion time to determine which of two strings to generate. As well as choice forms, the replacement text can contain iteration, either explicitly with jump statements or implicitly with nested (recursive) calls. Powerful macros can be very compact.

Letters generated by macroprocessors (for example those in Fig. 6.11) may appear badly laid out. This is because it is sometimes difficult to prevent stray spaces and newlines passing from the input to the output. A solution is to pass the output from the macroprocessor through a text formatting program. In this way, extra blank lines can be eliminated, lines can be justified and the appearance of the text generally improved. In the next chapter we look at categories and the operation of formatting programs.

Exercises

(1) Devise a way in which an M4 macro could take more than 9 parameters.

(2) Devise a macro which allows a user to include comments in the input to ML/I. Naturally, the comments should not appear in the output.

(3) Write an ML/I macro which generates the verses of "Old Macdonald had a farm". Give a typical call of your macro, parameters should be limited to names of animals and appropriate noises.

(4) Write an ML/1 macro which takes as parameter an integer in the range -1000 to 1000 and outputs the cardinal form of the number.

(5) Write an ML/1 macro which takes as parameter an integer in the range 1 to 1000 and outputs the ordinal of the number.

(6) Using your solution to exercise 4, or otherwise, write an ML/1 macro that generates the verses of "Ten green bottles". Generalize it to "N green bottles" (for parameter N).

(7) Using your solutions to exercises 4 and 5, or otherwise, write an ML/1 macro that generates the verses of "The twelve days of Christmas" Parameters of your macro should be limited to the names of the object given: partridge in a pear tree, calling birds and so on.

(8) Compare the power of ML/I and M4. (Remember recursion.)

(9) A local TV station sends out form letters of various kinds in connection with their fund-raising drives. They have created a file of macro definitions and another file of macro calls. They use the Unix M4 macroprocessor. Shown below are the letters output as a result of the following macro calls:

letter(Mr Brown,existing,renewal,the establishment of a script archive)
letter(Mr Nixon,existing,reminder,a new tape editing system)
letter(Mr DeLorean,prospective,a collection of silent movies)
letter(Ms Reagan,donor,$125,25th March,a set of Star Wars outtakes).

Write appropriate macro definitions.

KCET

March 1993

Dear Mr Brown,

Thank you for renewing your subscription to the station.

We are grateful for your support in the past. A station
such as ours relies on contributions of time and money from the public.
Your gifts are appreciated.

In the past,fund-raising has enabled us to increase the
power of our transmitter and buy much-needed equipment for our studio.
This year, one of our goals in which you may be particularly interested
is the establishment of a script archive.

Yours sincerely,

Station Manager

KCET

March 1993

Dear Mr Nixon,

We are grateful for your support in the past. A station
such as ours relies on contributions of time and money from the public.
Your gifts are appreciated.

We go on the air twice a year asking for donations.
Our next fund-raising period is April 1st to 8th 1993. As usual,
exciting and valuable premiums are offered to subscribers.

In the past,fund-raising has enabled us to increase the
power of our transmitter and buy much-needed equipment for our studio.
This year, one of our goals in which you may be particularly interested
is a new tape editing system.

Yours sincerely,

Station Manager

KCET

March 1993

Dear Mr DeLorean,

KCET is a subscriber-sponsored public television station
broadcasting on channel 28. It has a large number of volunteer employees.
As well as retransmitting programs produced by other public TV stations,
the station produces a number of its own documentaries.

In the past,fund-raising has enabled us to increase the
power of our transmitter and buy much-needed equipment for our studio.
This year, one of our goals in which you may be particularly interested
is a collection of silent movies.

We go on the air twice a year asking for donations.
Our next fund-raising period is April 1st to 8th 1993. As usual,
exciting and valuable premiums are offered to subscribers.

May we invite your support? Looking forward to hearing from you.

Yours sincerely,

Station Manager

KCET

March 1993

Dear Ms Reagan,

Thank you for your communication of 25th March and contribution of
$125 towards the running of the station.

In the past,fund-raising has enabled us to increase the
power of our transmitter and buy much-needed equipment for our studio.
This year, one of our goals in which you may be particularly interested
is a set of Star Wars outtakes.

Yours sincerely,

Station Manager

References

1. C. Strachey, "A general purpose macrogenerator," *The Computer Journal*, vol. 8, no. 3, pp. 225-241, 1965.

2. C. N. Mooers and L. P. Deutsch, "TRAC, A text handling language," *Proceedings ACM National Conference*, pp. 229-246, 1965.

3. C. N. Mooers, "TRAC, A procedure-describing language for the reactive typewriter," *Communications of the ACM*, vol. 9, no. 3, pp. 215-219, March 1966.

4. A. J. Cole, *Macro Processors*, Cambridge University Press, 1981. Cambridge Computer Science Texts #4. Second Edition.

5. M. Campbell-Kelly, *An introduction to macros*, Macdonald, London, 1973.

6. P. J. Brown, *Macro processors and techniques for portable software*, Wiley, 1974.

7. B. W. Kernighan and D. M. Ritchie, *The M4 macro processor*, Bell Laboratories, 1977. Unix Programmer's Manual, Seventh Edition.

8. B. W. Kernighan and P. J. Plauger, *Software Tools*, Addison-Wesley, Reading, Mass., 1976.

9. B. W. Kernighan and P. J. Plauger, *Software Tools in Pascal*, Addison-Wesley, Reading, Mass., 1981.

7

Text Formatting

In addition to the content of a document, its appearance is also important. Text is normally arranged (or formatted) on a page to help readers; presentation can also influence a reader's perception of the importance of the material [1]. We define **markup** as information present in a text file that directs the arrangement of the text. In this chapter we look at ways in which text can be marked up and how markup can be processed by programs. Coombs *et al.* [2] define four levels of markup: *punctuational, presentational, procedural* and *descriptive*.

Punctuational is the lowest level of markup; words are separated from one another by white space and punctuation is added to assist in phrasing. Presentational is the next level; horizontal and vertical spacing is used to assist the reader with larger text objects. For example, paragraphs are separated by blank lines, page numbers are added and lists of items may have hanging indents with bullets or item numbers. A person creating a document on a typewriter enters presentational markup along with the text. For example, when centering a heading, the typist enters an appropriate number of leading spaces.

Beyond presentational markup we have notation typically intended for programs to interpret. Procedural markup commands are embedded in a text file and direct a formatter reading the file to act in a certain way to produce an image of the text with appropriate presentational information on a screen, on a printer or in a file. In WYSIWYG systems the commands are embedded control codes, normally invisible, and the effects of the commands are seen immediately on the screen. In a batch system, the commands are typically more or less legible sequences intermixed with the text. Their effect is not apparent until the file is processed by the batch formatter.

An example of embedded commands are those necessary to offset a long quotation from the user's own text. In a batch oriented system the quotation might be preceded by:

```
.ne .8i
.in + 1i
.ll -1i
.ls 1
.sp 3
```

These are examples of directives to *troff* [3] that cause it to bring in the margins one inch, single space the text and offset it from the preceding text, starting a new page if necessary (if less than .8" available on the current page). A similar sequence, resetting the margins and restoring line spacing would appear at the end of the quotation. Although we can define macros to avoid having to write detailed directives at each point where they are required, the detailed directives are still present in the macro definition.

The final level of markup is descriptive. Here a user identifies logical components of the text independent of how they are to appear on the final document. In the case of the long quotation, the source file might look like:

```
<lq>
first line of quotation

...

last line of quotation
</lq>
```

The quotation tags in the above example are similar to those used in the Standard Generalized Markup Language (see 7.3.2). Coombs *et al.* make a strong case for the use of descriptive over procedural markup. Not only does it make the document more portable but the semantic tags can be used by programs such as intelligent document retrieval systems. Example requests to such a system might include:

Find documents containing "points of light" in a quotation
Find documents containing "trademark of AT&T" in a footnote
Find documents containing "Fermat's last theorem" in the abstract.

Batch processing vs WYSIWYG Documents with embedded procedural or descriptive markup are typically processed in a batch manner to produce a document representation that can then be viewed or printed. Alternatively, there are many programs (e.g. Wordstar, WordPerfect, MacWrite) that combine editing with formatting. A user of such a program sees the current text on the screen and, within the limitations of the display, the text is shown as it will look when printed. Such systems are termed WYSIWYG (What You See Is What You Get). A WYSIWYG system normally results in few surprises when a document is printed. In contrast, fundamental errors in embedded commands (e.g. line spacing) may only be detected in a batch system when the document is run through the formatter. Parallels can be drawn between document processing and program processing. A batch formatter is similar to a compiler, a WYSIWYG system is like an interpreter.

It can be argued that WYSIWYG editor/formatters are a return to presentational markup - the typewriter mode of operation. A writer is forced to be concerned with the appearance of the document rather than just its content at the time the text is being input. Additionally, WYSIWYG systems have been described as What You See Is All You've Got. Consider the problem of making global changes in a WYSIWYG system, for example modifying the spacing of long quotations from single to double. It is generally not correct to change all the single-spacing codes in the document to double-spacing codes because there may be other document components that have to remain single-spaced.

In this chapter we look at three classes of formatting system:

1. WYSIWYG
2. Batch procedural
3. Batch descriptive

The intention is to give a feel for the ways in which the different types of system operate without getting too bogged down in markup details. Furuta *et al.* [4] survey a number of systems including many of those discussed here.

7.1 WYSIWYG

In section 3.4 we briefly discussed the editor/formatters Bravo and STAR that run on Xerox workstations. In this section we will look at WordPerfect [5] and MacWrite [6]: two packages that can run on more modest personal computers. Packages such as these are updated frequently, any deficiencies noted here may well have been corrected in more recent releases.

7.1.1 WordPerfect

WordPerfect runs on micros, minis and mainframes. The discussion here is based on the author's experiences with version 5.0 running on IBM PCs and compatibles under MS-DOS.

A user enters text as if using an editor. There are reasonable initial values for left and right margins, page length and line spacing (the defaults give 1.25 inch margins on letter-size paper). At appropriate points as the user enters text, the system will insert a soft break (line break or page break); a user can force a line or page break by inserting the appropriate "hard" code.

In text formatting, a "widow" is the last line of a paragraph appearing as the first line of a page and an "orphan" is the first line of a paragraph appearing as the last on a page. With widow/orphan protection enabled, orphans and one line preceding a widow are moved to the next page.

At any time, the user can insert codes to change document parameters; the effect is seen instantly on the screen. For example, the margins can be changed resulting in a change to the positions of the soft (but not the hard) breaks. Formatting codes are normally invisible but can be revealed in a split-screen display.

WordPerfect has cut and copy facilities based on text units - sentence, paragraph and page. In detecting end-of-sentence, the software can be fooled by abbreviations, e.g. that one, and also (!) by inserts like that.

WordPerfect's abilities to handle multi-font documents depend on the printer and the printer driver. However, the typical screen can only show normal and boldened text accurately. There are similar limitations on line justification. A user can specify limits on the compression and expansion between words and characters but the justification cannot be shown on the screen.

There is an integrated spelling checker and thesaurus; the spelling checker is discussed in Chapter 10.

7.1.2 MacWrite

The main difference between WordPerfect and MacWrite is that the latter takes advantage of the MacIntosh bit-mapped screen. This hardware makes it feasible to allow graphics to be cut and pasted into a document. In addition, no matter what the selected type style and point size, appropriate representations of characters can be displayed on the screen. The user thus gets an accurate preview of the printed text. Other differences, for example the use of a mouse and pull-down menus in contrast to WordPerfect's function keys, are likely to disappear as future versions of WordPerfect appear.

7.2 Batch procedural

Because of the nature of the computing hardware and systems at the time, the earliest systems for formatting text were batch processes. Typical input was a card deck containing text cards and directive cards. The formatted document could be sent to the line printer or perhaps a typewriter-quality device. In this section we will look first at some ideas introduced in early systems, then we look at the *troff* program move on to the larger environment of Unix document processing tools and finally look at T$_E$X.

7.2.1 Early systems
First generation formatters date from the middle and late 1960s; two pioneering systems are RUNOFF [7] developed at MIT and the IBM FORMAT program [8]. RUNOFF introduced many ideas found in later systems, for example command lines beginning with a period were interspersed with the text to be formatted. RUNOFF commands were typically concerned with the physical form of the output rather than the logical components of the input. For example, it was easy to specify that the next five lines should be underlined (.SCORE 5) but not that the next five sentences should be.

FORMAT was a free-format system that distinguished between text control (e.g. tab over) and layout control (e.g. set tabs). Command words embedded in the text were responsible for text control, control cards controlled layout. Multi-column output could be generated.

A command word followed a right parenthesis and was delimited by a space. In the following example, the command word causes *underlined section* to appear underlined, then underlining is switched off, two newlines are generated, and a new paragraph started.

....)u underlined section)ullp Next paragraph begins with this ...

Lines were justified by the program inserting spaces alternately from the left and right. No hyphenation was done unless a hyphen appeared in the input. FORMAT had some features for assisting in the preparation of indexes. For example, it was possible to have the program produce an alphabetically ordered list of those words longer than three characters appearing in the text. Words could be listed with their frequency. In addition, a user could supply a list of words and have the program list the locations where each occurred.

Systems dating from the early and middle 1970s can be categorized as second generation. Typically they made use of techniques from other areas of Computer Science such as macros (see chapter 6), nested environments, conditionals, and variables. At this time, aids for writers began to appear, for example, automatic numbering of sections, footnote handling, and index construction. Examples of second generation systems are PUB [9] and *troff* [3]. *Troff* and programs based on it are widely used; derivatives for microcomputers (e.g. eroff [10]) are common. Because of this, we examine *troff* in some detail in the next section. Emerson and Paulsell [11] give detailed examples of *troff* capabilities.

7.2.2 *troff*
Troff is designed to accept input, possibly containing formatting directives, and send an appropriate stream of bytes to a phototypesetter. *Nroff* is a similar program that differs in that its output appears on the standard output as an ASCII stream that can be piped to a post-processor, viewed or

sent to a printer. As might be expected, *nroff* and *troff* have a large part of
their command languages in common. Like the first generation systems,
input is a mixture of text and directives. While *troff* commands can be
embedded in a line, most directives appear on lines by themselves and
begin with a period or quote in the first column. Kernighan and Plauger
[12, 13] describe implementations of a formatter that is a simpler version
of *nroff*.

The file listed in Fig. 7.1 contains examples of typical *nroff/troff* directives.

Figure 7.1 Text and *nroff/troff* directives

```
.nf
.na
   This first paragraph is neither filled nor justified
 so  it should appear on the output exactly as it appears
         in the source file.
.sp
.fi
The second paragraph of the document has
been preceded by a command to fill each line with as many
words as possible. If we have some long words it is possible that
hyphenation will take place (though it can be suppressed).
.sp
.ad r
     The third paragraph is preceded by a command which causes the
right margin only to be tidied, you can see the strange results when this
is formatted. This extra text at the end is designed to exaggerate the
effect a little.
.sp
.ad n
The fourth paragraph has been preceded by a command which
restores the normal alignment of margins. This results in much more
reasonable output. Once again extra text is added to ensure that the
result is large enough.
```

The output from passing this file through *troff* is shown in Fig. 7.2. This
example illustrates one of the simplest actions of a formatter, producing
filled and justified output lines from arbitrarily arranged input text. Line
filling can be switched on (fi) and off (nf); justification is termed "adjust-
ment" hence the commands for switching on (ad) and off (na).

Figure 7.2 Text generated from Fig. 7.1

This first paragraph is neither filled nor justified
so it should appear on the output exactly as it appears
    in the source file.

The second paragraph of the document has been preceded by a command
to fill each line with as many words as possible. If we have some long
words it is possible that hyphenation will take place (though it can be
suppressed).

The third paragraph is preceded by a command which causes the right
margin only to be tidied, you can see the strange results when this is
formatted. This extra text at the end is designed to exaggerate the effect a
little.

The fourth paragraph has been preceded by a command which restores the
normal alignment of margins. This results in much more reasonable
output. Once again extra text is added to ensure that the result is large
enough.

Macros Basic *troff* formatter commands are primitive; however, a user can
define and invoke macros. This can both reduce the length of the input
and make it more readable. It also allows the user to identify the logical
elements of the text; for example, macro call .pp could precede a paragraph, macro call .qu a quotation and so on. Appropriate directives are in
the replacement text in the macro definition.

Figure 7.3 contains text with macro definitions and calls. A macro
definition begins with .de and ends with a line containing two periods. In
this example we define four macros: for a new paragraph (pp), for a sub-
heading (sh), for the beginning of an indented section (se), and for the end
of a section (es). The sub-heading macro takes a single parameter - the
text of the heading - \\\$1 indicates its substitution point in the replace-
ment text. The output when Fig. 7.3 is run through *troff* is shown in Fig.
7.4.

Font control Because it is designed to drive a typesetter rather than be a
general filter, the principal capabilities that *troff* has in addition to the *nroff*
ones are selection of fonts and character size. Figure 7.5 contains *troff*
input with some examples of these additional commands. The size of the
characters in *points* (1 inch is slightly more than 72 points) can be changed
by means of a .ps command or by embedding a \s command in the text.
Macro WW in our example takes size as parameter. We can change font
in a similar way by using the .ft command or by embedding \f in a line.
Fonts available include Roman (R), italic (I), bold (B) and special. This

Figure 7.3 Macro definitions and calls

```
.de pp
.br
.sp 2
.ti 7
..
.de sh
.sp 2
.ul
\\$1
..
.de se
.sp 2
.in +6
.ti -4
..
.de es
.sp
.in -6
..
.sh "A test"
.np
This is only a test. Had this been real troff input you would see
instructions for doing real stuff.
.se
1. This is section one. It will have a sub-section coming up.
.se
1.1 And this should be indented, user has to put his/her own section
number in though
.es
Now we should be back to one level of indentation. The same as the line
which has "This is section one" on it.
.es
Here back to normal?
```

last is a set of characters useful for math notation and special purposes.
The output generated by Fig. 7.5 is shown in Fig. 7.6.

Diversions In both *nroff* and *troff* we can divert text into the replacement
text of macros to be called later. Footnotes can be handled in this way.
Another use of this capability is a macro that processes headings. The
heading macro could both display the heading and append to a macro a
copy of the heading and the current page number. At the end of the text, a

Figure 7.4 Output resulting from Fig. 7.3

A test This is only a test. Had this been real troff input you would see instructions for doing real stuff.

    1. This is section one. It will have a sub-section coming up.

        1.1 And this should be indented, user has to put his/her own section number in though

        Now we should be back to one level of indentation. The same as the line which has "This is section one" on it.

Here back to normal?

call of this macro generates a table of contents.

    Figure 7.7 lists a definition of a heading macro XX. It takes three parameters: the first is the level of the heading (0,1,2, or 3; where 0 is most important) the second parameter is the section number and the third is the title of the section. Typical calls of the macro are:

    .XX 0 5 "The relational model"
    .XX 1 5.1 "Relational Algebra"
    .XX 2 5.1.3 "Join operators"
    .XX 3 "Examples of equijoin"

Text is appended to macro CO, a typical initialization of which is shown in Fig. 7.8 (the .ta command establishes tab settings). Figure 7.9 lists a small test file that includes calls to XX. Appendix B shows the results of passing this file and the definitions of Figs. 7.7 and 7.8. through *nroff*.

    Several macro packages have been developed for *nroff/troff*. The *man* package is used for formatting on-line manual pages. More general packages are: the *mm* (memorandum macros) package, used as standard for Bell labs documentation, the *ms* package [14] and the *me* package from UC Berkeley [15]. The last two are oriented towards the preparation of technical documents. A macro package is invoked by means of a flag, for example:

troff -me filename ...

This causes *troff* to read the contents of the *me* package before the normal input. In the next section we look briefly at the *ms* macros.

Figure 7.5 Input for *troff*

```
.de WW
.sp 2
.ps \\$1
\\$1 point: Pack my box with five dozen liquor jugs
..
.sp 3
Point sizes
.WW 12
.WW 8
.WW 20
.ps 10
.sp 2
We can change size inside a line too \s12 like \s8 this \s20 see?\s10
.sp 2
Fonts
.de Fn
.sp 2
.ft \\$1
this text produced using .Fn \\$1
.br
abcdefghijklmnopqrstuvwxyz
.br
ABCDEFGHIJKLMNOPQRSTUVWXYZ
..
.Fn B
.Fn I
.sp 3
.ft R
We \fBcan \fRchange font \fIinside \fRa line too!
.sp 2
There is a fourth (special) font available. Let's see what it can do. An
example from the manual:
.sp
.ce
\(*S (\(*a \(mu \(*b) \(- > \(if
```

The ms macro package Identifiers of built-in *nroff*/*troff* commands and
variables consist of two lower case letters; *ms* macro names consist of
upper case letters to avoid clashes. Macro calls typically delimit logical
components of a text. For example, PP introduces a paragraph, FS and FE
delimit a footnote, NH n is a numbered heading at level n. In the latter
case, variables keep track of the appropriate section number to generate.

Figure 7.6 Output from the input of Fig. 7.5

Point sizes

12 point: Pack my box with five dozen liquor jugs

8 point: Pack my box with five dozen liquor jugs

20 point: Pack my box with five dozen liquor jugs

We can change size inside a line too like this see?

Fonts

this text produced using .Fn B
abcdefghijklmnopqrstuvwxyz
ABCDEFGHIJKLMNOPQRSTUVWXYZ

this text produced using .Fn I
abcdefghijklmnopqrstuvwxyz
ABCDEFGHIJKLMNOPQRSTUVWXYZ

We **can** change font *inside* a line too!

There is a fourth (special) font available. Let's see what it can do. An example from the manual:

$$\Sigma\,(\alpha \times \beta) \to \infty$$

In order that certain registers are initialized, a call of an *ms* macro must precede the first line of normal text.

Sections of text can be identified as "displays" (not to be formatted) and "keeps" (to be kept on the same page). A "floating keep" may be moved down through the text to avoid leaving empty space at the foot of a page. This last capability has been used in this text; the macros shown in Fig. 7.10 are used to delimit figures in the source file. Fs (figure start) opens a keep and a display and inserts the caption; Fe (figure end) closes the keep and display after the body of the figure. The reader may notice,

Figure 7.7 Heading macro

```
.de XX
.if \\$1=0 \{\
.   ce
.   ul
Chapter \\$2  \\$3
.   ls 2
.   nh
.   sp 3  \}
.if \\$1=1 \{\
.   sp 3
.   ne 4
\\$2 \\$3
.   sp 1  \}
.if \\$1=2 \{\
.   sp 2
.   ne 4
\\$2 \\$3
.   sp 1  \}
.if \\$1=3 \{\
.   sp 2
.   ne 4
.   ul
\\$2
.   sp 1  \}
.if \\$1<3 \{\
.da CO
.if \\$1=0 \{.sp 2\}
.if \\$1=0 \{Ch \\$2 \\$3  \\a \\n% \}
.if \\$1=0 \{.sp 1\}
.if \\$1=1 \{ \t \\$2 \\$3  \\a \\n% \}
.if \\$1=2 \{ \t \t \\$2 \\$3  \\a \\n% \}
.br
.di
\}
.if \\$1=1 \{ .ti 5 \}
.if \\$1=2 \{ .ti 5 \}
.if \\$1=3 \{ .ti 5 \}
..
```

particularly in this chapter, that if there are many floating keeps, some of them may float quite a distance down the text.

Figure 7.8 Initialization of macro for diversions

```
.de CO
.bp
.ta 7 12 52R
.nf
.na
Table of Contents \t Page
.ls 1
..
```

Figure 7.9 Text file with calls to heading macros

```
.XX 0 3 "Some more adventures with macros"
```
This is the introduction, it comes before all the text in the chapter. It
should be quite long enough now to test the macros.
```
.XX 1 1.1 "Part 1"
```
This is a section of text. We might need quite a lot of text to test the
macros, at least so one of the headings appears on page 2. Not much of
it will make any sense at all though.
```
.XX 2 1.1.1 "Level 2 sub-head"
```
This is really just filler to make sure that we don't have 2 headings next
to each other. Nothing bad happens if we do, it just doesn't look good.
```
.XX 3 "Level 3 sub-head"
```
We can define the XX macro to do anything we like with the parameters it
is given. One possibility is for it to put only the first 2 levels of
sub-heading into the table of contents.
```
.XX 2 1.1.2 "Level 2 sub-head"
```
Some more filler. What more can I say. Hope we are getting close to the
bottom of the page now.
```
.XX 3 "Level 3 sub-head"
```
This is text following another third level header. By now we must be on the
second page so let's throw in one last top level header
```
.XX 1 1.2 "Part 2"
```
Just a couple of lines here just so that we don't end with a header. Then
we can invoke the macro (CO) we have been appending text to all this time.
And see what's in it.
```
.CO
```

Figure 7.11 is a listing of a file (*mstest*) containing text plus calls to *ms*
macros. Macros used include: TL before the title, AU before the author,
and AB before the abstract. Appendix C contains the output from:

Figure 7.10 Figure macros

```
.de Fs
.KF
.DS L
\fBFigure \\$1\FR  \\$2
..
.de Fe
.DE
.KE
..
```

nroff -ms mstest

7.2.3 The Unix environment

In keeping with Bell Labs' philosophy, the Unix text processing environment consists of a number of interconnectable programs rather than one large one (see also the Writer's Workbench in chapter 11). Figure 7.12 shows the usual interconnection of some of the programs. It is difficult for a typical *nroff/troff* user to devise the sequence of low-level directives necessary to produce a complex object such as a table or graph. The Unix environment includes pre-processors that translate high-level descriptions of such objects into appropriate sequences of directives.[1]

Each of the pre-processors in Fig. 7.12 deals with a particular part of the input; for example, *pic* handles simple line drawings, *refer* processes references, and *tbl* handles tables. Each translates the input marked for its attention and passes the remainder of its input unchanged to the output. In theory, the pre-processors can be piped together in any order.

One advantage of dividing the functions between separate programs is that new components can be developed and plugged in, transparently replacing old ones, as long as the interfaces remain constant. In addition, depending on the run-time environment, there may be an advantage in running several small programs in tandem rather than one large one. A disadvantage of the modular approach is that a user may have to become familiar with several descriptive languages. In the following sections we look at three of the pre-processors: *refer*, *tbl* and *eqn*. See Bentley [17] for

---

1. In addition to those shown, other pre- and post-processors have been developed. For example, Buchman *et al.* [16] describe pre-processors and a post-processor than enable a user to mix left-to-right and right-to-left languages in the same document.

Figure 7.11 Text and ms macro calls

```
.TL
Some thoughts on teaching night classes
.AU
Peter Smith
.AI
Department of Computer Science
C.S.U.N., Northridge, CA 91330
.AB
Some advantages and disadvantages of night classes are presented and some
conclusions drawn.
.AE
.NH
Introduction
.PP
CSUN offers many sections of courses at night. This is so that students who work during
the day can come to school. In addition, it gives people a chance to teach part-time.
.NH
Some advantages and disadvantages of night classes
.NH 2
Advantages
.NH 3
Parking
.PP
Parking is usually easier than during the day (the most difficult time to
find a parking place is in the morning). The campus police are less likely
to come round and check decals in the dark.
.NH 3
Students
.PP
Students tend to be sleepier at night and not give you such a hard time.
However, this may mean that classes are not as lively as those during the day.
.NH 2
Disadvantages
.NH 3
Candy
.PP
The store in the student union closes around 7pm which may make it difficult
to get a quick fix of candy. Machines are available but charge outrageous prices.
.NH 3
Mountain lions
.PP
The existence of mountain lions on campus has not been proven. It is likely that this rumor
originated in one of the local colleges wishing to attract our better, but more timid, students.
.NH
Summary
.PP
On balance the availability of parking and the comparatively quiet
atmosphere at night outweighs the threat of attack from wildlife.
```

examples of *pic* picture descriptions; the line drawings in this text were
produced using *pic*.

Figure 7.12 Interconnection of Unix text formatting programs

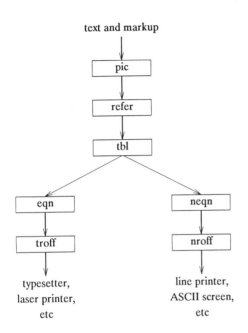

refer Authors of scholarly texts are expected to include precise references to their sources so that others may verify or criticize their work. However, two problems might arise. First, an author might not have all the required details of a particular paper or book being cited. Second, different publishing organizations have different formats for references at the end of a text and for citations in the body of the text. If a document is being prepared for two or more publications, for example an internal report, a journal paper and a conference proceedings, the author is faced with the difficulty of generating multiple versions of it.

The *refer* program solves the first problem by comparing possibly incomplete document specifications with the entries in a file of bibliographic data. If there is exactly one match, it is assumed that details of the intended document have been found. The second problem is solved by providing a number of ways in which citations can be output and by outputting reference details in the form of macro calls and assignments to string and number variables, thus enabling further customization.

Figure 7.13 shows typical entries in a bibliographic file used by *refer*. This example is an extract from the file used in preparing this text. The notation is fairly straightforward. Each line starts with a % followed by a key character (A for author, T for title, I for issuer, and so on). Blank lines

Figure 7.13 Extract from bibliographic file

%A M. Campbell-Kelly
%T An introduction to macros
%I Macdonald
%C London
%D 1973

%T Webster's New World Misspellers Dictionary
%I Simon and Schuster
%D 1983
%C New York

%A J. Bentley
%T Programming pearls: a spelling checker
%J Communications of the ACM
%V 28
%N 5
%D May 1985
%P 456-462

separate entries. The *indxbib* utility can be used to create indexes into the bibliographic file or an inverted file. If the bibliographic file is large, the indexes speed up searching considerably.

Figure 7.14 shows the section of the inverted file corresponding to the bibliographic entries of Fig. 7.13. The key comprises the name of the bibliographic file, the byte address where the entry begins, and its length (in bytes). Index fields are mapped to lower case and truncated at 6 characters. Common words and numbers (other than 20th century dates) are discarded.

Figure 7.14 Fragment of inverted file

biblio:1775,82 campbe kelly introd macros macdon london 1973
biblio:1857,89 webste world misspe dictio simon schust 1983 york
biblio:1946,120 bentle progra pearls spelli checke commun acm 1985

The bibliographic file can be searched both in an interactive manner and by *refer* processing embedded citations.

The *lookbib* program takes a list of keywords from the standard input and outputs all the bibliographic entries that contain all the keywords. If there are no indexes, it calls *indxbib* to create an inverted file.

Figure 7.15 Input to refer

```
.PP
This is a test of the refer program it should put in
references. Let's see if this one works. We will try and pick up the paper
by Kernighan
.[
kernighan document preparation
.]
on document preparation. Now try and get the book he wrote
.[ (
programming language kernighan
.])
on C. Just to see that refer really works we will try for a paper by
Deutsch about editors.
.[ [
deutsch editor
.]]
.PP
The refer program can be called with various flags. One (-e) causes
references found to be collected and only inserted into the text when a
$LIST$ indicator is encountered. In this way we can form a bibliography.
Here's another reference to the C book
.[ [
language 1978 ritchie
.]]
using different keys.
.PP
The refer program does reasonable things given a list of references. For
example, there are a couple of papers about B-trees
.[
B-trees Held
.]
.[
Comer B-tree
.]
which it should find. Finally, as
.[ Ref.
waltz goodman natural language
.]
comes out, let's see what it looks like.
.[
$LIST$
.]
```

A citation for *refer* is also a list of keywords, set off typically between
lines of the form .[and .]. When the program encounters such a list, it
checks that the citation matches exactly one entry in the bibliographic file.
If there are multiple matches or none at all it outputs a warning. It is a
good idea to overspecify a reference, putting in more than the minimum

number of keywords to identify it uniquely in the current file. In this way, there is less chance of later additions to the file making the reference ambiguous. *Refer* replaces the citation by an appropriate string and creates a sequence of macro calls and assignments of the bibliographic elements to string and number variables. The user has many options as to the form of the reference "number" and the location, format, and ordering of the bibliography. Figure 7.15 lists a file (*refertest*) containing text and typical incomplete citations. Figure 7.16 contains the output from the command:

refer -e -P -p biblio refertest | troff -ms

Figure 7.16 Formatted bibliographic data

This is a test of the refer program it should put in references. Let's see if this one works. We will try and pick up the paper by Kernighan[1] on document preparation. Now try and get the book he wrote (2) on C. Just to see that refer really works we will try for a paper by Deutsch about editors [3].

The refer program can be called with various flags. One (-e) causes references found to be collected and only inserted into the text when a $LIST$ indicator is encountered. In this way we can form a bibliography. Here's another reference to the C book [2] using different keys.

The refer program does reasonable things given a list of references. For example, there are a couple of papers about B-trees[4,5] which it should find. Finally, as Ref. 6 comes out, lets see what it looks like.

References

1. B. W. Kernighan, M. E. Lesk, and J. F. Ossanna, "UNIX Time-Sharing System: Document Preparation," *Bell System Technical Journal*, vol. 57, no. 6, pp. 2115-2135, 1978.

2. B. W. Kernighan and D. M. Ritchie, *The C Programming Language*, Prentice-Hall, Englewood Cliffs, New Jersey, 1978.

3. P. Deutsch and B. W. Lampson, "An online editor," *Communications of the ACM*, vol. 10, no. 12, pp. 793-799, 803, December 1967.

4. G. D. Held and M. R. Stonebraker, "B-trees re-examined," *Communications of the ACM*, vol. 21, no. 2, pp. 139-143, February 1978.

5. D. Comer, "The ubiquitous B-tree," *ACM Computing Surveys*, vol. 11, no. 2, pp. 121-137, June 1979.

6. D. L. Waltz and B. A. Goodman, "Writing a natural language data base system," *Proceedings of the Fifth International Joint Conference on Artificial Intelligence*, pp. 144-150, Cambridge, Mass., August 22-25, 1977.

The -e flag causes *refer* to collect bibliographic date and output it at the end of the output or when $LIST$ is encountered within citation delimiters. Without this flag, bibliographic information is inserted as footnotes. The -P flag causes a citation to appear correctly before rather than after punctuation. The -p flag allows a user to specify a personal file of information to be searched (*biblio* in this case) either in addition to or as well as the default file.

Citations are, for the most part, converted directly into appropriate text. Figure 7.17 shows the output from *refer* for the first reference in the example of Fig. 7.16.

Figure 7.17 refer output

```
.ds [F 1
.]-
.ds [T U\s-2NIX\s0 Time-Sharing System: Document Preparation
.ds [K unix bstj
.ds [A B. W. Kernighan
.as [A ", M. E. Lesk
.as [A ", and J. F. Ossanna
.ds [J Bell Sys. Tech. J.
.ds [V 57
.ds [N 6
.ds [P 2115-2135
.nr [P 1
.ds [D 1978
.nr [T 0
.nr [A 0
.nr [O 0
.][ 1 journal-article
```

While the user is free to write his or her own definitions for the macros called here (]- and][), a macro package such as *ms* (see 7.2.2) contains definitions that are appropriate for most circumstances. The macros are responsible for formatting the bibliography. They determine, for example, whether journal volume and number appear as "Vol. X, No. Y" or as "X(Y)", and whether the date appears in parentheses. On the other hand, the *refer* program is responsible, for example, for determining whether "&" or "and" is used in a list of authors.

Note in Fig. 7.16 that the default citation format, as evidenced by the first example, is a superscripted integer. We can change this, as shown by the second citation, if we use different delimiters for the partial citation in the source file. If we only redefine the opening delimiter, the closing one becomes null (see the final citation in the example). In the third citation *refer* recognized the sentence delimiter and arranged for the citation to appear before the period. The references to the C book illustrate how two or more citations to the same work, even if they use different keys, collapse into one bibliographic entry. A list of citations (to B-tree papers) is also handled in a reasonable way. The "internal" delimiters must be just .[and .].

Figure 7.18 shows the output from the command

refer -e -s -l4,2 -P -p biblio refertest | troff -ms

Figure 7.18 Formatted bibliographic data

This is a test of the refer program it should put in references. Let's see if this one works. We will try and pick up the paper by Kernighan[Kern78a] on document preparation. Now try and get the book he wrote (Kern78b) on C. Just to see that refer really works we will try for a paper by Deutsch about editors [Deut67a].

The refer program can be called with various flags. One (-e) causes references found to be collected and only inserted into the text when a $LIST$ indicator is encountered. In this way we can form a bibliography. Here's another reference to the C book [Kern78b] using different keys.

The refer program does reasonable things given a list of references. For example, there are a couple of papers about B-trees[Held78a, Come79a] which it should find. Finally, as Ref. Walt77a comes out, lets see what it looks like.

References

Come79a.
  D. Comer, "The ubiquitous B-tree," *ACM Computing Surveys*, vol. 11, no. 2, pp. 121-137, June 1979.

Deut67a.
  P. Deutsch and B. W. Lampson, "An online editor," *Communications of the ACM*, vol. 10, no. 12, pp. 793-799, 803, December 1967.

Held78a.
  G. D. Held and M. R. Stonebraker, "B-trees re-examined," *Communications of the ACM*, vol. 21, no. 2, pp. 139-143, February 1978.

Kern78a.
  B. W. Kernighan, M. E. Lesk, and J. F. Ossanna, "UNIX Time-Sharing System: Document Preparation," *Bell System Technical Journal*, vol. 57, no. 6, pp. 2115-2135, 1978.

Kern78b.
  B. W. Kernighan and D. M. Ritchie, *The C Programming Language*, Prentice-Hall, Englewood Cliffs, New Jersey, 1978.

Walt77a.
  D. L. Waltz and B. A. Goodman, "Writing a natural language data base system," *Proceedings of the Fifth International Joint Conference on Artificial Intelligence*, pp. 144-150, Cambridge, Mass., August 22-25, 1977.

The source file is the same as in our previous example but here we invoked *refer* with two additional flags. The -s flag indicates that the bibliography is to be sorted by the last name of the principal author. The -l flag controls the format of the citations: in this example a citation comprises 4 characters from the author's name and 2 from the year. (This is not really appropriate for the last citation in our example.) Notice that a letter is appended to the year. This is to distinguish between two or more works written in the same year having the same (principal) author. In our example, this produces different tags for the book and the paper authored by Kernighan.

The *refer* program provides a very simple mechanism for processing citations and bibliographies; its output can be tailored for many different bibliographic formats and its existence encourages the maintenance of shareable bibliographic files.

tbl Tables are two-dimensional structures; producing a nicely formatted table is non-trivial if the entries vary in size or the table has an irregular shape. The *tbl* program [18] translates table descriptions written in a high-level notation into sequences of *nroff/troff* directives. Other input is passed through unaltered. In this section we briefly examine some of the capabilities of *tbl*; see Ref. 18 for more details.

A table description is delimited by .TS and .TE directives and has two parts: a description of the table format and a listing of the table contents. The description of the table format first specifies options for the table as a whole and then information about the format of table lines. Consider the example of Fig 7.19 which lists the contents of a file (*tbl1*) containing a table description taken from Ref. 18.

Options for the table as a whole are listed on a single line delimited by a semi-colon. In this example we want the table centered and enclosed in a box. We also indicate that we will use ">" to separate fields in the data; by default the tab character serves this purpose.

Line format directives are delimited by a period. Each of the lines in this section describes the format of a table line, except that the last description line is used as often as necessary to complete the table. In the example of Fig. 7.19 we indicate that the first line is to be a centered entry (c) spanning (s) three columns. The second line is to be three centered entries separated by vertical bars (|). The third and subsequent lines are to have two left-justified entries (l) and a numeric entry (n). Numeric entries are aligned on the units digits.

In the data section, each line corresponds to a line in the table. The ">" character specified in the global options section is used to separate fields. A line containing only an equals sign or an underscore generates a double or a single line the width of the table. An equals sign or an underscore appearing in place of a table entry results in an appropriate line filling the

Figure 7.19 Table description for *tbl*

```
.TS
box,center,tab( > );
c s s
c |c |c
l |l |n.
Major New York Bridges
=
Bridge > Designer > Length

Brooklyn > J. A. Roebling > 1595
Manhattan > G. Lindenthal > 1470
Williamsburg > L. L. Buck > 1600

Queensborough > Palmer & > 1182
> Hornbostel

> > 1380
Triborough > O.H. Ammann > _
> > 383

Bronx Whitestone > O.H. Ammann > 2300
Throgs Neck > O.H. Ammann > 1800

George Washington > O.H. Ammann > 3500
.TE
```

entry only.

The output from the command

                    tbl tbl1 | troff

is shown in Fig. 7.20.

The .TS and .TE lines are passed unaltered through to the output and can thus be used to trigger macro calls. For example, we can add a label and a caption to the .TE line thus:

                .TE 12.6 "1930-50 Population changes"

Now a macro such as the following:

Figure 7.20 Output generated from Fig. 7.19

Major New York Bridges		
Bridge	Designer	Length
Brooklyn	J. A. Roebling	1595
Manhattan	G. Lindenthal	1470
Williamsburg	L. L. Buck	1600
Queensborough	Palmer & Hornbostel	1182
Triborough	O.H. Ammann	1380
		383
Bronx Whitestone	O.H. Ammann	2300
Throgs Neck	O.H. Ammann	1800
George Washington	O.H. Ammann	3500

```
.de TE
.ce 2
Table \\$1
\\$2
.sp 2
.da CO
Table \\$1 \\n%
.br
.da
..
```

causes the table to be followed by a centered label and caption and also appends the label and current page number to a table of contents.

Tbl allows a user to redefine the format of a table by means of the .T& directive. Figure 7.21 contains an example description (from Ref. 18) in which this is done twice. The \^ notation in the data indicates that the table entry immediately above extends into this row. Figure 7.22 shows the output after Fig. 7.21 has been passed through *tbl* and *troff*.

Our examples have illustrated only some of the capabilities of *tbl* but they should be sufficient to indicate the ease with which tables can be described.

eqn Mathematical notation is more complex than normal text and more difficult to set in type. There are several reasons for this. First, there are conventions as to where certain fonts (roman, bold, italic) are used. Second, there is a greater variety of character sizes (for example, super and subscripts) and the size of some characters (for example, summation and integral signs) depends on other text components. Third, different

Figure 7.21 Table with format redefined

```
.TS
box,tab(>);
c s s s.
Composition of Foods
.T&
c |c s s
c |c s s
c |c |c |c.
Food>Percent by Weight
\^>
\^>Protein>Fat>Carbo-
\^>\^>\^>hydrate
.T&
l |n |n |n.
Apples>.4>.5>13.0
Halibut>18.4>5.2>...
Lima beans>7.5>.8>22.0
Milk>3.3>4.0>5.0
Mushrooms>3.5>.4>6.0
Rye bread>9.0>.6>52.7
.TE
```

Figure 7.22 Output derived from Fig. 7.21

Composition of Foods			
Food	Percent by Weight		
	Protein	Fat	Carbo-hydrate
Apples	.4	.5	13.0
Halibut	18.4	5.2	...
Lima beans	7.5	.8	22.0
Milk	3.3	4.0	5.0
Mushrooms	3.5	.4	6.0
Rye bread	9.0	.6	52.7

alphabets are used (Greek, Roman and special symbols). Finally, there is the two-dimensional nature of objects such as matrices and sets of equations.

The *eqn* program [19] is a pre-processor designed to make it easy to include mathematical notation in a document, either in-line or set off in displays. The program converts mathematical notation, described in a simple language, into appropriate *troff* directives (*neqn* is a similar preprocessor for *nroff*).

The designers of *eqn* envisaged a typical user reading from a handdrafted version of the intended mathematical notation and entering a description of it on a conventional keyboard. Because no special keys are assumed, symbols have to be spelled out, e.g. "sum", "pi", "int". The descriptive language is small (the authors claim that it can be learned in an hour or so), is defined by a context free grammar of about 70 rules and has about 50 special keywords. Semantic rules define precedence and associativity of operators.

Figure 7.23 is a listing of file *eqn1*. If we wish the mathematical notation to be set off from the surrounding text we enclose it between .EQ and .EN directives. Like .TS and .TE these two lines are passed through to *troff* where they may trigger calls to macros to offset the notation. We can also include notation in-line as shown in the first example. We specify the delimiters for in-line notation with the *delim* directive. In our case, text between $ and $ delimiters is translated by *eqn*.

The first part of the input shows how super and subscripting work. Following that is a series of expressions that illustrate how spaces are treated as symbol delimiters by *eqn* and otherwise discarded. A visible space character (ˉ) can be used to force a space.

The EQ macro can take parameters enabling equations to be labelled in the usual way. Some special symbols (such as integral signs and square roots) are supported and can be referenced by simple mnemonics. The size of the symbol is adjusted to fit the following text.

Figure 7.24 contains the output from the command

eqn eqn1 | troff -ms

Note how *eqn* uses spaces to delimit symbols (an unwary user may find closing parentheses attached to preceding characters) and uses braces to change precedence. Equation numbers are right justified by the EQ macro in the *ms* package.

Figure 7.25 lists a file (*eqn2*) that uses some of the two-dimensional capabilities of *eqn*.

We can line up a series of expressions by marking a location in the first one and specifying which location in the others should fall vertically underneath it. However, *eqn* is a one-pass process and the user is responsible for ensuring that there is enough horizontal room for successful alignment.

Matrices are specified column by column. The manual warns users to be very careful to have the same number of objects in each column. The user can specify whether the columns are to be centered, left-justified or right-

Figure 7.23 Contents of file eqn1

```
.EQ
delim $$
.EN
```
This is an example of the use of the "eqn" program. We can include quite
complicated mathematical bits and pieces, in with normal text or set off in
displays.
```
.sp 1
```
Here is some in-line stuff $T sup 5 ˜ = ˜ X sub 1 + ˜X sub 2 + ... + ˜X sub k .$
That illustrates super- and sub-scripting. It also shows the need to be
careful with spaces and bracketing. Consider the following attempts to get
```
.sp
.EQ
```

˜˜˜˜{a˜ + ˜b} over 2c˜ = ˜1

```
.EN
```
Braces allow us to modify priorities. A tilde (˜) is a visible space.
```
.EQ
```

a + b over 2c = 1
a + b over 2c = 1
˜˜˜˜(a + b) over 2c = 1
˜˜˜˜(a˜ + ˜b) over 2c˜ = ˜1
˜˜˜˜{a˜ + ˜b} over 2c˜ = ˜1

```
.EN
```
The next example illustrates the equation numbering option handled by the
ms macro definition of EQ.
```
.EQ I  (3.1a)
```

t = x sup 2 + y sub k

```
.EN
```
Finally, some of the special symbols.
```
.EQ
```

1 over sqrt { ax sup 2 + bx + c }

```
.EN
.EQ
```

prod from k = i to k = n x sub k˜ = ˜ int from i = 1 to i = b f(x)

```
.EN
```

justified. Piles are defined in a similar way. Figure 7.26 shows the result of
processing file *eqn2* through *eqn* and sending the result to *troff*. Note how
the size of the curly brace in the pile is adjusted to suit the pile.

Figure 7.24 Math notation

This is an example of the use of the "eqn" program. We can include quite complicated mathematical bits and pieces, in with normal text or set off in displays.

Here is some in-line stuff $T^5 = X_1 + X_2 + ... + X_k$. That illustrates super- and sub-scripting. It also shows the need to be careful with spaces and bracketing. Consider the following attempts to get

$$\frac{a + b}{2c} = 1$$

Braces allow us to modify priorities. A tilde (˜) is a visible space.

$$\frac{a+b}{2c} = 1a + \frac{b}{2c} = 1 \quad (a + \frac{b)}{2c} = 1 \quad (a + \frac{b)}{2c} = 1 \quad \frac{a + b}{2c} = 1$$

The next example illustrates the equation numbering option handled by the ms macro definition of EQ.

$$t = x^2 + y_k \qquad\qquad (3.1a)$$

Finally, some of the special symbols.

$$\frac{1}{\sqrt{ax^2 + bx + c}}$$

$$\prod_{k=i}^{k=n} x_k = \int_{i=1}^{i=b} f(x)$$

Appropriate use is made of italic fonts.

We can have a table containing mathematical notation. In that case the source file would be processed by both *tbl* and *eqn*. The user guide recommends that *tbl* be run first. Figure 7.27 is a listing of a file (*tbleqn*) containing a description of a table of information about integral approximations. Figure 7.28 shows the output from

tbl tbleqn | eqn | ditroff

7.2.4 TₑX

In some ways TₑX is *troff* taken to extremes. A TₑX user can exercise very close control over the printed form of a document. TₑX is "intended for the publication of beautiful books – and especially for books that contain a lot of mathematics" [20 p. 1]. The development of TₑX was motivated by Knuth perceiving a degradation in journal print quality and problems with producing the second edition of Volume 2 in his Art of Computer Programming series. TₑX enables users to be concerned about low levels of detail of the appearance of the output document. "With TₑX the goal is to

Figure 7.25 Contents of file eqn2

It is possible to "mark" parts of an equation and to have subsequent lines
lined up. This is demonstrated in the following examples.
.EQ I (12.a)
x sup i sup 2˜-˜y sub i sup 2˜ + ˜z sub i sup 3˜mark = ˜t sup n
.EN
.EQ I (12.b)
x˜ + ˜y ˜lineup = ˜ 2
.EN
.EQ I (12.c)
x˜lineup = ˜1
.EN
.sp 1
It is possible to display matrices quite easily - need to take care that
there are the same number of elements in each column.
.EQ
matrix {
  ccol {x sub i above y sub i}
  ccol {x sup 2 above y˜ + ˜x}
  ccol {a˜-˜b above 4809}
}
.EN
An extension of this idea allows one to build piles, in the example below
the left hand one is right-justified and the right hand one is left-justified!
.EQ
sign (x)˜ = ˜
    left {
    rpile { 1 above 0 above -1}
    ˜˜˜ lpile   {if˜x>0 above if˜x=0 above if˜x<0}
.EN

produce the finest quality; this requires more attention to detail" [20 p. 4].
TeX is notable for its conceptual model and for the innovative algorithms
it uses in solving various formatting problems. As with *troff*, many users
may prefer to use a macro package rather than raw TeX commands.
LATeX [21] is one of the most widely used.

Conceptual model The conceptual model behind TeX is one of boxes and
glue. A box contains an object such as a character, a word, a line or a
page. The alignment of two boxes produces a box that encloses them. The
space between boxes contains glue. A particular element of glue has both
a natural size and stretchability and compressibility coefficients. For
example, we can specify that the glue between sentences is more

Figure 7.26 Math notation

It is possible to "mark" parts of an equation and to have subsequent lines lined up. This is demonstrated in the following examples.

$$x^{t^2} - y_i^2 + z_i^3 = t^n \qquad\qquad (12.a)$$

$$x + y = 2 \qquad\qquad (12.b)$$

$$x = 1 \qquad\qquad (12.c)$$

It is possible to display matrices quite easily - need to take care that there are the same number of elements in each column.

$$\begin{matrix} x_i & x^2 & a - b \\ y_i & y + x & 4809 \end{matrix}$$

An extension of this idea allows one to build piles, in the example below the left hand one is right-justified and the right hand one is left-justified!

$$sign(x) = \begin{cases} 1 & \text{if } x > 0 \\ 0 & \text{if } x = 0 \\ -1 & \text{if } x < 0 \end{cases}$$

stretchable than that between words. Now when we stretch a line to right justify it, TeX will tend to increase any space between sentences more than the spaces between words.

Algorithms TeX has noteworthy algorithms for hyphenation and for finding the best points at which to break a paragraph into lines. The latter can also be applied to find the best points at which to paginate a document. We consider the hyphenation algorithm in more detail in Chapter 9 and look at the line-breaking problem here.

One strategy for formatting a paragraph is to read in as many words as possible into a line buffer, output it, then process the next linefull. Proceed in this way until the end of the paragraph. However, this approach (used by *troff* for example) may result in a wide variety of line lengths in the paragraph. This means either a very ragged right margin or, if the lines are right-justified, in widely differing amounts of white space from one line to another.

The algorithm used by TeX takes a paragraph-wide view. It reads the whole paragraph, determines the best points at which to break it into lines, then outputs the lines. Knuth and Plass [22] describe the way in which the best break-points are determined and how TeX's conceptual model can solve related problems such as forcing a page to end at a certain word and setting an index.

TeX first determines the location of the feasible break-points. A break-point is feasible if the text from the beginning of the paragraph to the point can be set and not exceed certain badness criteria. The feasible break-

Figure 7.27 Table with math notation

```
.EQ
delim @@
.EN
.TS
box,center,tab( > );
c s s.
Approximation of Integrals

.T&
c |c |c
c |c |c.
> >
> >
> Mid-point > @ h˜times˜sum from i=0 to n-1 ˜f(x sub i + h over 2 )@
> >
> >[ h = (b-a)/n ]
@ int from a to b f(x) @ > _ > _
> >
> >
> Trapezium > @h over 2˜times˜sum from i=0 to n-1 f(x sub i ) + f(x sub i+1 )@
> >
> >[ h = (b-a)/n ]
> >
.TE
```

points can be represented by a network in which the value on an edge joining two break-points is the number of "demerits" earned by the line
between them. Demerits are a function of the way in which the line's set
length differs from its natural length and certain properties of the line
break-point (e.g. a hyphenated line following another is considered very
bad). The problem of finding the optimum break-points reduces to the
problem of finding the shortest path through the network.

Additional sophistication is possible. For example, when computing the
score of a line, TEX can take into account properties of the preceding line.
Thus, for example, a line may have more demerits the more its natural
length differs from that of the previous line. The idea here is to avoid having a loosely set line follow a tightly set line. The network processing is
more complex but results look better.

TEX users expect to be able to direct the detailed operation of the formatter. As we saw at the beginning of the chapter, another approach is for
the user to describe the components of the document and let the

Figure 7.28 Output generated from Fig. 7.27

Approximation of Integrals		
$\int\limits_{a}^{b} f(x)$	Mid-point	$h \times \sum\limits_{i=0}^{n-1} f(x_i + \dfrac{h}{2})$ $[\, h = (b\text{-}a)/n \,]$
	Trapezium	$\dfrac{h}{2} \times \sum\limits_{i=0}^{n-1} f(x_i) + f(x_{i+1})$ $[\, h = (b\text{-}a)/n \,]$

formatting environment determine how different types of component are presented. We look at these *descriptive* systems next.

7.3 Batch descriptive

Earlier, we discussed advantages of a user describing the logical components of a document rather than issuing directives to the formatter. Here we look at the Scribe document compiler and SGML.

7.3.1 Scribe

Scribe [23] is designed for users who, for the most part, wish to leave low-level details of document format to the system; thus it is at the other end of the spectrum from TEX. Rather than giving low-level positioning details of how a document is to appear, Scribe users identify the logical components of the text. Scribe uses a database of "document format definitions" which contains rules for formatting particular types of document. This approach greatly increases the portability of documents across systems and printing devices. Scribe knows about the capabilities of printing devices and will do the best it can given the capabilities of the available device. For example, headings may appear in large letters on a laser printer and centered in capitals on a daisy wheel printer.

Figure 7.29 contains an example input to Scribe (taken from Ref. 23) and Fig. 7.30 shows the corresponding output. Note in Fig. 7.29 how the user is concerned solely with the logical components of the document and not with aspects of the printed form such as margins, centering and indentations.

Figure 7.29 Scribe input © Brian Reid

```
@Make(Wedding Program)
@Style(Font "Times Roman 10")
@begin(Introductory)
The Marriage of Loretta Rose Guarino and Brian Keith Reid
Saturday, May 12, 1979
The Church of St. Michael and All Angels,     Tucson, Arizona
@Separator()
@end(Introductory)
@Heading(Voluntary)
@Begin(Verse)
@i[Siciliano], from @i[Sonata #2 for Flute and Keyboard], J. S. Bach
@i[Prelude in Classic Style], Gordon Young
@i[Andante], from @i[Organ Concerto in F. Major], G. F. Handel
@end(Verse)
@Heading(Processional)
@begin(Verse)
@i[Adagio in A Minor], from the @i[Toccata, Adagio, and Fugue in C Major], J. S. Bach
@i[Rigaudon], Andre Campra
@end(Verse)
The text for the Marriage Ceremony may
be found in the @i[Book of Common Prayer] beginning on page 423.
@Heading(The Invocation@PageNum[p. 423])
@Heading(The Ministry of the Word@PageNum{p. 425})
@SubHeading(The Old Testament@>Tobit 8:5-8@\)
@SubHeading(The New Testament@>I Corinthians 13:1-13@\)
@SubHeading(Hymn 363)
@SubHeading(The Gospel@>John 15:9-12@\)
@SubHeading(Homily@>Fr. John Fowler)
@Heading(The Marriage@PageNum[p. 427])
@SubHeading(The Exchange of Vows)
@SubHeading(The Prayers)
@Heading(The Blessing of the Marriage@PageNum[p. 430])
@SubHeading(The Blessing)
@SubHeading(The Peace)
@Heading(The Holy Communion@PageNum[p. 361])
@SubHeading(The Great Thanksgiving)
@SubHeading(The Breaking of the Bread)
@SubHeading(The Prayer of Thanksgiving@>p. 432)
@SubHeading(Benediction and Dismissal)
@Heading(Processional)
@begin(verse)
@i[Toccata], from @i[Symphony #5 for Organ], C. M. Widor
@end(verse)
```

Environments The document type specified by the user provides a global environment of attributes for the document. Within the document, a user may establish local environments that may be nested. The definition of each of the built-in environments consists of a list of attribute-value pairs. Generally, a nested environment inherits from the outer level the values of those attributes not explicitly given values in its specification.

In case a user does not like the built-in environments, Scribe provides mechanisms for modifying them, either locally or globally. Figure 7.31(a) shows the built-in definition of Itemize (for itemized lists, from Ref. 24). Figure 7.31(b) shows the delimiters for an itemized list that has the same attributes as the original except that the "spread" (extra inter-line spacing) is 0. The modification of Fig. 7.31(b) is local, Fig. 7.32 shows what we

Figure 7.30 Output generated by Scribe from Fig. 7.29 ⊚ Brian Reid

The Marriage of Loretta Rose Guarino and Brian Keith Reid
Saturday, May 12, 1979
The Church of St. Michael and All Angels,   Tucson, Arizona

∗∗∗   ∗∗∗   ∗∗∗

Voluntary
   Siciliano, from *Sonata #2 for Flute and Keyboard*, J. S. Bach
   Prelude in Classic Style, Gordon Young
   Andante, from *Organ Concerto in F. Major*, G. F. Handel

Processional
   Adagio in A Minor, from the *Toccata, Adagio, and Fugue in C Major*, J. S. Bach
   Rigaudon, Andre Campra

           The text for the Marriage Ceremony may be
           found in the *Book of Common Prayer* beginning
           on page 423.

The Invocation   p. 423

The Ministry of the Word   p. 425
   The Old Testament   Tobit 8:5-8
   The New Testament   I Corinthians 13:1-13
   Hymn 363
   The Gospel   John 15:9-12
   Homily   Fr. John Fowler

The Marriage   p. 427
   The Exchange of Vows
   The Prayers

The Blessing of the Marriage   p. 430
   The Blessing
   The Peace

The Holy Communion   p. 361
   The Great Thanksgiving
   The Breaking of the Bread
   The Prayer of Thanksgiving   p. 432
   Benediction and Dismissal

Processional
   Toccata, from *Symphony #5 for Organ*, C. M. Widor

would put at the beginning of the document file if we wished our new definition to take effect over the whole file.

Alternatively, a user can define a completely new environment. This can be done by specifying the attribute list completely (as in the built-in definition of Itemize in Fig. 7.31(a) or by specifying the difference between the new and an existing environment. Figure 7.32 shows a definition of a

Figure 7.31 Local and global environment changes

(a) @Define (Itemize, Break, Continue, Fill, LeftMargin +5,
     Indent -5, RightMargin 5, Numbered <- @,* >,
     NumberLocation lfr, Blanklines break, Spacing 1,
     Above 1, Below 1, Spread 1)

(b) @Begin(Itemize, Spread 0) ... @End(Itemize)

(c) @Modify(Itemize, Spread 0)

new environment based on Itemize. The difference between this
specification and the Modify of Fig. 31(c) is that this time the old environment definition is still available.

Figure 7.32 Definition of new environment

@Define(SpacyItemize = Itemize, Spacing 2, Above 2, Below 2, Spread 2)

Writer's Workbench features Scribe has a number of what Reid terms
"Writer's Workbench" features though these do not have anything in common with the Bell Labs product of the same name (see Chapter 11).
Among the features are citation and reference processing, cross-reference
handling and facilities for processing large texts.

Citations and References In section 7.2.3 we noted the problem of producing bibliographies in documents and saw how the Unix *refer* program
solved them. Scribe's solution is to enable users to insert bibliographic
information from external files (that can be shared between users) and to
enable both citations and references to be formatted in a variety of ways.
Scribe also knows about the formats required by certain professional
organizations.

In the text, a command of the form @cite(keyword) will initiate a search
of the bibliographic file (user-specified or default) for the entry with the
given keyword. The @cite command is replaced by an appropriate citation
and a reference is added to the bibliography. Scribe users have to know
the appropriate keyword to identify a reference whereas *refer* users can
supply a list of index terms. On the other hand, Scribe permits null citations; documents can appear in the bibliography without being cited in the
text. Scribe also enables a user to have bibliographies (under arbitrary
headings) output at more than one point in a document, for example at the
end of each chapter of a book. A bibliography will contain at least those
works cited since the preceding bibliography.

Figure 7.33 shows a typical entry in the bibliographic file. The first field is the unique key chosen by the user. This key must be known in order to retrieve the entry. The field designated "Key" is the key by which the entry is to be sorted in a sorted bibliography.

Figure 7.33 Typical entry in the Scribe bibliography database

```
@Book (ckmacro, Title = "An introduction to macros",
    Author = "Campbell-Kelly, M." Key="Campbell-Kelly",
    Series = "Macdonald/Elsevier Computer Monographs",
    Publisher = "Macdonald", Year = "1968", Address = "London")
```

Cross-referencing Cross-references in a document are phrases such as "see page 65", "see Fig. 8.9", "see section 5.1.2". References to pages are difficult to get correct when a document is formatted by a batch program because typically the user cannot know in advance the number of the page on which the target of the reference will be placed. Even references to figures and sections may be awkward to determine if such objects are numbered automatically by the formatter. Scribe users can embed (unique) labels in the source text and have references to them translated into, for example, page or section numbers.

There are two types of label depending on whether you want the location of the object or its number (e.g. a figure or footnote number). Locations are labelled with @Label(label) and Scribe associates the current page number and section number with the label. The association produced by @Tag(label) depends on the type of object tagged, for example, a figure, an element in an enumerated list, or a footnote.

There are two types of reference. @Pageref(label) is replaced by the page number associated with the label and @Ref(label) is replaced by the other number (section, figure, list element, footnote and so on).

What about forward references? As the text is compiled, Scribe generates formatted text and, if necessary, updates an auxiliary file containing label information. This file is analogous to the symbol table of an assembler but is retained between document compilations. If no changes were made to the file during compilation then references in the text are correct. If there were changes then forward references may be incorrect and the text will be correct after a second pass through Scribe. Like an assembler, Scribe detects references to undefined labels.

Large texts Scribe has some capabilities designed to facilitate the processing of large texts such as books. A large document may be broken up into a hierarchical structure of files; directives in non-root files specify the root. When the structure is processed by Scribe, information about the individual parts is recorded in an auxiliary file. Subsequently, a particular sub-part can be processed and the corresponding output will have correct cross-references, page and section numbers. In addition, a file containing part of a larger document can be processed as if it were a stand-alone document. Certain commands ignored when it is processed as part of a larger whole (such as specification of the output device), take effect when it is processed alone.

7.3.2 SGML

Standard Generalized Markup Language (SGML) [25] is notation for describing classes of documents and for coding documents belonging to described classes. An SGML document has two parts: a document type definition (DTD) that describes a class of document, and a document instance. The DTD may be incorporated by reference. SGML identifies elements of a document; it is the responsibility of the application program, e.g. the viewer, retrieval program or formatter, to display elements in an appropriate way. A good introduction to the uses of generalized markup with particular reference to SGML, can be found in Smith [26]; Bryan [27] is a well-illustrated guide to SGML.

The DTD contains production rules that describe the contents of elements. Figure 7.34 shows an example DTD based on the discussion in Ref. 28.

Figure 7.34 Example SGML DTD

```
<!doctype letter [
<!element letter    -- (opening, paragraph+,closing)>
<!element opening   -- (address&date)>
<!element address   -- (name,(streetnum+ |PObox),citystate>
<!element name      -- cdata>
<!element streetnum -- cdata>
<!element PObox     -- cdata>
<!element citystate -- cdata>
<!element date      -- cdata>
<!element paragraph -- cdata>
<!element closing   -- (postscript+ |carboncopy)>
<!element postscript -- cdata>
<!element carboncopy -- cdata>
]>
```

In this definition, a *letter* consists of an *opening* followed by one or more *paragraph*s, followed by a *closing*. The *opening* consists of an *address* and a *date*; the *address* in turn consists of a *name* followed by either a *PObox* or one or more *streetnumber* lines followed by a *citystate*. The terminal elements (those not defined further) are just sequences of characters (*cdata*).

In the document instance, SGML tags identify structural elements of a document such as the abstract, an unordered list and a long quotation. Typical tags are of the form <element> to begin and </element> to close an element. Some tags may be omitted if the results are unambiguous though Heath and Welsch [29], in suggesting improvements to SGML, argue that tag minimization may make a document more difficult to parse. Figure 7.35 contains an instance of the *letter* document class that was defined in Fig. 7.34.

Figure 7.35 Example letter

```
<name> John Doe
<streetnum> The Larches
<streetnum> 7601 Shady Lane
<citystate> Northridge, CA 91330
<date> 10-30-91
<paragraph>
Dear Dad,
How are you doing? Hope you can come to lunch Sunday.
<paragraph>
Best wishes,
<carboncopy> Mom, Grandpa
```

SGML is already being adopted as a standard in order to increase the portability of documents within organizations. Tools for creating both DTDs (see, for example Ref. 28), and tagged documents will become increasingly common.

Summary

A variety of document formatting tasks can be handled easily by programs. These range from simple pagination, through line justification to typesetting of mathematical notation. Many formatting systems also relieve writers of the burden of numbering text elements such as figures and footnotes; some make it easy to insert cross-references and construct indexes.

Formatters can be classified broadly as WYSIWYG or batch. The former are interactive and display an approximation of the file as it would appear when printed. The latter read a file containing text and directives and create a formatted document. There are advantages in marking up a text by identifying its logical components (e.g. lists, headings, and quotations) rather than by inserting output-oriented commands (e.g. change to italic, indent 10 spaces). Logical tags add more information and make the document more device independent.

Exercises

(1) Determine, by formatting appropriate data files, the algorithm that your batch formatter uses to justify lines.

(2) Appendix D lists a (fake!) resume generated by *troff* from a certain text file. Create a file that will cause *troff* to output this resume. Aim to make your source file as compact as possible through the use of macros.

(3) This book was formatted using a *troff*-like formatter and various pre-processors. What deficiencies do you find in the formatting that you would not expect to find in a book that was set by hand.

(4) WYSIWYG and batch formatters each have their advantages and disadvantages. For each type of formatter, give an example of a formatting problem where it would be the more convenient of the two to use.

References

1. G. Koren, "A simple way to improve the chances for acceptance of your scientific paper," *The New England Journal of Medicine*, vol. 315, no. 20, p. 1298, November 13th, 1986. Letter to the Editor.

2. J. H. Coombs, A. H. Renear, and S. J. DeRose, "Markup systems and the future of scholarly text processing," *Communications of the ACM*, vol. 30, no. 11, pp. 933-947, November 1987.

3. J. F. Ossanna, "NROFF/TROFF user's manual," Comp. Sci. Tech. Rep. No. 54, Bell Laboratories, Murray Hill, New Jersey, October 1976.

4. R. Furuta, J. Scofield, and A. Shaw, "Document formatting systems: survey, concepts and issues," *ACM Computing Surveys*, vol. 14, no. 3, pp. 481-472, September 1982.

5. *WordPerfect Version 5.0 Reference manual,* WordPerfect Corporation, Orem, Utah, 1988.

6. *MacWrite II,* Claris Corporation, Mountain View, CA, 1988.

7. J. Saltzer, "Manuscript typing and editing: TYPSET, RUNOFF," in *The Compatible Time-Sharing System: A programmer's guide*, ed. P. A. Crisman, The MIT Press, Cambridge, MA, 1965. Section AH.9.01.

8. G. M. Berns, "Description of FORMAT, a text-processing program.," *Communications of the ACM*, vol. 12, no. 3, pp. 141-146, March 1969.

9. L. Tesler, "PUB: the document compiler," Operating note 70., Stanford Artificial Intelligence Project, Stanford University, California., September 1972.

10. *Eroff desktop typesetting system,* Elan Computer Group Inc., Los Altos, CA, 1987.

11. S. L. Emerson and K. Paulsell, *Troff typesetting for UNIX systems,* Prentice Hall, 1987.

12. B. W. Kernighan and P. J. Plauger, *Software Tools,* Addison-Wesley, Reading, Mass., 1976.

13. B. W. Kernighan and P. J. Plauger, *Software Tools in Pascal,* Addison-Wesley, Reading, Mass., 1981.

14. M. E. Lesk, "Typing documents on the Unix System: Using the -ms macros with troff and nroff," in *UNIX Time-sharing system: UNIX programmer's manual (Volume 2)*, Bell Laboratories, Murray Hill, NJ, November 1978. Seventh Edition.

15. E. P. Allman, *-ME Reference Manual,* April 1986. Unix 4.3 BSD: Supplementary documents.

16. C. Buchman, D. M. Berry, and J. Gonczarowski, "DITROFF/FFORTID, an adaptation of the Unix DITROFF for formatting bidirectional text," *ACM Transactions on Office Information Systems*, vol. 3, no. 4, pp. 380-397, October 1985.

17. J. Bentley, "Programming pearls: little languages," *Communications of the ACM*, vol. 29, no. 8, pp. 711-721, August 1986.

18. M. E. Lesk, "Tbl - a program to format tables," Comp. Sci. Tech. Rep. No. 49, Bell Laboratories, Murray Hill, New Jersey, September 1976.

19. B. W. Kernighan and L. L. Cherry, "A System for Typesetting Mathematics," *Communications of the ACM*, vol. 18, pp. 151-157, Bell Laboratories, Murray Hill, New Jersey, March 1975.

20. D. E. Knuth, "Tau Epsilon Chi: A system for technical text," in *TEX and Metafont: New directions in typesetting*, Digital Press and the American Mathematical Society, Bedford, MA and Providence, RI, 1979. Part 2.

21. L. Lamport, *LATEX User's guide and reference manual,* Addison-Wesley, Reading, MA, 1986.

22. D. E. Knuth and M. F. Plass, "Breaking paragraphs into lines," *Software Practice and Experience*, vol. 11, no. 11, pp. 1119-1184, November 1981.

23.   B. K. Reid, "Scribe: A document specification language and its compiler," CMU-CS-81-100, Department of Computer Science, Carnegie-Mellon University, October 1980.

24.   B. K. Reid and J. H. Walker, *Scribe: Introductory user's manual*, Unilogic, Pittsburgh, May 1980. Third Edition, Preliminary draft.

25.   American National Standards Institute, *Information Processing – Text and Office Systems – Standard Generalized Markup Language (SMGL)*, ANSI, New York, 1986. ISO 8879.

26.   J. M. Smith, "The implications of SGML for the preparation of scientific publications," *The Computer Journal*, vol. 29, no. 3, pp. 193-200, June 1986.

27.   M. Bryan, *SGML : An author's guide to the Standard Generalized Markup Language*, Addison-Wesley, Reading, MA, 1988.

28.   W. T. Polk and L. E. Bassham III, "A window and icon based prototype for expert assistance for manipulation of SGML document type definitions," *Proceedings of the ACM Conference on document processing systems*, pp. 79-84, Santa Fe, New Mexico, December 5-9, 1988.

29.   J. Heath and L. Welsch, "Difficulties in parsing SGML," *Proceedings of the ACM Conference on document processing systems*, pp. 71-77, Santa Fe, New Mexico, December 5-9, 1988.

Concordances and Collocations

A typical concordance of a text is a list of the words in the text arranged in alphabetical order. With each word there is normally some summary information, such as total number of occurrences and relative frequency, and a list of the occurrences of the word each shown in the context of a small fragment of surrounding text. A concordance thus makes it easy to see how a writer used a particular word in a particular piece of text.[1] A good concordance will also include frequency tables of various kinds ordered in a variety of ways, for example alphabetically, reverse alphabetically and by frequency.

Concordances are useful in many ways. For example, if you were writing a paper on Shakespeare's use of sun imagery, it would be very tedious to go through the collected works finding the places where he used the word. In a Shakespeare concordance the 254 occurrences are arranged together; this is illustrated in Fig. 8.1, an extract from Spevack [1].[2] In the preface to his Kyd concordance [3] Crawford indicates that his main objective in compiling the concordance was to allow others to test his theory that Kyd wrote the anonymous work *Arden of Faversham*. Yule [4] in his investigations into the authorship of *De Imitatione Christi* (see Chapter 12), used Storr's concordance [5] to make certain word counts easier to compute.

Before computerization, concordances were produced by hand and took a considerable amount of time. For example, Bartlett's Shakespeare

---

1. The most frequent words may be omitted. For example, Spevack [1] has only summary information for the 43 words most frequently used by Shakespeare and Ellison [2] omits the 131 most common words in the Bible - accounting for 59% of the text.
2. The heading for a word gives the total occurrences of the word, its relative frequency (the percentage of text it accounts for), the number of occurrences in verse and the number of occurrences in prose. Text extracts are sorted by line number within Scene within Act within work. The first extract from a particular work is tagged with a mnemonic. Prose extracts are marked "P".

Figure 8.1 Extract from Spevack Shakespeare concordance
Reprinted by permission ⊙ 1973 by Marvin Spevack.

SUN	254 FR	0.0287 REL FR 232 V 22 P
can have no note, unless the sun were post –	TMP	2.01.248
all the infections that the sun sucks up | from		2.02. 1
the sun will set before i shall discharge | what		3.01. 22
i have bedimm'd | the noontide sun, call'd forth		5.01. 42
which now shows all the beauty of the sun, | and	TGV	1.03. 86
star, |but now i worship a celestial sun.		2.06. 10
the sun begins to gild the western sky, | and		5.01. 1
then did the sun on dunghill shine.	WIV	1.03. 63 P
i rather will suspect the sun with / cold | than		4.04. 7
have i laid my brain in the sun and dried it,		5.05.135 P
it is i | that, lying by the violet in the sun,	MM	2.02.165
ere twice the sun hath made his journal greeting		4.03. 88
my woes end likewise with the evening sun.	ERR	1.01. 27
at length the sun, gazing upon the earth,		1.01. 88
town, | dies ere the weary sun set in the west		1.02. 7
when the sun shines, let foolish gnats make		2.02. 30
for gazing on your beams, fair sun, being by.		3.02. 56
bower, | where honeysuckles, ripened by the sun,	ADO	3.01. 8
forbid the sun to enter, like favorites | made		3.01. 9
study is like the heaven's glorious sun, | that	LLL	1.01. 84
"so sweet a kiss the golden sun gives not | to		4.03. 25
then thou, fair sun, which on my earth dost		4.03. 67
ay, as some days, but then no sun must shine.		4.03. 89
o, 'tis the sun that maketh all things shine!		4.03.242
in conflict that you get the sun of them.		4.03.366
the sun was not so true unto the day | as he to	MND	3.02. 50
hecat's team | from the presence of the sun,		5.01.385
the shadowed livery of the burnish'd sun, | to	MV	2.01. 2
a day, | such as the day is when the sun is hid.		5.01.126
if you would walk in the absence of the sun.		5.01.128
ambition shun, | and loves to live i' th' sun,	AYL	2.05. 39
who laid him down and bask'd him in the sun,		2.07. 15
a great cause of the night is lack of the sun;		3.02. 28 P

concordance [6] was begun in 1876; the preface is dated 1894. Ellison estimated that it would take 25 years to produce an exhaustive Biblical concordance by hand and this in fact is the length of time it took Young to produce her concordance to Byron's poetry [7].

A typical hand-made concordance is produced by writing out overlapping fragments of the text on index cards or slips of paper, perhaps with the word of interest highlighted. The cards are sorted by the highlighted word and tallied to produce the concordance. Using this method to produce a concordance to a large text, for example the Bible or the complete works of Shakespeare, is tedious as well as time-consuming.

The Spevack Shakespeare concordance was produced using an IBM 360/50, the Fuger concordance to James Joyce's *Dubliners* [8] used the COCOA package [9, 10] on a TR440. While the manual algorithm for producing a concordance can be implemented reasonably easily on a computer, there are some aspects that may require human intervention. For example, markers of some kind would be necessary to enable a program to discriminate between homographs, that is, distinct words with the same spelling such as pen (writing instrument) and pen (pig holder). Markers would also be used to allow verse and prose to be distinguished. Such indicators were inserted into the Shakespeare input to Spevack's program so that separate totals for verse and prose could be computed (see Fig. 8.1). We look at text markup in section 8.1. Although a computer-generated concordance can be exhaustive, it cannot be analytical, for example listing the Greek or Hebrew sources for words in the Bible.

Breaking a text into overlapping fragments is non-trivial. In his preface, Spevack outlines the procedure used in his concordance, including the punctuation hierarchy used to determine fragment boundaries. Fragments can be labelled with a suitable reference (for example the line number in the input text, or an act-scene-line triple) and the keyword tagged in some way.

While fragments would be sorted by tagged word, there are many ordering possibilities within a word group. Spevack sorted by reference, Fuger sorted by the context following the tagged word.

Collocations In addition to the study of particular words, it is often of interest to see how an author used particular pairs of words. A program that can generate a concordance to an arbitrary text will typically be capable of reporting places where a particular pair of words appear together.

Generating a complete concordance of a document is relatively simple. A simple package to do this is described in section 8.2. Oakman [11, ch. 4] presents a good overview of concordances from a mainly literary perspective and gives top-level flow charts for concordance production. Day [12 ch. 12] shows briefly how concordances might be produced using FORTRAN, Pascal and SNOBOL.

Perhaps of greater interest than the generation of complete concordances are packages that allow users to select particular parts of the text or particular words of interest. In addition, such packages may be able to find those words or pieces of text satisfying some arbitrary condition. In sections 8.3 and 8.4 we look at OCP [13, 14] and CLOC [15, 16, 17, 18]: two general purpose concordance/collocation packages.

One of the first problems facing a user of a package is how to represent the source text in computer-readable form. We look at this problem in the next section.

8.1 Coding of text

While concordance construction is amenable to computerization, clearly it requires the text to be available in machine-readable form. The number of machine-readable texts is growing rapidly and archives are established at several centers.[3] If a document is produced on a computer-controlled printing device then much of the information necessary to describe it is available. Difficulties arise however, when a text exists only in hard copy form, for example a 16th century manuscript. What do we code and how do we code it?

Deciding what aspects of the document to capture is a problem of knowing what aspects of the document will be of interest to researchers. For example, suppose that the letter "F" was written in two slightly different forms in the manuscript; is it worth recording the distinctions? Will future researchers be interested in knowing where page breaks occurred in a manuscript or where there was a clear change of hand-writing?

Although the conventions used by packages such as COCOA have been widely adopted, not every coder uses them. Therefore a concordance program must be very flexible in the ways that it allows users to specify markers, alphabets, delimiters, punctuation and so on. Examples of the types of information that may have to be encoded (taken from the OCP User's Manual [13]) are shown in Table 8.1.

Table 8.1 Document information that may have to be coded

Proper names
Accents
Foreign words vis-a-vis the base language
Font changes
Editorial marks
Grammatical categories
Numerals
Punctuation
Hyphenation
Layout of text
Non-Roman characters
References (chapters, authors, speakers etc.)

Figure 8.2 shows an example (from Ref. 13) of some of the simpler codes

3. For example, there is an archive of modern English at the University of Bergen, a large collection of Greek texts at the University of California, Irvine, and the Oxford Archive at Oxford University contains texts in a variety of languages.

used at the beginning of Shakespeare's *The Merchant of Venice*. This text uses COCOA references: P for author, T for title, A for act, S for scene and C for speaker. Stage directions are enclosed in double parentheses, a # precedes an italicized word.

Figure 8.2 Coded text

```
<P Shakespeare>
<T Merchant>
<A 1>
<S 1>
((Venice. #A #Street.))
((#Enter Antonio, Salarino, #and Salanio.))
<C Antonio>
In sooth I know not why I am so sad:
It wearies me; you say it wearies you;
But how I caught it, found it, or came by it,
What stuff 'tis made of, whereof it is born,
I am to learn;
And such a want-wit sadness makes of me,
That I have much ado to know myself.
<C Salarino>
Your mind is tossing on the ocean;
There, where your argosies with portly sail,--
Like signiors and rich burghers on the flood,
```

In the next three sections we look at three example packages: first a comparatively simple implementation of manual concordance techniques, second a sophisticated machine-independent program (OCP) and finally we examine CLOC, with particular attention to its data structures.

8.2 Example package: kwic and format

While at U. C. Berkeley, Bill Tuthill wrote a package of programs that produces a concordance in a manner similar to the manual method. *Kwic* and *format* have limited capabilities for special alphabets but can produce a keyword-in-context concordance on text using standard alphabets. There appear to be no facilities for producing summary tables such as word lists.

Kwic reads a file and outputs a record for each symbol. The record consists of the symbol, a page/line reference and a fragment showing the keyword in context. Page breaks are marked in the source by a user-specifiable character (default ' ='). Figure 8.3 shows a fragment of the output from *kwic* applied to Chapter 4 of Smith and Barnes [19].

Figure 8.3 Output from *kwic*

prohibits	5,95	this book was prepared	prohibits users from having
users	5,95	was prepared prohibits	users from having more/than
from	5,95	prepared prohibits users	from having more/than 16
having	5,95	prohibits users from	having more/than 16 files
more	5,95	users from having	more/than 16 files open
than	5,96	users from having more/	than 16 files open at a
16	5,96	from having more/than	16 files open at a time.
files	5,96	from having more/than 16	files open at a time./
open	5,96	more/than 16 files	open at a time./ /We will
at	5,96	more/than 16 files open	at a time./ /We will consider

System utilities, such as *grep*, can be used to remove unwanted entries from the output of *kwic*, for example those beginning with non-alphabetic characters, and to sort the entries by keyword. Fig. 8.4 shows a fragment of the Chapter 4 data after this step.

Figure 8.4 Sorted *kwic* records

can	12,95	algorithms we examined	can be termed external sorting
cannot	200	file. If the new record/	cannot be part of the current
cannot	3,55	records. These records	cannot contribute to the
capacities	12,139	a variety of/main memory	capacities./ /Modify the
capacity	67	a given total storage	capacity. A/disadvantage
capacity	127	is the extreme case./The	capacity is large enough
capacity	3,72	memory/have the same	capacity and both can hold
capacity	12,148	Keeping the main memory/	capacity constant, tabulate
carefully	7,43	initial/distribution are	carefully chosen.) We assume
case	126	This is the extreme	case./The capacity is large
case	128	Of course, in this	case sorting would take

Finally, the *format* program reads the sorted records and produces a con- cordance. A Unix shell command for producing the concordance is:

deroff *source* | kwic - | grep *pattern* | sort | format > *concordance*

Figure 8.5 shows the section of the concordance of Chapter 4 containing the words of Fig. 8.4.

8.3 Example package: OCP

OCP (Oxford Concordance Program) was intended as a successor to the COCOA package. Version 2 is written in FORTRAN-77 and is designed to be machine independent. If efficiency is a consideration, some parts can be recoded in assembler.

Figure 8.5 Concordance produced by *format*

12,95	algorithms we examined	can be termed external sorting
CANNOT	(2)	
200	file. If the new record/	cannot be part of the current
3,55	records. These records	cannot contribute to the
CAPACITIES	(1)	
12,139	a variety of/main memory	capacities./ /Modify the
CAPACITY	(4)	
67	a given total storage	capacity. A/disadvantage
127	is the extreme case./The	capacity is large enough
3,72	memory/have the same	capacity and both can hold
12,148	Keeping the main memory/	capacity constant, tabulate
CAREFULLY	(1)	
7,43	initial/distribution are	carefully chosen.) We assume
CASE	(11)	
126	This is the extreme	case./The capacity is large
128	Of course, in this	case sorting would take

A user gives OCP a text and a list of directives. Some of the directives tell OCP how to interpret the text, others specify the actions to be performed on it. For example, a user can indicate how accents are coded in the text and request a concordance of all words beginning with M.

Kwic has some capabilities for handling foreign alphabets; OCP has considerable flexibility in processing text in which characters, accents and punctuation have been coded in various ways. Non-Roman alphabets can be processed: a user maps each character in the alphabet onto a sequence of one or more Roman characters. Alphabetic order is established when the mapping is specified to OCP. The example of Fig. 8.7 illustrates this.

OCP can produce concordances, word lists and indexes. Vocabulary statistics can be produced in parallel with any of these. A user can specify subsets of the full output in a variety of ways and has control of many aspects of the output format.

Fig. 8.6 shows an example taken from the OCP User's Manual. The first part lists directives input to OCP and the second is the output produced. The text used is the first 70 lines of Shakespeare's *The Merchant of Venice* (Fig. 8.2 lists the first few lines). In the directives, the user indicates that text enclosed in double parentheses is to be ignored (these are stage directions) and that all text is to be processed except that spoken by Salanio. Padding is part of a word to be ignored when sorting is done. Recall that in this text the # symbol is used indicate italics. Only a partial concordance is required - various forms of the verb "to be"; these are to be grouped under the headword "be". The References command controls the format of the fragment tags.

Figure 8.6 OCP Example 1

```
*input
references cocoa.
text continue "+".
comments between "((" to "))".
select except where C = "Salanio".
*words
padding "#".
punctuation ".,::;?!--"
*action
do concordance.
references T = 3, A = 1, S = 1, L = 3, C = 5.
pick words "is was am were are be being been".
headwords "be" = "is was am were are be being been".
*go
```

```
                                               be   16
Mer  1  1     3 Anton        In sooth I know not why I  am so sad
Mer  1  1     6 Anton    What stuff 'tis made of, whereof it  is born
Mer  1  1     7 Anton                            I  am to learn
Mer  1  1    10 Salar            Your mind  is tossing on the ocean
Mer  1  1    13 Salar     Or, as it  were, the pageants of the sea
Mer  1  1    42 Salar          Is sad to think upon his merchandise
Mer  1  1    44 Anton        My ventures  are not in one bottom trusted
Mer  1  1    45 Anton    Nor to one place; nor  is my whole estate
Mer  1  1    48 Salar        Why, then, you  are in love. Fie! Fie
Mer  1  1    49 Salar  Not in Love neither? Then let's say you  are sad
Mer  1  1    50 Salar         Because you  are not merry: and 'twere as easy
Mer  1  1    51 Salar  For you to laugh, and leap, and say you  are merry
Mer  1  1    52 Salar         Because you  are not sad. Now, by two-headed Janus
Mer  1  1    58 Salar      Though Nestor swear the jest  be laughable
Mer  1  1    65 Anton           Your worth  is very dear in my regard
Mer  1  1    70 Bassa     You grow exceeding strange: must it  be so
```

Figure 8.7 shows another example from the user's manual. The first part is a listing of a small Russian text mapped onto Roman characters, the second is a listing of OCP directives. The main point of interest here is the specification of the alphabet mapping. Double angle brackets are padding characters. The output generated by OCP is shown in Fig. 8.8.

Collocations OCP requires users to specify the order of the collocates. A typical request is:

PICK COLLOCATES "BINARY" UPTO 4 "ALGORITHM"

Figure 8.7 OCP Example 2

Stala ona odyevat*sya: pal*to, kaloshi... Vyeshchi nam yeye
pokazali, -- pravilo znachit: po instruktsii my vyeshchi smo-
tryet* obyazany. < <Dyen*gi, sprashivayem, s vami kakiye budut?> >
Rubl* dvadtsat* kopyeyek dyenyeg okazalos*, -- starshoi* k syebye
vzyal. < <Vas, baryshnya, govorit yei*, ya obyskat* dolzhyen> >.
Kak ona tut vspykhnyet. Glaza zagoryelis*, rumyanyets yeshchye
gushchye vystupil. Guby tonkiye, syerdityye... Kak posmotryela
na nas, vyeritye orobyel ya i podstupit*sya ne smyeyu.

*input
text hyphen "-".
*words
alphabet "A = a B = b V = v G = g D = d Ye = ye Zh = zh Z = z I = i I* = i* K = k L = l
M = m N = n O = o P = p R = r S = s T = t U = u F = f Kh = kh Ts = ts Ch = ch Sh = sh
Shch = shch ** Y = y * E = e Yu = yu Ya = ya".
padding "< < > >".
punctuation "-- . :: , ?".
*action
do concordance.
references L = 3.
maximum context span L and upto ".".
*format
layout length 80.
*GO

which would detect "binary search algorithm" but not "algorithm for binary
search". To detect the latter an OCP user would need to request

> PICK COLLOCATES "BINARY" UPTO 4 "ALGORITHM",
> "ALGORITHM" UPTO 4 "BINARY"

8.4 Example package: CLOC

In this section we look at some aspects of the design and capabilities of
CLOC. Although it has been superceded in some respects by packages
such as OCP, it is in some ways (for example, the analysis of collocations)
more powerful. Figure 8.9 shows an example of CLOC output taken from
the User's Manual. The only words selected in this example are those ending "ed"; each such word occurs once in the data file.

Figure 8.8 Output from Fig. 8.7

```
                          baryshnya    1
5  Vas, baryshnya, govorit yei*, ya obyskat* dolzhyen> >

                          budut    1
3  Dyen*gi, sprashivayem, s vami kakiye budut?> > Rubl* dvadtsat* kopyeyek

                          vami    1
3  Dyen*gi, sprashivayem, s vami kakiye budut?> > Rubl* dvadtsat* kopyeyek

                          Vas    1
5  Vas, baryshnya, govorit yei*, ya obyskat* dolzhyen> >

                          vyeritye    1
8  Kak posmotryela na nas, vyeritye orobyel ya i podstupit*sya ne smyeyu

                          Vyeshchi    2
1  Vyeshchi nam yeye pokazali, -- pravilo znachit: po instruktsii my vyeshchi
2  nam yeye pokazali, -- pravilo znachit: po instruktsii my vyeshchi

                          vzyal    1
5  Rubl* dvadtsat* kopyeyek dyenyeg okazalos*, -- starshoi* k syebye vzyal

                          vspykhnyet    1
6  Kak ona tut vspykhnyet

                          vystupil    1
7  Glaza zagoryelis*, rumyanyets yeshchye gushchye vystupil

                          Glaza    1
6  Glaza zagoryelis*, rumyanyets yeshchye gushchye vystupil

                          govorit    1
5  Vas, baryshnya, govorit yei*, ya obyskat* dolzhyen> >

                          Guby    1
7  Guby tonkiye, syerdityye

                          gushchye    1
7  Glaza zagoryelis*, rumyanyets yeshchye gushchye vystupil

                          dvadtsat*    1
4  Dyen*gi, sprashivayem, s vami kakiye budut?> > Rubl* dvadtsat* kopyeyek

                          dyenyeg    1
4  sprashivayem, s vami kakiye budut?> > Rubl* dvadtsat* kopyeyek dyenyeg

                          Dyen*gi    1
3  Dyen*gi, sprashivayem, s vami kakiye budut?> > Rubl* dvadtsat* kopyeyek

                          dolzhyen    1
5  Vas, baryshnya, govorit yei*, ya obyskat* dolzhyen> >

                          yeye    1
1  Vyeshchi nam yeye pokazali, -- pravilo znachit: po instruktsii my vyeshchi
```

Overview of CLOC Rather than using the "manual" algorithm like *kwic*, CLOC holds an exact representation of the input text in a series of data structures. Using these it can answer *ad hoc* queries efficiently and process

Figure 8.9 Example CLOC concordance

concordance of 8 nodes
= = = = = = = = = = = =

node accomplished occurs 1 times
12   Draining the saturated ground was accomplished by widening a natural

node consisted occurs 1 times
9   12 postgraduates.   The site consisted of 190 acres of marshy

node constructed occurs 1 times
13   around which the University was constructed.

node destined occurs 1 times
10   mansion, Heslington Hall, destined to become the

node followed occurs 1 times
5   University for York. This was followed by a petition to Parliament

node opened occurs 1 times
7   1947. The University officially opened in 1963 with a student

node received occurs 1 times
4   Plan).   In 1617 James I received a petition requesting a

node saturated occurs 1 times
11   building. Draining the saturated ground was accomplished by

both concordance and collocation requests.

8.4.1 Itemization
CLOC breaks up the input text into items. A user controls the location of item boundaries by specifying an alphabet of characters; the order in which the alphabet characters are listed is used in sorting output. Characters not listed in the alphabet are treated as separators between words. Thus the input becomes a sequence of items each of which is either a word (sequence of one or more characters in the alphabet) or a separator (sequence of one or more characters not in the alphabet). The input is clearly an alternating sequence of words and separators.

8.4.2 Data structures
CLOC creates two data structures from the input in such a way that the input text could be recreated exactly from the contents of the structures. Thus the input is no longer needed once the data structures are set up. The data structures used are a randomly accessible file of records and a symbol table with an associated character string. The file of records,

symbol table and string can be saved in a permanent file for later use.

The file of records There is a one-to-one correspondence between records in the file and items in the input text. Each record contains a pointer to a symbol table entry that in turn points to a segment of the character string and yields the text of the item. If the record represents a word item then it contains a pointer to the record representing the next occurrence of the word. If the record represents a separator item then instead it contains a symbolic address of the item in the input.[4] The symbolic address (for example Act-Scene-Line in a play) can be used to tag the context in the concordance.

The symbol table Items are hashed into the table for fast retrieval. If output is required to be ordered in some way, sorting is done in a scratch area. Rather than containing the text of an item, a symbol table entry contains a pointer to a segment of an associated character string. This is so that CLOC does not need to impose an upper bound on the length of word or separator a user can process. Instead there is a (large) limit on the total length of all the symbols that can be represented concurrently in a table. The string lengths are stored in the symbol table, they are used when sorting in length order.

If a symbol table entry represents a word item then in addition to the pointer to the string segment three other fields are used. These fields are not used if the table entry is for a separator symbol. The fields are: a count of the number of times the word appears in the text and two pointers to the file of records: one to the record representing the first occurrence of the word and one to the record representing the last occurrence.

Figure 8.10 is a pseudocode representation of the algorithm used by CLOC for processing an input item. Figure 8.11 shows a short example text and the CLOC data structures as they might appear after the word "great" has been processed. An arbitrary hash function is used in this example.

8.4.3 Production of a concordance
The general form of a CLOC concordance request is:

CONCORDANCE sorting criterion, style, citationwidth, reference

In addition, there may be control lines specifying the set of words of interest. Example requests are shown in Fig. 8.12. If a concordance for

4. The assumption is that nobody would be interested in all occurrences of a particular separator.

Figure 8.10 Item-processing algorithm

if item is in symbol table

then if the item is a word
    then Add 1 to the frequency count.
        Append a new record to the file of records
        and link it to the end of the appropriate list.
        Update "last" pointer.
    else Append a record containing line reference
      to the file of records.

else if the item is a word
    then Create a new symbol table entry with count = 1.
        Append record to file of records and point
        to it with "first" and "last" pointers.
    else Create a new symbol table entry
        Append a record containing line reference
        to the file of records.

more than one keyword is requested, the *sorting criterion* determines the order in which the keywords are presented. The *style* parameter governs the display of text fragments. For example, if KWIC is selected the keyword is centered on the output line (see Fig. 8.9.) and the left and right margins will probably be ragged. The other option for this parameter is LEFT. It results in fragments being printed as far to the left as possible; the Spevack extract (Fig. 8.1) is in this style.

Citationwidth allows a user to control the amount of context displayed for each word occurrence. The user can specify the number of words to be displayed before and the number of words to be displayed after the keyword. Alternatively the user can specify a pair of characters, the first delimits the context before the keyword, the second delimits the context after it.[5]

The *reference* parameter controls the tagging of fragments. A typical label comprises parts of references embedded in the text, for example, author, title, act, scene.

Figure 8.13 contains an algorithm for outputting a concordance of a single word. It assumes that a representation of the text is held in the data structures described above and that the user has specified that in each

---

5. Oakman [11] discusses the problem of choosing the best fragment to display for a word occurrence. The criteria may be subtle and best handled by inserting markers into the source text.

Figure 8.11 Text and resulting CLOC data structures

Text: the whale, the great white whale!

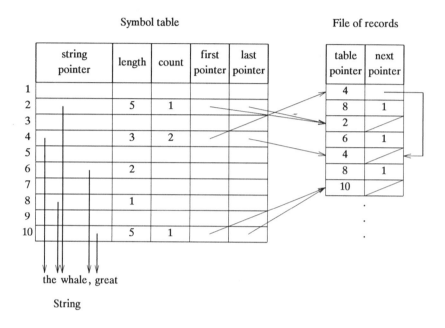

Symbol table   File of records

	string pointer	length	count	first pointer	last pointer		table pointer	next pointer
1							4	
2		5	1				8	1
3							2	
4		3	2				6	1
5							4	
6		2					8	1
7							10	
8		1					.	
9							.	
10		5	1				.	

the whale, great

String

Figure 8.12 Example CLOC concordance requests

CONCORDANCE
CONCORDANCE REVALPHA
CONCORDANCE KWIC, CITE 6 BY 5
CONCORDANCE LEFT, CITE FROM;TO;EXCLUSIVE
CONCORDANCE LEFT, REFS A4 P6
CONCORDANCE DFREQ, LEFT, CITE 6 BY 6, REFS C6 L4

fragment the keyword be preceded by N words of context and followed by M words.

Producing a fuller concordance involves extracting from the symbol table the words that match a user-specified pattern, sorting them by the sorting criterion, and then carrying out the algorithm of Fig. 8.13 on each in turn.

Figure 8.13 Algorithm for single-word concordance

Get symbol table entry for word.
Print word and total number of occurrences
For each record on the list rooted in the table entry
(assume record number p)
 do for k from max(1,p-N*2) to min (p+M*2, record in file)
    do Put item pointed to from record k into buffer
       If k=p (* key word *)
          then note location of keyword
       If item is a separator
          then note line reference
    Output line reference
    If style=KWIC
       then output spaces to center keyword
    Output buffer

8.4.4 Collocations

A user of OCP specifies the collocates of interest and the order in which
they occur. In contrast, a CLOC user can also specify a word of interest
(the node word) and a region of interest (the span) around each
occurrence of this word. The words occurring in these regions are tallied
and the user can choose to have displayed information about all collocates
or just those satisfying certain frequency constraints. The general CLOC
collocation request is of the form:

COLLOCATIONS sorting criterion, style, citationwidth, reference
*SPAN spanwidth
*FREQUENCY expression
< collocate selection and rejection criteria >

The parameters of the COLLOCATION command are similar to those of
the CONCORDANCE command (see 8.4.3). *Spanwidth* specifies an area
around each occurrence of one of the words of interest (a typical collocation request restricts node words to those on a specified list). The FRE-
QUENCY command allows users to select collocations based on frequency of occurrence. Consider the following example.

SELECT WORDS
*LIST OF WORDS SUN MOON EARTH
COLLOCATIONS KWIC, CITE 6 BY 6
*SPAN 4 BY 5
*FREQUENCY > 7

This request indicates that we are interested in those words that occur
more than 7 times in the parts of the text that are up to 4 words before or

up to 5 words after an occurrence of "SUN", "MOON" or "EARTH". Figure 8.14 shows an example, taken from the CLOC manual, of output from a COLLOCATIONS command.

Figure 8.14 Example CLOC collocations

```
collocate analysis of 1 nodes (cited about node)
========================
node  university  occurs 6 times
collocate  the  occurs 9 times
node-collocate pair occurs 6 times
1                                        The University ; "A society of
3                    the dissemination of knowledge". (University of York Development Plan
6                          and a deputation to the University Grants Committee in
6                          and a deputation to the University Grants Committee in
7                    Grants Committee in 1947. The University officially opened in
13                   artificial lake around which the University was constructed.

node  university  occurs 6 times
collocate  a  occurs 9 times
node-collocate pair occurs 4 times
1                                        The University ; "A society of
4                    received a petition requesting a University for York. This was
4                    received a petition requesting a University for York. This was
6                          and a deputation to the University Grants Committee in

node  university  occurs 6 times
collocate  of  occurs 6 times
node-collocate pair occurs 3 times
1                                        The University ; "A society of
3                    the dissemination of knowledge". (University of York Development Plan
3                    the dissemination of knowledge". (University of York Development Plan

node  university  occurs 6 times
collocate  in  occurs 4 times
node-collocate pair occurs 3 times
6                          and a deputation to the University Grants Committee in
7                    Grants Committee in 1947. The University officially opened in
7                    Grants Committee in 1947. The University officially opened in
```

Collocation computation Consider the problem of finding the collocates of a single node word. The algorithm in Fig. 8.15 uses a scratch symbol table and a scratch file of records. It assumes that the span is P BY Q.

The occurrences of the node word are found by traversing the list rooted in the symbol table entry of the word. The record file is randomly accessible so we can easily scan the words within the user-specified SPAN of each node word occurrence. Words encountered in these scans are entered and tallied in the scratch symbol table. For each table entry we form a list of

Figure 8.15 Algorithm for collocations of a single word

Find the node word in symbol table(s).

For each record on the list rooted in the table entry
(assume record number p)
do for k from max(1,p-P*2) to min (p+Q*2, item count) excluding p
    do If word in scratch symbol table
        then Add 1 to frequency count
        else Make entry with count = 1
        Append p to list pointed to from table entry.

Remove all entries from the dynamic symbol table not satisfying the
FREQUENCY expression.
For each word remaining in the dynamic symbol table
do Output frequency of node word
    Output frequency of word in text
    Output frequency of word in span of node word
    For each word with address on the list rooted in the scratch table entry
    do Output context (see Fig. 8.13)

node word locations using the scratch file of records. For example, if item record 500 represents an occurrence of node word "sun" and an occurrence of "fair" is within its span, then the list for "fair" includes 500.

Having completed our examination of regions round occurrences of the node word we remove from the scratch symbol table those words not satisfying any FREQUENCY constraint. Remaining words are the collocations of interest.

To produce output like that shown in Fig. 8.14, we take each node word in turn and process its collocates one by one. For each node-collocate pair we output the frequency of the node word (from the main symbol table) the frequency of the collocate in the entire text (from the main symbol table), its frequency within the specified span of the node word (from the scratch symbol table) and the contexts. The contexts are found by following the list of pointers to node word occurrences and printing an appropriate amount of surrounding context.

8.4.5 Large texts
The symbol table and string used by CLOC are static, that is they are of a certain fixed size. If a text causes either to overflow, the current version of CLOC terminates with an invitation to the user to recompile the package with larger table limits. In this section we outline a way in which CLOC might be modified to enable it to process arbitrarily large texts.

When the space used in the symbol table or character string reaches a predefined limit, CLOC could continue to process input items but change the action taken for items not in the symbol table. It could append an empty record (the kth in the file) to the file of records and write the pair:

$$(item, k)$$

to an overflow file.

If the overflow file is non-empty when all the input text has been read then the contents of the symbol table and character string are saved to disc (as table-string 1) and both are cleared. The pairs in the overflow file are now read. The item component is hashed into the symbol table and the record indexed by the integer component is updated as in the algorithm of Fig. 8.10.

It is possible that a second hash table or string will become full before the overflow file has been completely read. This is dealt with by having an "overflow overflow" file to which pairs that could not be processed are written. When the overflow file has been completely read the second table and string are saved and cleared and the "overflow overflow" file read and processed in a similar manner.

If the input file is very large it might produce a series of tables (and associated strings). Therefore, in general, the fields in the file of records that point to symbol table entries will consist of a table number and a position within the table.

8.5 Future trends

Literary software is following other areas and migrating to microcomputers. Current microcomputers are comparable in power with the systems on which the first computer-generated concordances were produced. Micro-OCP is a version of OCP that runs on IBM PCs and compatibles [14]. Oxford University Press publishes a machine-readable version of the complete works of Shakespeare coded for Micro-OCP.

Summary

A concordance can be viewed as an index into a text. It enables someone to identify quickly the locations of a particular word and also the places where certain words are used together. Producing a concordance of a text by hand is a tedious and error-prone task. The difficulties encountered in producing one by computer tend to be literary problems rather than computer ones. For example, there are decisions as to what of the input text to encode and how to determine the best context to be displayed. For the most part, the computing techniques involved are well-established.

Packages are available that, in addition to producing full concordances, can supply the answers to *ad hoc* queries involving perhaps only a small fraction of a text or vocabulary. We looked at *kwic*, OCP and CLOC. In the case of CLOC, its data structures were described and algorithms presented for producing concordances and reporting collocations.

This is the end of the section of the text that considers a text file as a sequence of symbols. In the next two chapters we look at a higher level of processing where the text is treated as a stream of words. The fact that words have a structure is used in hyphenation and spelling checking and correction.

Exercises

(1)   Implement the hand concordance algorithm. If possible use an existing sort package rather than write your own. What problems do you encounter?

(2)   Comment on the usefulness of concordance and collocations for texts which are not natural language, for example programs in a high-level programming language.

(3)   Criticize the CLOC data structures. What alternatives can you suggest that would allow queries of the same power?

References

1.   M. Spevack, *The Harvard Concordance to Shakespeare,* The Belknap Press of Harvard University Press, Cambridge, Mass., 1973.

2.   J. W. Ellison, *Complete concordance of the Revised Standard Version Bible,* Thomas Nelson and Sons, New York, 1957.

3.   C. Crawford, *A concordance to the works of Thomas Kyd,* Kraus Reprint Ltd., Vaduz, 1963.

4.   G. U. Yule, *The statistical study of literary vocabulary,* Archon Books, 1968.

5.   R. Storr, *Concordantia ad quatuor libros latine scriptos De Imitatione Christi,* Oxford University Press, 1911. Altera editio.

6.   J. Bartlett, *A complete concordance to Shakespeare,* MacMillan, London, 1956.

7.   *A concordance to the poetry of Byron,* Pemberton Press, Austin, TX, 1964. Ed. I. D. Young (4 vols).

8.   *Concordance to James Joyce's Dubliners,* Georg Olms Verlag, Hildesheim, 1980. Ed. W. Fuger.

9.   G. L. M. Berry-Rogghe and T. O. Crawford, *COCOA--A word count and concordance generator,* Atlas Computer Laboratory, Chilton, England, 1973.

10. G. L. M. Berry-Rogghe, "COCOA: A word count and concordance generator," *ALLC Bulletin,* vol. 1, no. 2, pp. 29-31, 1973.

11. R. L. Oakman, *Computer methods for literary research,* The University of Georgia Press, Athens, GA, 1984.

12. A. C. Day, *Text Processing,* Cambridge University Press, 1984. Cambridge Computer Science Texts #20.

13. S. Hockey and J. Martin, *Oxford Concordance Program - Version 2: User's Manual,* Oxford University Computing Service, 1988.

14. S. Hockey and J. Martin, "The Oxford Concordance Program Version 2," *Literary and Linguistic Computing,* vol. 2, no. 2, pp. 125-131, 1987.

15. A. Reed, *CLOC mark 2O: A collocations and concordance package,* Birmingham University Computer Centre, March 1988.

16. A. Reed, "CLOC: a collocation package," *ALLC Bulletin,* vol. 5, no. 2, pp. 168-173, 1977.

17. A. Reed, "Anatomy of a text analysis package," *Computer Languages,* vol. 9, no. 2, pp. 89-96, 1984.

18. A. Reed and J. L. Schonfelder, "CLOC - a general-purpose concordance and collocation generator," in *Advances in computer-aided literary and linguistic research,* ed. D. E. Ager, F. E. Knowles and J. Smith, pp. 59-72, University of Aston, 1978.

19. P. D. Smith and G. M. Barnes, *Files and databases: an introduction,* Addison-Wesley, Reading, Mass., 1987.

IV

Word-by-Word Processing

Formatting Revisited - Hyphenation

In our earlier look at formatting (chapter 7) we considered words as indivisible symbols. In practice, when choosing the line-breaks in a paragraph, we can bring end of a line closer to the right margin if we allow the last word to be hyphenated and broken over two lines. The problem is that there are conventions as to what words may be split in this way and where they may be broken. In addition, conventions vary. For example, British English (as represented by Ref. 1) hyphenates *eight-een* whereas American English (see, for example, Ref. 2) has *eigh-teen*.

Hyphenation should hinder the reader as little as possible. Thus, the last line of a page should not end with a hyphen and if a word is hyphenated, pronunciation of the first half read alone should be same as when it appears in the whole word. This means, for example, that we cannot have *ra-vine*, *ra-ther* or *ra-cing* because the first half cannot be pronounced correctly without knowledge of the whole word. The following example of this pronunciation rule being violated may be apocryphal:

> completing the project required many many-
> ears more than originally estimated.

We look at the hyphenation problem for English in this chapter; the problem for other languages is discussed elsewhere (see, for example, Ref. 3).

What may be hyphenated In theory, any multi-character symbol can be split over two lines but, in order to help readers, we can place limits on our formatter. For example, we could forbid the hyphenation of symbols such as 10/21/95, 32,768 and PDP-11/70. We could define a word to be a sequence of characters delimited by white space or punctuation (including hyphens) and hyphenate only those words where every character is a letter.

The results of hyphenation must be readable. We cannot therefore hyphenate a short word leaving a single character on either line. An accepted convention is that a hyphenatable word must be at least five characters long and that each half after hyphenation must be at least two characters long. The following are therefore not normally allowed: *ex-am*, *bead-y*, *A-pril*.

Since we must be able to read the hyphenated text, each half of the word must contain a vowel group. Thus, *goodni-ghts* is not acceptable and single vowel words such as *knights* and *strengths* cannot be hyphenated at all. The character "y" causes problems because sometimes it acts as a vowel (as in *symphony*) and sometimes not (as in *leapyear*).

In order to count as a separate vowel group, a vowel cluster must be separated from the next by at least one consonant. A word like *through* only has one vowel group so cannot be hyphenated. In counting vowel groups to determine the number of syllables, most algorithms discount a "silent e" at the end of a word (like *mouse*) and some will discount a penultimate e when the last character is s or d (as in *paged* or *moves*). However, this is not foolproof, consider *jagged* and *passes*.

Where may we hyphenate We have seen how some words can be rejected as unhyphenatable. What about the remainder? How do we decide where a word can be split? In English we hyphenate between syllables, so the problem becomes one of identifying syllable boundaries. There are three main approaches: use an algorithm, use a lexicon, or use both an algorithm and a lexicon.

The worst cases for any method that processes words out of context are homographs, that is two or more words that are spelled the same but are hyphenated differently. Consider, for example, the words listed in Table 9.1.

Table 9.1 Homographs with different break-points

rec-ord	(noun)	re-cord	(verb)
des-ert	(noun)	de-sert	(verb)
proj-ect	(noun)	pro-ject	(verb)
rec-reation	(sport)	re-creation	(make again)
tend-er	(ship)	ten-der	(verb)
add-er	(person)	ad-der	(snake)

Examining the context of a word and identifying its part of speech helps in some cases (but not all, see *adder*).

9.1 Algorithm only

We need an algorithm that can take an arbitrary word and identify at least some of the legal hyphenation points. Most algorithms use information derived from a lexicon in which hyphenation points have been identified.

Moving window A simple approach is to consider 4-character windows into the word and apply tests to see if a hyphen could be inserted in the middle of the window. Suppose our formatter is filling a paragraph line by line, that the input is

> ... the Los Angeles Times photographer who took the ...

and that after putting *Times* into the line buffer, we have 9 spaces remaining in the buffer. The last two characters that we could fit into the buffer, remembering to allow for the hyphen itself, are *gr*. So the first window we try is *grap*.

For each window, we need to test three conditions:

> can the last two characters begin a syllable?
> can the middle pair of characters be broken by a hyphen?
> can the first two characters end a syllable?

All must yield true for a hyphen to be put in the middle of the window. We could implement the tests using three 26*26 boolean matrices. Alternatively, the matrices could contain probabilities and we could accept the break-point if the product of the probabilities exceeds some threshold. Liang [4] refers to this approach as the "Time magazine algorithm". The probabilities are derived from a marked lexicon in a simple way. For example, in the first matrix, the entry for *ex* is

$$\frac{number\ of\ occurrences\ of\ ex\text{-}}{number\ of\ occurrences\ of\ ex}$$

We would expect certain entries to be 0.0; e.g. that for *qu* in the second matrix.

In the case of our example, *ap* would be an acceptable beginning to a syllable and there is no reason why we should not split r and a. However, we cannot have a syllable ending in *gr*. This test having failed, we move the window one place to the left and test *ogra*. In this case we pass all three tests: *-og*, *g-r* and *ra-* are all acceptable. So *photog-* is put in the buffer (the line now needs to be padded by a single space) and the next line begins with *rapher*.

Notice that if we had had only seven spaces in the buffer, the next place would also have passed the window test and we would have *photo-grapher*.

But this serves to illustrate the limitations of the window approach. While *to-gr* is acceptable in *photo-graphic*, it is not acceptable in *photo-grapher* because of the principle that the pronunciation of the first half of the word must not mislead the reader. Liang gives the example of *dem-on-stra-tion* versus *de-mon-stra-tive* to show that we may need to look as many as 10 characters ahead when deciding if a break-point is legal.

Word structure A more promising approach might be to analyze the structure of the word; after prefixes and before suffixes are good hyphenation points. But remember we are assuming that we have no lexicon, thus it is difficult to identify affixes reliably. Consider the following examples:

dis-favor	but	dish-washer
in-edible	but	inn-keeper
sudden-ly	but	melan-choly
start-ing	but	duck-ling

We can often split a double consonant, but notice the difference between *pass-ing* and *let-ting*. In addition, rules on doubling a final letter when adding a suffix is another place where British and American English sometimes diverge.

A brute-force solution to hyphenation would use a (large) lexicon. We look at that solution next.

9.2 Lexicon only

In a lexicon entry we can represent all the legal break-points of a word and perhaps give each a weight to indicate preferences. An advantage of using only a lexicon is that it makes the formatter a little more language-independent; the rules for hyphenating vary a lot from language to language (see, for example Ref. 5).

Normal dictionaries may not be suitable unless they contain variations on the head words (for example *computes* and *computed* in addition to *compute*). Peterson [6] describes how a machine-readable copy of Webster's Seventh New Collegiate Dictionary was processed and compared with other machine-readable dictionaries in attempt to form a definitive hyphenation word list. In a considerable number of cases (2,011 out of 108,190) the hyphenation varied from source to source.

The lexicon will be large (the Atex system uses a list of 100,000 words) but addressable memories are also becoming very large. Even if the lexicon has to be held on secondary storage, there are techniques for organizing it (for example, dynamic hashing [7] or table-assisted hashing [8]) such that any word can be retrieved in a single disc access. In addition, assuming a simple formatting strategy that fills each line with as many words as possible from the beginning of the paragraph, at most one word on a line is

a candidate for hyphenation. Of these, perhaps two-thirds can be eliminated from further consideration by the screening process outlined earlier.
Thus, we may actually look up only about 2% of the tokens in the source.

Homographs can be identified as such in the lexicon. However, even if
the part of speech of a word occurrence could be determined from its context, this may not be sufficient to identify which homograph it was. The
formatter could make an arbitrary choice and advise the user to check its
decision.

A system relying solely on a lexicon has to have a fall-back if the word is
not present. A possible strategy is to leave the word un-hyphenated and to
write it to a log for the system administrator to deal with.

Scribe Scribe [9] uses a lexicon-only approach. A document can have a
document-specific hyphenation list associated with it; that list is used when
the document is formatted. If Scribe finds a word that should be
hyphenated but is not in the list, the word is written to a log file. Such
words can be looked up in a master hyphenation lexicon and added to the
document specific list. Alternatively, the user can mark hyphenation
points directly in the text.

9.3 Combination lexicon and algorithm

Typically, a system using both an algorithm and a lexicon uses the lexicon
to store those words that would be broken incorrectly by the algorithm.
Any new exceptions to the algorithm found by proof-reading the output
can be added to the lexicon. This approach is used by TeX [10, Appendix
H], by the Autologic hyphenation system, and by *troff* (though with a very
small lexicon).

TeX As noted in section 7.2.4, TeX takes a paragraph-long view when
breaking a paragraph into lines. Penalties associated with hyphenation
mean that it only hyphenates if there is no better alternative. A word is
considered for hyphenation when it would straddle the end of a line following a feasible break-point. To be a candidate for hyphenation, the word
must be entirely lower case, in a single font, preceded by glue (see 7.2.4)
and followed by glue or punctuation.

TeX takes a cautious approach to hyphenation; it is relatively simple and
almost always safe. Because of the wider view that TeX takes, it is
sufficient for the algorithm to find a sub-set of the legal break-points in a
word rather than all of them. The algorithm is applied if the word is not
found in an exception list of about 350 words.

The TeX algorithm uses patterns to indicate where hyphens may and
may not be placed. Examples of the former are -less, con-s, and ex-;

examples of the latter (termed "inhibiting" patterns) are b=ly, =cing, and =tly. Table 9.2 gives examples of the effect of these patterns.

Table 9.2 Effects of hyphenation patterns

-less	enables	care-less
con-s	enables	con-struction
ex-	enables	ex-actly
b=ly	prohibits	notab-ly
=cing	prohibits	enti-cing
=tly	prohibits	silen-tly

Liang [4] describes how five levels of pattern matching are carried out, and how each level, apart from the first, deals with exceptions to the previous level. Liang also describes how the patterns were derived from a word list and how they are stored in a compact form.

In assessing the goodness of a set of line breaking points, TEX imposes user-settable penalties for hyphens, for two consecutive hyphenated lines and for hyphenating the penultimate line of a paragraph. These penalties tend to cause TEX to avoid such configurations except in extreme situations such as fitting text in very narrow columns. A user can correct mistakes that TEX might make by marking hyphenation points in a word; in TEX these are called "discretionary hyphens".

Autologic The Autologic program (reprinted with permission in Appendix E) was used in both the Autologic Newspaper and Commercial Printing systems; note that current company products are more advanced. The initial Autologic exception lexicon contained 39,455 words; it was indexed on the combination of first letter and word length giving an average of about 100 words in each search segment.

The Autologic algorithm has two sets of rules. "Last character" rules identify the rightmost hyphenation point. "Other times" rules identify any remaining points. Figure 9.1 shows how the algorithm operates for the word *hyphenated*.

WordPerfect WordPerfect uses left and right hyphenation bounds to determine if a word should be hyphenated or put completely on the next line. The user specifies the bounds as percentages of the line length. By default, the left bound is 10% of the line length to the left of the right margin and the right bound is 4% to the right.

When hyphenation is on, a word that starts at or before the left bound and continues past the right bound must be hyphenated. A word that starts after the left bound and continues past the right margin is wrapped to the next line. When hyphenation is off, a word that does not fit between

Figure 9.1 Processing of *hyphenated*

Last character rule (for "D")
    The preceding character is an E
    The character before that is a T or a D

    This yields hyphenat-ed

Other times rule
    Scan right to left for vowel   hyphenat-ed
    Scan left to find a consonant   hyphenat-ed
    Apply appropriate rule (for "N") hyphen-at-ed

Again
    Scan right to left for vowel   hyphen-at-ed
    Scan left to find a consonant   hyphen-at-ed
    Apply appropriate rule (for "H") hy-phen-at-ed

the bounds is put on the next line.

A WordPerfect user can choose between manual and automatic hyphenation. In manual mode the user is prompted for a hyphenation position. In automatic hyphenation, a set of rules is applied; the user is prompted only if the rules fail to hyphenate the word. For a nominal sum, WordPerfect Corporation provides a large lexicon that makes automatic hyphenation more precise.

troff A *troff* user can disable hyphenation altogether (.nh) or enable it with various flags set. The flags determine whether the first (last) two characters of a word can be split off and whether a line that will cause a trap (typically the last line on a page) can end with a hyphen. In addition, a user-settable hyphenation indicator character can be embedded in a word to specify desired hyphenation points. The default indicator is \%. If this marker appears before the first character then the word will not be hyphenated. Figure 9.2(a) shows the result of formatting without markers, Fig. 9.2(b) is the same text with the marker inserted before the first character of Catherine.

If the user finds that *troff* is making errors in hyphenation (e.g. transparent is hyphenated incorrectly as you can see), words with break-points marked can be added to a small (128 character) exception list. If there is not enough room in the list, one solution is to pre-process the text through a macro-processor like M4 (see 6.1) replacing problem words with words containing explicit hyphenation markers. An example macro definition is:

Figure 9.2 Hyphenation of a word can be suppressed

```
This is a test  of  the  hyphenation  algorithm
used  by troff. A proper name may be hyphenated
by the program  unless  we  specify  otherwise.
Let's  try a few right here: Christopher, Cath-
erine, Margaret, Elizabeth.
```

(a)

```
This is a test  of  the  hyphenation  algorithm
used  by troff. A proper name may be hyphenated
by the program  unless  we  specify  otherwise.
Let's   try   a   few   right   here:  Christopher,
Catherine, Margaret, Elizabeth.
```

(b)

define(transparent,trans\%par\%ent)

While *troff* can be prevented from hyphenating the last line on a page, it has no qualms about hyphenating successive lines. See Fig. 9.3 for an extreme example of this.

Figure 9.3 Excessive hyphenation

```
To get troff to hyphenate con-
secutive   instances   of output
lines we'll cause  the   inclu-
sion  of numerous lengthy col-
lections of characters  subse-
quently  manipulating  parame-
ters controlling line length.
```

Comparisons of the three methods The output from a system relying totally on an algorithm is likely to require careful proof-reading unless the occasional bad break is acceptable; as might be the case with a newspaper column for example. The lexicon required by a lexicon+algorithm approach is smaller than that of a lexicon-only scheme but if the larger lexicon can be organized to fetch a word in one access, the latter may be faster overall. Homographs are a problem; a method with a lexicon at least has a means of detecting them. A reasonable strategy is not to hyphenate such words at all. Overall, the tendency is to strive for better algorithms and use an exception list to catch exception words.

Summary

Allowing words to be split over lines enables text to be set tighter; if the lines are justified, less white space is needed. A word cannot be broken at an arbitrary point; typically, English words are broken between syllables. The rules for hyphenation are difficult to embody into an algorithm because, in the worst case, they may depend on the part of speech which requires contextual analysis. Even the best algorithms use a lexicon of exceptions to the rules they implement. Algorithms that do not try to find every possible break-point can be quite compact. A method based solely on a lexicon, while requiring a lot of storage, can be quite fast, but it needs a way of dealing with words not in its word list.

Exercises

(1)   Obtain a word list with hyphenation points marked and create the matrices used by the Time magazine algorithm. For various threshold values, compare the break-points selected by the algorithm with those in the original word list. Record the number of correct points found and the number of erroneous points.

(2)   Conflation is the process of reducing a word to its root form and, in some ways, is a similar problem to hyphenation. Try developing a conflation algorithm. See section 3.9 of Winograd [11] for some ideas.

(3)   This text was prepared using a *troff*-like formatter. Can you find any hyphenation errors?

References

1.   *Collins Dictionary of the English Language,* William Collins Sons & Co., Glasgow, 1979.

2.   *Webster's Ninth New Collegiate Dictionary,* G. & C. Merriam, Springfield, Mass., 1984.

3.   J. A. Manas, "Word division in Spanish," *Communications of the ACM,* vol. 30, no. 7, pp. 612-616, July 1987.

4.   F. M. Liang, "Word hy-phen-a-tion by computer," STAN-CS-83-977, Department of Computer Science, Stanford University, California, August 1983.

5. *Style Manual,* U.S. Government Printing Office, Washington D. C., 1973. Revised Edition.

6. J. L. Peterson, "Use of Webster's Seventh New Collegiate Dictionary to construct a master hyphenation list," *Proceedings of the NCC,* vol. 51, pp. 665-670, AFIPS Press, June 1982.

7. P.-A. Larson, "Dynamic hashing," *BIT,* vol. 18, pp. 184-201, 1978.

8. P.-A. Larson and A. Kajla, "File organization: Implementation of a method guaranteeing retrieval in one access," *Communications of the ACM,* vol. 27, no. 7, pp. 670-677, July 1984.

9. B. K. Reid, "Scribe: A document specification language and its compiler," CMU-CS-81-100, Department of Computer Science, Carnegie-Mellon University, October 1980.

10. D. E. Knuth, "Tau Epsilon Chi: A system for technical text," in *TₑX and Metafont: New directions in typesetting,* Digital Press and the American Mathematical Society, Bedford, MA and Providence, RI, 1979. Part 2.

11. T. Winograd, "Understanding natural language," *Cognitive Psychology,* vol. 3, no. 1, pp. 1-191, January 1972. Also published in book form by Academic Press, 1972.

Spelling Checking and Correction

In this chapter and the next we look at programs that assist writers. Rather than considering utilities that help during document composition (brainstorm aids, outliners and so on), we examine those that can be applied to a completed text. Generally, such programs compare various aspects of a document against sets of standards. In this chapter we look at spelling checkers: programs that typically process the input one word at a time. In the next chapter we look at programs that take a wider view of a text.

A spelling checker is one of the most useful and conceptually simple aids for a writer. Checking the spelling in a large document by hand is tedious and error-prone. Checking by hand without reference to a standard word list means that checking will be with respect to the checker's ideas of spelling. A program using a lexicon establishes a common spelling standard.

Spelling checkers typically look at words in isolation and are therefore limited in the type of errors they can detect. They are unable to detect misuse of words (for example, use of *too* where *to* or *two* is correct) or errors of syntax or semantics. Table 10.1 list some errors found by the author while proof-reading documents. The first error may be detectable by a program knowing about letter patterns in English. Detection of the second error probably requires a lexicon with a stop list. The stop list (a list of known errors) prevents *presenation* being accepted as *pre-senate-ion*. The last four examples would not be found by a simple spelling checker and require increasingly sophisticated detection methods.

Checking programs can be categorized in many ways: for example, is checking applied as the document is typed or only when it is complete? Is there any assistance with error correction? Is the checking and/or correction performed interactively or in batch mode? Is checking based on a lexicon? In this chapter we consider some aspects of spelling checking and correction and look at example systems. Bentley [1] and Peterson [2] have good discussions of the topic.

Table 10.1 Example textual errors

1   ...**betwwen** three and four...
2   ...the **presenation** of the material...
3   ...the user **cold** enter more than...
4   A warning of deadlocks **if** given, but no solution.
5   ...extend this **ideas** so that several...
6   ...characters into the **lime** buffer.

10.1 The lexicon

Most spelling checkers, and any program that aspires to correct spelling, needs a word list of some form. In this section we look at some aspects of lexicon size, derivation, and storage.

10.1.1 Lexicon size
There are two kinds of errors a spelling checker may make. First, it may flag as incorrect a word which is correct. Second, it may accept as correct, a word which is not the one the user intended to enter. Errors of the first kind are a nuisance but not serious. The author can skip over erroneous entries in a "List of misspellings" and no action is needed on the source text.

Errors of the second kind are more serious since they are unlikely to be detected unless the document is proof-read by hand. In a lexicon-based system, errors of this kind are caused when a mis-spelling or mis-typing transforms a word into one that is represented directly or indirectly by a lexicon entry. While it may seem attractive otherwise to have as large a lexicon as possible, Peterson [3] observes that the larger the lexicon, the larger the probability that a mistyping may transform a word into an entry in the lexicon and thus make it an undetectable error. He recommends the use of a core lexicon of modest size together with a facility that enables "errors" detected using the core to be compared with users' specialized word lists. Thus, the errors of an engineer, mis-typing *cam* as *cwm* and a geographer mis-typing *cwm* as *cam* will both be detected, provided neither word appears in the core.

10.1.2 Lexicon derivation
The problem of forming a core lexicon is one of finding a set of words that are both in common use and are correctly spelled. Machine-readable dictionaries are available (see, for example, Peterson [3]) but in the absence of such ready-made word lists, machine-readable texts are a natural source of words. One can begin with a completely empty lexicon, run the texts through the spelling checker and add to the lexicon the correctly spelled

words appearing in the "misspellings" lists.

10.1.3 Type of entry
In the lexicon we could store all variants of a root word: for example, *match, matches, matched, matching, mismatched* and so on. An alternative is to save space by storing only root words (*match* in our example) and, with each one, a list of valid affixes (prefixes and suffixes) and affix combinations. In the case of *match, un-* is legal combined with *-ed* (yielding *unmatched*) but probably illegal in combination with *-es* (*unmatches*). We now need a conflation process that takes an arbitrary word and reduces it to its root together with a list of the affixes stripped. This is a non-trivial problem in English where addition of a suffix often modifies the end of a word, for example *handy* + *ly* = *handily* and *knife* + *s* = *knives*.

A third alternative is to save even more space and store only the root words and a general list of legal affixes. However, in this case we will have to guard against erroneous words being considered to be in the lexicon. For example, *bisecter* might be accepted because it can be formed by adding prefix *bi-* and suffix *-er* to lexicon entry *sect*. A solution to the problem is to have a "stop list" containing known erroneous words. A word found in such a list is flagged as an error no matter what is in the lexicon.

The choice between the three alternatives outlined above depends on factors such as the error rate we are prepared to tolerate, the amount of available memory, and the way in which we check words. For example, if checking is performed character by character as text is entered, then a full lexicon will allow faster response.

10.1.4 Lexicon storage
In theory, it does not matter how fast a spelling check runs as long as it gives the correct results. However, a user will typically want the results as soon as possible. In a lexicon-based system the storage problem is one of designing a data structure that will indicate as quickly as possible whether or not a given string is in the lexicon.

Solutions are likely to depend on the lexicon size, the available primary and secondary memory and the way in which words are checked. For example, if checking proceeds in parallel with the entry of a word, as in the case of some typewriters equipped with dictionaries, then a trie structure is appropriate (see, for example, Knuth [4]). The trie is traversed as characters are entered. An error indication can be given as soon as no legal word is possible.

If the complete word is known in advance, a variety of structures is possible. Turba [5] has a good survey. If primary memory is limited, a hierarchical structure may be adopted with the most frequent words being held in main memory and the least frequent on disc. In addition, some space can be saved if the user is prepared to accept a certain error rate in look-ups. That is, with a certain probability, an erroneous string will be accepted as a lexicon entry. This is illustrated in the next section. For an interesting technique using logic programming, see Berghel [Ref. 6 and 10.4.5 below].

10.1.5 Case study: spell
McIlroy [7] describes how the lexicon used by the Unix *spell* program began with the intersection of a word lists from the Brown Corpus (representing words in common use) and words from on-line dictionaries.[1] A variety of proper names were added to this list to form the final lexicon; on a local system, 4,682 of 24,473 entries in the *spell* lexicon are proper names.

In order to save space, the lexicon used by *spell* contains only root forms and general affix stripping is performed before look-up. A stop list is used to catch erroneous combinations of root and affixes; any word in the stop list is flagged as an error. The local version of *spell* has about 1,450 words in its stop list, some of them are shown in Table 10.2.[2]

Table 10.2 Examples of stop list entries

abducter	atter	bisecter	compeler	counterto
hesitator	inflictor	lober	nely	overseven
pipper	preson	recommited	reoh	sandbaged
standed	thier	undelicate	unmoral	unprobable

The method used to store the lexicon used by *spell* is, in part, a consequence of the architecture of the PDP-11 which has a small (64K byte) data space. The lexicon is represented by a bit vector using Bloom filters [9] as follows.

Assume there are N bits in our vector, initially all zero. An M-word lexicon is represented by the vector that results from the following process:

For each of the M words
do Apply K independent hash functions to it yielding $A_1, A_2, \cdots A_K$
(where $1 \leq A_i \leq N$)
Set bits $A_1, A_2, \cdots A_K$ to 1.

---

1. The Brown Corpus [8] is a set of 500 samples of about 2000 words each drawn from different text genres. Each of the samples is an example of the English language that was first generated (spoken, written, printed) in 1961. The corpus is thus a snapshot of American English at a particular time.
2. For example, *preson* is in the stop list because this common mis-typing of *person* would otherwise be accepted as pre+son.

To see if an arbitrary word is in the lexicon we apply the same K hash functions to it and examine the bits indexed by the hash values. If all are 1, we assume that the word is in the lexicon. If any is zero we assume it is not. Clearly there is the possibility of a non-word being accepted as a lexicon entry (for example, on the local system *aniversery* is thought to be in the lexicon). On discovering such a non-word, it can be added to the stop list. McIlroy shows how to choose the best value of K for given N and M.[3] The rate of errors produced by the fuzzy nature of the lexicon is comparable with the rate produced by typos that transform a word into another lexicon entry.

10.2 Spelling error detection

The simplest strategy for detecting errors is to compare words in the document with the contents of a lexicon. As we have seen, this look-up may have a certain error rate associated with it due to the number of lexicon entries (too many or too few), the nature of the entries (if a general affix list is used with root words) or the way in which they are stored (for example using Bloom filters).

Some systems have tried to reduce the need for a large lexicon by analyzing constituent parts of a word, comparing them with statistics of the language and computing a "wierdness" measure of the word. What they are looking for is the characteristics of some misspellings that appear to make them "leap off the page" when a document is being proof-read.

As we saw in Chapter 4, natural languages are redundant. That is, for any value of N, the possible N-letter groups do not occur with equal frequency. The larger the value of N, the larger is the percentage of possible groups that does not occur at all. Thus, a word can be scored according to the *a priori* probability of its constituent parts.

Typically, scoring also takes into account statistics of the document itself: a wierd word occurring often enough in a particular text will probably be accepted. However, this leads to the problem of "spellos" - where the user has consistently entered what he believes is a correct spelling but which in fact is in error.[4]

In summary, checking for errors cannot be exact. Some errors slip through because words are examined in isolation. Even at the word level, the size of the lexicon and the way it is stored introduce errors. Reliance

---

3. *Spell* uses a 400,000 bit vector and a typical lexicon has 24,000 words; the best value of K is 11.
4. This is in contrast to "typos" where there has been some typing error made in entering a word. An example of a typo is entering "fisrt" for "first". An example of a spello is entering "fobia" for "phobia". The categories overlap; for example, entering "beleive" for "believe" could be either.

on probabilistic measures adds further to the error rate.

10.3 Spelling correction

Ideally, a spelling checker will both detect and correct spelling errors without user intervention. In theory, such an ideal is not possible because a mis-spelled word p can be the result of mis-spelling or mis-typing more than one distinct correct word q.[5] In practice, however, some candidate words q are much more likely than others. In this section we look at some approaches to error correction.

Table 10.3 may give an indication of some of the difficulties faced by a spelling corrector operating on words in isolation. It contains a sample of the errors logged by a spelling checker; with each word is a count of the number of times it was recorded.[6] A few of the entries are correct words or symbols. In only about half of the remaining cases is it possible to be confident what the intended word was.

10.3.1 Correction strategies
A number of correction strategies are possible. At one extreme, a program could ask the user to enter the correct word and could then remember it in an "errors" list for future reference. At the other extreme, a program could replace an error by its best guess as to the correct word. A third strategy is to have the program generate a list of likely candidates from which a user is asked to choose. In the case of the last two options, we need to be able to generate a list of candidate words (in order of likelihood) given the misspelling and the lexicon.

A simple correction technique is to maintain a list of common errors each with its correct spelling. On locating an error in a list, the program substitutes the correct word. Lists of common spelling errors are available (see, for example Ref. 11), but the entries should probably be user-specific and be built up dynamically. In addition, the majority of data entry errors are likely to be typographical. An entry in the common errors list must be both common and unambiguous, that is, it must always be a mis-spelling or mis-typing of the same word. It is likely that most entries will be longer words and that the list will be comparatively small. Pollock [12] noted that the SPEEDCOP system used fewer than 300 entries in its common errors table and that such lists could be expected to correct 10% of errors in a text.

---

5. Pollock [10] reports that 10-15% of misspellings can plausibly be corrected to more than one lexicon word.
6. Errors were recorded by the Unix *spell* program running on two separate multi-user systems over an 18-month period. In that time 19,129 errors were logged, representing 7,231 different strings.

Table 10.3 Sample spelling errors

5	Acct	1	Bacscrew	1	Caal
1	DBF	5	Deducation	1	Dosting
1	Eida	1	Goodtimme	1	Industies
1	Linkletter	3	Mordor	1	Org
4	Quux	7	SS142	1	Suwel
1	Tu	1	Wr	1	acase
1	adver	2	ammounts	1	argos
1	availiable	6	befgore	2	buisiness
2	ccou	1	circul	1	compaany's
2	continuiu	3	curr	1	deletetions
1	difgf	6	dost	2	edgetrigger
6	employement	1	esential	1	extracuricular
1	fina	1	fullfills	3	gradution
2	helieve	2	ica	2	inb
2	insructed	1	itemes	1	knw
1	lless	1	mardeting	3	mmet
1	nand	12	northridge	2	ofg
1	opportunti	1	palced	1	persephone
1	possi	1	professiom	10	questiona
2	reconcidered	1	researchfor	1	researh
1	reseatchrch	2	resentfuol	4	reshearch
1	resi	2	resme	2	reso
2	resorces	1	resourses	7	respondants
1	rrerefinancing	1	seeked	4	sizeof
1	sssssssssssssssssss	2	succes	1	t'row
1	thenm	1	toa	1	trunc
2	ungetl	1	vestors	8	wikth
1	yearxwith				

Pollock and Zamora [13] classify the use of a common errors dictionary as an "absolute" correction technique. A "relative" technique on the other hand, selects from the lexicon a set of words that are plausible corrections with respect to the mis-spelling and some model of how errors are generated. The correct word is selected from this set.

Pollock and Zamora computed a "similarity key" for each word in their lexicon and sorted the lexicon by this key. The key is designed to be as insensitive as possible to common typographical errors. Thus, making a single error in a word typically leaves its key largely unchanged. A search for the key computed from a mis-spelling provides a starting point for a search of the lexicon.

The SPEEDCOP researchers found that 90-95% of errors in initial data entry contained only one error. Damerau [14] found that occurrences of four single error types accounted for over 80% of errors. These errors are: insertion of an extra character, omission of a character, typing the wrong character, and transposition of adjacent characters. Pollock and Zamora took as the correct word the first one encountered (scanning outwards from the entry point) that could be transformed into the mis-spelling by a single Damerau error. (Peterson's corrector [15] also reverses Damerau errors.)

The SPEEDCOP system corrected 85-95% of the misspellings for which it was designed, 75-90% of mis-spellings where the correct word was in the lexicon, and 65-80% of all errors [12].

10.4 Example systems

In this section we consider briefly some example spelling error detection/correction systems.

10.4.1 spell

The Unix utility *spell* can be categorized as an after-the-fact, detection only, batch, lexicon-based system.[7] It makes use of general Unix utilities as illustrated in Fig. 10.1.

Figure 10.1 Operation of spell

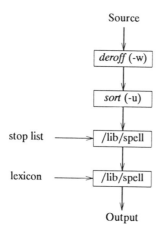

Text is passed through a series of "filters": *deroff* removes formatting

---

7. See Bentley [1] for a description of the evolution of *spell*.

directives and arranges words one to a line, *sort* sorts the words into alphabetical order and removes duplicates. There is no mapping onto a single case: both "Dog" and "dog" may be present in the output from *sort*. This is so that proper names with improper first characters (such as "texas" and "knuth") can be flagged as errors.

The two remaining filters are special purpose components. The first compares the words against a "stop list" of known errors. Affix stripping is performed if appropriate; words that match a stop list entry are flagged by having a hyphen appended. The final filter screens its input against the lexicon and outputs both the previously tagged errors and those words not transformable into a lexicon entry by conflation. More recent versions of *spell* (for example the *spellwwb* component of the Writer's Workbench - see 11.1) enable users to have words screened against their own lexicons in addition to the standard one.

Figure 10.2 lists a short text file (*spelltest*) and Fig. 10.3 shows the results of

            spell spelltest

Figure 10.2 Text with errors

This is a shot piece of text. It should ,however
be long enough to ilustrate some of the
shortcomings of spell. It should, for example,
ilustrate that information about the number of
ocurences of an error is missing. There are some
common words, like adrenalin, which one would need
to add to a personnel dictionary. This sentence
gives the programme a flavour of British spelling.
Here are some affixes: antifreeze, antidefrosted
and unhappily.

Figure 10.3 Output from *spell*

adrenalin
flavour
ilustrate
ocurences
progiamme

This example illustrates some of the deficiencies of *spell*. After the text has passed through *deroff* we have lost information about the location of words in the original file. After text has passed through *sort* (at least as used by *spell*) we have lost information about the number of times each word occurs in the input. As a result we do not know where the errors are in the original document or how many times a particular error occurred.

A simple solution to the second problem is to remove the -u flag from *sort*. Now duplicates are not removed and each occurrence of a word is looked up in the lexicon. The second /lib/spell filter should now be followed by a *uniq* filter with the -c flag. This replaces successive occurrences of a word by a line containing a count and the word. The results of applying this modified version of *spell* to the file of Fig. 10.2 are shown in Fig 10.4.

Figure 10.4 Output from modified *spell*

1 adrenalin
1 flavour
2 ilustrate
1 ocurences
1 programme

Spell has various options. Figure 10.5 shows the results of

spell -v -b spelltest

The -b flag uses a lexicon in which British spelling is employed. The -v flag outputs those words that were not literally in the lexicon (i.e. did not match a root) together with the affixes that were stripped.

Figure 10.5 Output from spell with -v and -b flags

adrenalin
ilustrate
ocurences
+es   affixes
+anti+ed   antidefrosted
+anti   antifreeze
+s   gives
+mis   missing
+s   shortcomings
+ing   spelling
+un-y+ily   unhappily
+s   words

10.4.2 typo

Strictly speaking, *typo* [16] falls into the same categories as *spell*. However, it uses a much smaller lexicon (fewer than 3,000 words) and instead of flagging a non-lexicon word as an error, it computes a "wierdness" score for it. The higher the value of this score, the more likely it is that the word is an error.

The wierdness score is based on the trigrams (3-letter groups) making up the word. In normal English only about 22% of the 21,952 trigrams occur.[8] A single-character error affects three trigrams and is likely to turn one of them into one of the 78% that does not normally occur. *Typo* goes to great lengths to compute the wierdness scores of the words not found in its dictionary and then presents the words sorted by this score. The only reason for this ordering appears to be psychological - the most likely errors appear early in the list and encourage the reader to continue reading. Figure 10.6 (reprinted, with permission, from Ref. 16) shows example *typo* output; each word is preceded by its (normalized) wierdness score. The success of the wierdness formula can be judged by the locations of the words tagged by bullets. The bullets (not generated by the program!) identify the actual spelling errors.[9]

10.4.3 Intspell

Hsu [17] used the components of *spell* (Fig. 10.1) as the basis of an interactive checker/corrector. *Intspell* reads the source file a screenfull at a time and each segment is run through *spell* to identify possible errors. If any errors are found, *Intspell* moves the cursor to each in turn. The user has an opportunity to correct the errors before the segment is appended to an output file. At each mis-spelling, the following five options are available:

replace:	replace by user input
replace and remember:	replace this and all future occurrences of the same word by user input
accept:	accept as correct
accept and remember:	accept as correct this and all future occurrences of the word
look-up:	suggest possible correct words

The "replace and remember" feature uses a list of pairs of words against which the output from *spell* is compared. The "accept and remember" option adds the word to a supplementary dictionary.

---

8. Assume a 28-character alphabet: A-Z, space and newline. 21,952 = 28^3

9. Space does not permit inclusion of the final two columns of the output. In addition to the words shown, there were 114 words with scores of 3, 2 and 1. Four of these were identified as errors: one had a score of 3, the others had scores of 2.

Figure 10.6 Example *typo* output © 1975 I.E.E.E

- 17 nd
17 heretofore
- 17 erroronously
- 16 suer
16 seized
- 16 poiter
16 lengthy
16 inaccessible
16 disagreement
- 16 bwirte
15 violating
15 unaffected
15 tape
15 swapped
15 shortly
- 15 mutiliated
15 multiprogramming
15 likewise
15 datum
- 15 dapt
15 cumulatively
15 consulted
15 consolidation
15 checking
- 15 accordinng
- 14 typpical
14 tabular
14 supplying
14 subtle
14 shortcoming
14 pivotal
14 invalid
14 infrequently
14 flexible
14 flags
14 conceptually
- 14 bwaite
14 broadly
- 14 amy
14 adds
14 accompanying
13 overwritten
13 occupying
13 lookup
13 flagged
- 9 inn
- 8 subrouutine
8 adjunct
7 drawbacks
- 6 thee
- 6 odification
- 6 od
6 indicator
6 imminent
6 formats
6 cetera
5 zeros
5 virtually
5 ultimately
5 truncate
5 therewith
5 thereafter
5 spectre
5 rewritten
5 raises
5 prefix
- 5 pesudonym
- 5 neames

- 5 namees
5 multiplied
5 interrelationship
5 inefficient
5 icalc
5 handler
5 flag
5 exercised
- 5 erroreous
5 dumped
5 dump
5 deficiency
5 controller
5 contiguous
5 changing
5 bottoms
- 5 bitis
5 ascertain
- 5 accomodate
4 unnecessarily
4 traversing
4 tracing
4 totally
4 tops
4 thirteen
- 4 tallyed
4 summarized
4 strictly
4 simultaneous
4 retrieval
4 quotient
4 proceeding
4 proceeded
- 4 preceeding
4 popularity
4 periods
4 owners
4 owner
4 occupies
4 nonzero
4 nonowners
4 nonexistence
4 miscellaneous
4 messages
4 legs
4 iread
4 interconnections
4 integrity
3 intact
4 incorporating
4 illustratively
4 illustrates
4 guarded
4 exhausted
4 eventually
4 erroneously
4 erroneous
4 denied
4 dedicated
4 decremented
4 corrected
4 complexities
4 circular
4 choosing
4 candidate
4 bulk
4 borrowing
4 borrow

4 arbitrarily
4 anew
4 wishes
3 verifying
3 verify
3 verifies
3 unused
3 undertaken
3 unallocated
3 treating
3 treat
3 traverses
3 traversed
3 traces
3 trace
3 therein
3 termed
3 tally
3 systematically
3 suffer
3 successfully
- 3 subroute
3 subdirectory
3 subdirectories
3 sub
3 structurally
3 simplify
3 simplified
3 sequential
3 separately
3 separated
3 searching
3 searches
3 searched
3 scheme
3 saved
3 salvage
3 retrieving
3 retrieved
3 retrieve
3 retained
3 respects
3 resides
3 reside
3 requests
3 requesting
3 renaming
3 rename
3 relieve
3 referring
3 referenced
3 recording
3 recorded
3 recalled
3 pseudonym
3 provisions
3 priorly
3 presumed
3 presently
3 preparation
3 precaution
3 preassigned
3 permitting
3 permission
3 permissible
3 outer
3 opens
- 3 occurance

3 necessity
3 manipulating
3 manipulate
3 itrunc
3 interprets
3 interpret
3 interference
3 interfere
3 interact
3 intends
3 initiation
3 indexing
3 indexes
- 3 independently
- 3 indentified
3 inconsistent
3 implementing
3 iget
3 identifying
3 identifies
3 hierarchy
3 hierarchal
3 grown
3 functionally
3 fixptr
3 findb
3 extension
3 extending
3 exits
3 exceptions
3 entering
3 ending
3 ended
3 encounter
3 elimination
3 discrepancies
3 diagrammatically
3 diagrammatical
3 determination
3 designating
3 deletion
3 deleting
3 deletes
3 deleted
3 default
3 dealt
3 dealing
3 dcheck
3 corrects
3 correctness
3 copy
3 copies
3 copied
3 consistency
3 consist
3 consequence
3 conjunction
3 computers
3 complements
3 closing
3 closes
3 clears
3 cleared
3 claimed
3 checks
3 charts
3 cautiously
3 bypassed

The "look-up" option generates a list of candidate words from a mis-spelling by reversing the four Damerau error types. The list is screened against the lexicon before being presented to the user. Reversing a supposed Damerau error in an N-letter word generates $53N+25$ candidate words.[10] *Intspell* records, for each user, the number of occurrences of each of the four error types. The counts determine the order in which candidate correct words are presented to the user. This technique was found to reduce the number of words presented before one was selected.

10.4.4 WordPerfect

A WordPerfect user can invoke the spelling checker on arbitrary parts of the current document. The checker also detects double word occurrences. The program first looks for a word in a small lexicon of common words. If the word is not there, it looks in the main lexicon. A user can also set up a supplementary lexicon to be searched.

A word not found in any lexicon is highlighted on the screen and the user is given a list of candidate replacement words and a set of options. The user can choose to skip all occurrences (or just this one) of the word, can add the word to the supplementary lexicon, can edit the word and can select from the candidate words. A user can also specify a pattern to be matched against the lexicons.

The number of candidate words found depends on the "non-word"; Table 10.4 shows some examples.

Table 10.4 Number of candidate replacement words presented.

Non-word	Number of candidates
nano	14
strat	17
frot	19
newe	26
corrie	40
ot	56
rute	79

Table 10.5 lists, in their order of presentation, the 19 words considered by WordPerfect to be possible replacements for *frot*. Examination of replacement lists for different words suggests that those at the beginning of a list are based on letter differences and transpositions and that these are

---

10. N result from reversing an insertion error, N-1 from reversing a transposition error, 25N from reversing a substitution error and 26(N+1) from reversing an omission.

Table 10.5 Possible replacements for *frot*

foot	fort	fret
frog	from	front
frost	froth	rot
fraud	fraught	frayed
fred	freed	freight
freud	fried	fright
fruit		

followed by an often longer list of words considered phonetically similar.

10.4.5 A logic approach

Berghel [18] describes an elegant Prolog-based approach to error detection and correction. In his system the lexicon is represented by a set of axioms, one for each lexicon entry. Thus, the following:

    w('C,'A,'T).
    w('D,'O,'G).
    w('F,'R,'O,'G).

asserts that *CAT*, *DOG*, and *FROG* are words. Full words are stored rather than roots plus affixes. Given an appropriately constructed string S, the Prolog mechanism indicates if w(S) is true.

A second set of axioms defines similarity relations between strings. In this way Prolog, given a word x, will identify the set of words that are similar to x as defined by the axioms. Because there are no intervening approximations or metrics, in information-theoretic terms the result is 100% precision and 0% fallout. Berghel presents the axioms corresponding to the four Damerau errors and also those for three categories of string similarity (material, positional, and ordinal) defined by Faulk [19].

Although the system does not order the candidate lexicon words in any way, it is elegant in that any similarity measures that can be expressed in Prolog can be implemented with minimal effort.

Summary

A program to verify the spelling in a document is a conceptually simple and useful writer's aid. It is not likely to be a complete substitute for a human proof-reader because of limitations in the view that such programs normally take of text (word at a time). In addition, selection and representation of entries in the lexicon may introduce errors.

Attempts have been made to automate correction of errors. A completely automatic system is theoretically impossible. However, in practice, a large proportion of errors introduced during text entry fall into a few categories, thus allowing the most probable correct word to be identified in many cases.

Exercises

(1) *Spell* (Fig. 10.1) eliminates duplicate words before lexicon look-up and thus only looks up a particular word once. Compare this with the strategy outlined in the text where compression of duplicates is performed after look-up. Run the two versions of *spell* on text files of various sizes and compare run-times.

(2) How would you rectify the first deficiency of standard *spell*, namely the lack of positional information about the errors it finds?

(3) Consider the revised checker of Exercise 1. How could you speed up the checking of words by taking advantage of the fact that input to the lexicon look-up is sorted? As a side project, analyze typical documents to see how many words occur only once, how many exactly twice and so on.

(4) Analyze the spelling errors you make. What proportion are typos rather than spellos? Detection of each is the same but good correction methods are likely to be different. What correction strategy can you devise for spellos? How can software distinguish a spello from a typo?

(5) Some typing errors, lik ethese, occur at word boundaries. Design a program that can perform the "obvious" correction.

(6) WordPerfect presents a user with a list of words that sound like the one it did not find in its lexicons. Devise a way in which the lexicons can be structured so that such words can be found quickly.

References

1. J. Bentley, "Programming pearls: a spelling checker," *Communications of the ACM*, vol. 28, no. 5, pp. 456-462, May 1985.

2. J. L. Peterson, "Computer programs for detecting and correcting spelling errors," *Communications of the ACM*, vol. 23, no. 12, pp. 676-687, December 1980.

3. J. L. Peterson, "A note on undetected typing errors," *Communications of the ACM*, vol. 29, no. 7, pp. 633-637, July 1986.

4. D. E. Knuth, *The Art of Computer Programming, Vol. 3: Sorting and Searching*, Addison-Wesley, Reading, Mass., 1973.

5.   T. N. Turba, "Checking for spelling and typographical errors in computer-based text," *ACM SIGPLAN Notices*, vol. 16, no. 6, pp. 51-60, June 1981. Proceedings of the ACM SIGPLAN/SIGOA Symposium on text manipulation, Portland, Oregon, June 8-10, 1981.

6.   H. Berghel, "Crossword compilation with Horn clauses," *The Computer Journal*, vol. 30, no. 2, pp. 183-188, April 1987.

7.   M. D. McIlroy, "Development of a spelling list," *IEEE Transactions on Communications*, vol. COM-30, no. 1, pp. 91-99, January 1982.

8.   C. K. Kucera and W. N. Francis, *Computational analysis of present-day American English*, Brown University Press, Providence, RI, 1967.

9.   B. H. Bloom, "Space/time trade-offs in hash coding with allowable errors," *Communications of the ACM*, vol. 13, no. 7, pp. 422-426, July 1970.

10.   J. J. Pollock, *SPEEDCOP: Final report*, Chemical Abstracts Service, Columbus, Ohio, November 1981. CAS Internal Report.

11.   *Webster's New World Misspellers Dictionary*, Simon and Schuster, New York, 1983.

12.   J. J. Pollock, *SPEEDCOP: Task B.1 - Automatic correction of common misspellings*, Chemical Abstracts Service, Columbus, Ohio, October 1981. CAS Internal Report.

13.   J. J. Pollock and A. Zamora, "Automatic spelling correction in scientific scholarly text," *Communications of the ACM*, vol. 27, no. 4, pp. 358-368, April 1984.

14.   F. J. Damerau, "A technique for computer detection and correction of spelling errors," *Communications of the ACM*, vol. 7, no. 3, pp. 171-176, March 1964.

15.   J. L. Peterson, *Design of a spelling program: an experiment in program design*, Springer-Verlag, New York, October 1980. Lecture Notes in Computer Science 96.

16.   R. Morris and L. L. Cherry, "Computer detection of typographical errors," *IEEE Transactions on Professional Communication*, vol. PC-18, no. 1, pp. 54-64, March 1975.

17.   Chin Ming Hsu, *Intspell - An interactive spelling checker/corrector*, Computer Science Department, CSUN, Northridge, CA, 1986. MS Thesis.

18.   H. Berghel, "A logical framework for the correction of spelling errors in electronic documents," *Information Processing and Management*, vol. 23, no. 5, pp. 477-494, 1987. Also available as research report CSAS-TR 86-05, Department of Computer Science, University of Arkansas, Fayetteville.

19.   R. Faulk, "An inductive approach to language translation," *Communications of the ACM*, vol. 7, no. 11, pp. 647-653, November 1964.

V

Natural Language Processing

Tools for Writers

Under the heading of tools for writers are both programs that assist in the creation of text and those that analyze a finished document. The former include tools that help arrange a writer's ideas and brainstorm organizers of various kinds. In this chapter we look at programs in the latter category, those that produce a report on a file of text. This type of software can give immediate, reliable and consistent feedback on a document.

Types of measurement In some sense, document analyzers compare a user's text against a set of standards. There is a spectrum of factors that can be measured, ranging from objective (e.g. spelling) to subjective (e.g. continuity). We look at two products: the Writer's Workbench from Bell Laboratories and IBM's CRITIQUE. The former assumes, for the most part, that the input is grammatically correct; the latter can accept a wider range of input and diagnose syntax errors. Wallroff [1] has an interesting commentary on editing by computer in general with particular reference to four programs (including the Writer's Workbench and CRITIQUE).

11.1 Bell Laboratories' Writer's Workbench

The Writer's Workbench (WWB) [2,3], developed from an internal product at Bell Labs [4,5], is a set of programs that produces a report on a file of text. The report can be divided broadly into two sections: "proofreading" and "style". The first section is concerned with more objective matters such as spelling, punctuation and split infinitives: areas where clear-cut rules exist. The second section contains various measures of the style of the document, for example variation in sentence type and length. The philosophy underlying the package is that documents that break accepted style rules are hard to read.

In keeping with Bell Labs' software engineering principles, WWB is a package of independent programs rather than one large one. Figure 11.1

shows the package components and their relationships.

Figure 11.1 Components of the Writer's Workbench

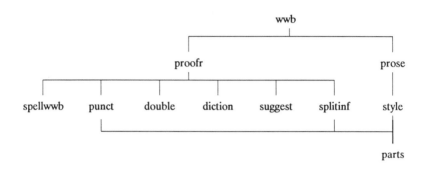

The higher-level components are typically Unix shell scripts that invoke the lower-level ones. The lower-level components (such as *spellwwb* and *diction*) can also be used in a stand-alone manner.

Figure 11.2 contains the text of a file (*gopher*) distributed as a test file with the WWB software. Before proceeding further, the reader should test his or her proof-reading skills and see how many errors can be found in the file. Appendix A contains the output from the command

wwb gopher

that produces a full report on the file.

Proofreading As can be seen from Fig. 11.1, the proofreading component *proofr* invokes *spellwwb* (spelling), *punct* (punctuation), *splitinf* (split infinitives), *diction* (wordy and hackneyed phrases), *double* (double words), and *suggest* (suggests replacements for the phrases found by *diction*).

Spellwwb is an improvement over the standard Unix *spell* (see Chapter 10) in that it can filter the list of misspellings output by *spell* through user-specified files. These files will typically contain specialized or personal word lists. A utility (*spelladd*) helps users set up these lists.

Punctuation checking includes counting the number of opening and closing "brackets" of various kinds (where the number of openers should be the same as the number of closers) and counting the quotation characters (where the total is normally an even number). The program also checks that the first word of a sentence is capitalized. *Punct* can output the punctuation rules it uses, in case the user is unsure why an "error" has been reported.

Figure 11.2 Test file for Writer's Workbench

.SA 1
.nr Pt 1
.nr Hy 0
.PH ""
.P
Many biological organisms cause damage to communication
wires and cables; bacteria, fungi, insects, rodents,
and marine borers are examples.
However, the most rapid and extensive damage is caused
by various species of rodents.
.P
It is generally recognized that gophers are attracted
to disturbed soil such as that found in a freshly buried
wire and cable trench.
one theory for gopher damage is that the animals believe
the soft lead cables to be roots from which they can expect water.
Generally, however, it is believed that rodents must chew to
keep their incisors sharp and to keep them from growing too long.
.P
Because of gopher damage experienced on less important
cables the first Bell System coaxial cable was protected by means
of .01-inch steel tapes covered with ashpalt impregnated jute.
This cable was installed between Stevens Point, Minnesota, and
and Minneapolis in 1940.
Gopher damage to the asphalt and jute (which presumably occurred
soon after installation) exposed the steel to the corrosive
enviorment of the soil and eventually resulted in failure of the cable.
Because of this experience, tests with live animals were
conducted by Livingston, to hopefully find what thickness of
material would prevent penetration, and in addition be
corrosion resistant.
These tests which used the cables as a barrier indicated that
a .01-inch copper tape was a reasonable choice.
This material was first utilized on Bell's Dallas - Los Angeles
coaxial toll cable.
.P
Because of the history of damage cited above, the Bell System
has in general applied some from of gopher protection to wires and
cables west of the Mississippi River and in some of the southern states.
Jute or polyethylene-covered thermoplastic-flooded steel has
been utilized for the cables while wire products were protected with
polyvinyl chloride (PVC jacketed galvanized steel.

Double words (unintended repetitions of a word) are easy to overlook,
particularly after a file has been edited and one occurrence of the word is
at the end of a line and the other is at the beginning of the next line. It is a
simple matter for *double* to report double words.

The *diction* component of WWB [4] was one of the first developed. It detects occurrences of phrases that are wordy or often misused or that have become cliches. Examples of such phrases are: "a number of", "during the time that" and "not in a position to". The list used by *diction* can be customized, thus allowing users to add their own pet peeves and remove favorite phrases. Offending pieces of the input file are highlighted between *[and]* delimiters. In the first few weeks of operation at Bell Labs, about 200 of the 450 phrases in the default file occurred at least once in the 35,000 sentences run through the program.

Suggest lists alternatives to the phrases found by *diction*. However, the program is very simple: it uses a stream editor to scan a file of about 600 lines each containing a word or phrase and suggested substitutions. Table 11.1 contains some examples from the file; some of the suggestions are not applicable in all contexts. Cherry and Vesterman report that authors appeared to make the suggested changes 50-75% of the time [4].

Table 11.1 Examples of phrases and suggested substitutions

and/or	X or Y or both
equally as good	as good as, equally good
in a very real sense	in a sense or OMIT WHOLE PHRASE
it is incumbent on me	I must
melt down	melt
miss out on	miss
situation	REWRITE
sufficient number of	enough
utilize	use

The final proofreading check is for split infinitives. Even though "to boldly go" may sound more dramatic than "to go boldly" it would be flagged as an error. The output from *parts* (see below) enables the program to detect infinitives split by adverbs.

Style evaluation Figure 11.3 is an example of the output from *style*; it shows the result of applying the program to the file of Fig. 11.2. The statistics are designed to enable a user to judge the readability of the text, to see if there is sufficient variety in the sentence forms and to decide if certain language elements are too common. In the case of many of the measures output by *style*, the user may be uncertain as to what a good value is. The *prose* component of WWB compares the measurements with a selected set of standards and outputs a narrative analysis of the user's document (see Appendix A).

Figure 11.3 Output from *style*

readability grades:
    (Kincaid) 13.6 (auto) 14.3 (Coleman-Liau) 13.4 (Flesch) 14.8 (37.9)
sentence info:
    no. sent 13 no. wds 294
    av sent leng 22.6 av word leng 5.19
    no. questions 0 no. imperatives 0
    no. content wds 180 61.2% av leng 6.57
    short sent (<18) 23% (3) long sent (>33) 8% (1)
    longest sent 36 wds at sent 12; shortest sent 13 wds at sent 7
sentence types:
    simple 23% (3) complex 62% (8)
    compound 8% (1) compound-complex 8% (1)
word usage:
    verb types as % of total verbs
    tobe 44% (14) aux 13% (4) inf 13% (4)
    passives as % of non-inf verbs 36% (10)
    types as % of total
    prep 12.6% (37) conj 4.4% (13) adv 4.8% (14)
    noun 29.3% (86) adj 17.7% (52) pron 3.1% (9)
    nominalizations 2 % (7)
sentence beginnings:
    subject opener: noun (2) pron (0) pos (0) adj (5) art (0) tot 54%
    prep 0% (0) adv 15% (2)
    verb 0% (0) sub_conj 23% (3) conj 0% (0)
    expletives 8% (1)

Prosestand produces a readable listing of the default standards used by *prose*; these are shown in Fig. 11.4. In addition, a *prose* user may choose to have the document compared against a set of standards based on training documents. Given the standards file, the output from *prose* is largely self-explanatory. It advises the reader why a certain aspect of a document is important and compares the measurements of the user's text with the standards.

A user can establish his or her own set of standards using *mkstand*. *Mkstand* is invoked with a list of files. It runs *style* on each of the files individually and creates a standards file based on the outputs from *style*. In fact, what it does is to compute the mean and standard deviation of each of the 10 features used by *prose*.[1] For each measure, the standards file will

---

1. Kincaid readability score, mean length of content words, percentage of short sentences, percentage of long sentences, passive verbs as percentage of non-infinitive verbs, percentage of nominalizations, mean sentence length (in words), percentage of expletives as sentence beginners, percentage of simple sentences

Figure 11.4 Default document standards

These are desirable ranges for technical documents based
on 30 technical memoranda judged good by managers in the
research area of Bell Labs:

Kincaid readability grades:.................... > 10.1 to 15.0 years

Average sentence length:...................... 16.7 to 25.3 words

Average length of content words:.............. 5.8 to 7.0 letters

Percentage of short sentences:................ 29.2% to 38.0%

Percentage of long sentences:................. 11.7% to 18.9%

Percentage of simple sentences minus
the percentage of complex sentences:........... -24.2% to 30.1%

Percentage of compound sentences plus
the percentage of compound-complex sentences:.. 5.7% to 35.2%

Passives should be fewer than:................ 28.6%

Nominalizations should be fewer than:.......... 4.2%

Expletives should be fewer than................ 5.7%

contain the mean ± 1 and 2 standard deviations. If a file has any score
more than 3 standard deviations from the mean, all its scores are excluded
from the calculations. The manual for *mkstand* recommends that at least
20 files be used to generate a standard and that each be at least 1900
words or 90 sentences long.

Readability Many formulae have been devised in an attempt to encapsu-
late the readability of a document in a single number (see, for example,
Ref. 6). One application of such numbers is in determining the grade level
of a school text: the numbers computed by *style* are output as grade-
reading scores. A typical formula involves average sentence length and
average word length (in characters or syllables). For example, the Flesch

minus percentage of complex sentences, and percentage of compound sentences
plus percentage of compound-complex sentences.

reading ease score [7] is:

206.835
- 1.015 * average words per sentence
- 0.846 * average syllables per word

It is usually reported in the range 0 (very difficult) to 100 (very easy). The WWB manual advises that of the four formulae computed by *style*, the Kincaid measure [8], derived from Navy training manuals, is the most applicable to technical documents. The Kincaid reading grade is:

11.8 * average syllables per word
+ 0.39 * average words per sentence
- 15.59

Note that the formulae measure only one aspect of readability. The grade level of a document can be decreased by the simple expedient of splitting long sentences into shorter ones. The number of syllables in a word is only one aspect of its readability - compare *minimum* and *psychosis*.

Other WWB utilities The Writer's Workbench package includes programs other than those shown in Fig. 11.1 and those mentioned above. For example, *abst* computes the abstractness of a document using a list of 314 words considered abstract by psychological researchers. *Sexist* is similar to *diction*; it detects sexist words and phrases (users can set up their own list). Finally, *org* gives a general indication of the organization of a document by printing just the significant parts of the text - headings and first and last sentences of paragraphs.

Parts *Parts* [5] was one of the first WWB components developed. It is generally used as a pre-processor by other utilities rather than as a stand-alone tool. The output from *parts* is a copy of the input file with each word tagged with its part of speech; Fig. 11.5 show the output from *parts* run on four sentences (the program routinely de-capitalizes words). The examples show both that *parts* is not 100% accurate and that many English words are potentially ambiguous.

In making class assignments, *parts* uses a small dictionary of function words and irregular verbs, knowledge of suffixes and finally, knowledge of English sentence structures. *Parts* assigns one of thirteen parts of speech to a word with about 95% accuracy.[2]

---

2. Internally, parts uses 29 word classes. These are collapsed to the following 13 on output: noun, verb, article, adjective, adverb, conjunction, preposition, interjection, auxiliary verb, pronoun, subordinate conjunction, to be, and passive.

Figure 11.5 Output from *parts*

```
I       saw     the     gray    cat     walking     slowly    .
pron    verb    art     adj     noun    noun        adv       .

I       love    flying  planes  .
pron    verb    adj     noun    .

see     ,   for     example     ,   the     text    above   .
noun    ,   prep    noun        ,   art     noun    adv     .

time    flies   like    an      arrow   .
noun    verb    prep    art     noun    .
```

The ability of *parts* to determine the part of speech of a word is useful in other applications. For example, when generating speech from text, the pronunciation of a word sometimes depends on its part of speech. Consider the difference between arithmetic (noun) and arithmetic (adjective), between record (noun) and record (verb) and between lead (noun) and lead (verb).

WWB goes beyond spelling checkers in performing simple proof-reading checks on a document. If the document is free of syntax errors, WWB can provide useful style analyses. Keifer and Smith [9] report that use of WWB speeded the learning of editing skills by their students. Because the *parts* component assumes that its input is free of syntax errors, WWB is perhaps most useful in the later stages of document development. In contrast, CRITIQUE can detect a variety of syntax errors; we look at this package next.

11.2 CRITIQUE

IBM's CRITIQUE program [10] is an extension of the earlier EPISTLE system [11, 12]. EPISTLE was designed to be an aid for businessmen, particularly middle management, in their interactions with text. One goal was for it to provide synopses of incoming mail, highlight features known to be of interest, and extract index terms to aid document filing. A second goal was for it to provide critiques of documents. As its name suggests, CRITIQUE performs this second function. Its scope is wider than EPISTLE; in addition to office environments, it has been tested in publication organizations and educational institutions.

The examples presented in Ref. 10 suggest that CRITIQUE is comparable with the *proofr* component rather than the *style* component of WWB. However, it is capable of more detailed criticism than *style* in that it can detect more than 100 style and grammar errors. CRITIQUE uses a parser that yields approximate parses for a large percentage of written English. Syntax errors can be diagnosed.

Operation CRITIQUE processes text in six steps. First, the labeller identifies surface features such as boundaries of paragraphs, headings and sentences. The program knows about certain forms of embedded formatting information and can be customized to ignore such embedded codes. It is able to skip non-text such as tables and figures.

The second step is lexical analysis. Here words are looked-up in the on-line dictionary. The dictionary, based mostly on Webster's 7th Collegiate, has about 100,000 entries and contains syntactic information and information about the structure of words. Most words not found in the dictionary are assumed to be singular nouns.

The output from the lexical analyzer is passed to the parser. The parser and grammar rules are written in PLNLP (Programming Language for Natural Language Processing). PEG, the Penelope English Grammar is largely the work of Karen Jensen (see, for example, Ref. 13). Like the earlier EPISTLE system, parsing may take one or two passes. In the first pass, constraints such as subject-verb agreement are enforced. If no parse is obtained, a second attempt is made, this time with constraints relaxed. The parser may also make substitutions, such as *whose* for *who's* in an attempt to obtain a parse.

A particular sentence may have many parses. Wallroff [1] gives the following example of a sentence in which every word can be tagged with more than one part of speech:

Test results show that sand filters produce more even results.

CRITIQUE has a mechanism for choosing between alternative parses and, if the parses are sufficiently different, it will report the sentence as being UNCLEAR.

In the fourth step the text is processed by STYLE RULES. Weaknesses of usage and diction are detected as are flaws such as split infinitives and faulty parallel construction.

The fifth and sixth steps are the collection and presentation of the information gathered by CRITIQUE. The interactive version offers three levels of help, the batch version outputs brief explanations of errors. Figure 11.6 shows an example of CRITIQUE output with the text generated by the program shown in italics.[3] Note the error that CRITIQUE missed.[4]

---

3. Figure 11.6 is a reproduction of Fig. 2 in Ref. 10 used by permission of the

Figure 11.6 Output from CRITIQUE

```
Lets contemplate how a president is elected.
*Let's
In many cases the best candidate in the eyes of
        |MISSING COMMA
the public is the one who has the most exposure.
This is no way to chose a president, but
                    *choose
unfortunately it is often true. The total package
of a candidates political ideas don't really make
                        *doesn't
an impression on the public. His appearance
                        |FRAGMENT
and mannerisms and the amount of exposure
that make him successful.
```

Implementation CRITIQUE appears to process sentences in isolation; there is no mention of inter-sentence checks such as might detect the possible error in:

The boy threw the ball to the girl. He nearly caught it.

Thus, in a multi-processor system, sentences can be assigned to different processors and analyzed in parallel. CRITIQUE saves information about a document so that the next time it is processed only changed sentences need be checked.

CRITIQUE users can classify advice as "correct", "useful", "missed" or "wrong". In this way, its developers get feedback on its performance.

Applications and testing At the time of writing, CRITIQUE has just been announced by IBM as part of the Processmaster/VM program. During its development, CRITIQUE was tested in educational institutions, publishing organizations and office environments. Different types of users have different requirements; for example, speed is more important in offices while accuracy is more important in composition classes. A pre-release version of CRITIQUE has been used in two university English departments: the interactive version at the University of Hawaii [14] and the

---

authors and the Association for Computational Linguistics; copies of the publication from which this material is derived can be obtained from Dr Donald E. Walker (ACL), Bellcore, MRE 2A379, 445 South Street, Box 1910, Morristown, NJ 07960-1910, USA.
4. "candidates" should be "candidate's"

batch version by Colorado State University [15, 16].

Chandler *et al.* [14] identify three factors in the success of CRITIQUE at Hawaii: its interactive nature, the recognition that usage had to be supervised, and the identification of CRITIQUE as a learning rather than just a correcting tool. All three of CRITIQUE's help levels were used and it was a successful teaching tool because it was operating on the students' own writing.

The parse trees produced by CRITIQUE proved surprisingly useful. Reference 14 describes, with many examples, ways in which the trees helped students; for example, in correcting punctuation, in reducing wordiness, and in determining when to ignore CRITIQUE's comments.

Colorado State University used CRITIQUE in a batch manner, sending essays to IBM over BITNET and getting CRITIQUEd essays returned in the same way. Smith reports that this configuration was frustrating at times but that students reacted positively to CRITIQUE and became adept at rejecting bad advice.

Summary

Spelling checking, as described in the previous chapter, is perhaps the simplest form of document evaluation. In this chapter we have looked at systems that go further in assessing the goodness of a document in objective ways. We have seen that simple punctuation checking can be done and that a system using a parser and wide-coverage grammar can detect many type of syntax error. In the case of more subjective measures, standards can be established against which to measure such aspects of a document as variation in sentence length and type.

Exercises

(1) A spelling checker will not normally detect typos that produce genuine words. For example, the author recently noted "form" typed as "from", "or" as "of", and "fur" as "fir" in a document. In many instances the new word is not syntactically valid in context, for example:

   fill in your name and salary in the application from.

Would *parts* be useful in detecting such errors? If so, describe how you would use it; if not, describe the methods you might use to detect this kind of error.

(2) A simple syntax checker could use a list of valid sentence forms in checking the syntax of an arbitrary sentence. Valid sentence forms include:

article noun verb
article noun adverb verb article noun.

Describe how the parts component of WWB could be used both in creating the list of valid forms and in checking a text file.

(3)   What are the limitations of the syntax checker of Exercise 2?

(4)   In Chapter 3 we discussed syntax-directed editors. Given that written documents tend to be more formal and well-formed than spoken utterances, how feasible do you think it is to develop such an editor for English? What problems do you foresee?

(5)   Unless used for rhetorical purposes, it is considered bad style to have many repetitions of the same word or phrase close together in a document or to have adjacent sentences with the same structure. Outline how a style checker could warn a user about this. What criteria would you use for "too many"?

References

1.   B. Wallroff, "The literate computer," *The Atlantic Monthly*, vol. 261, no. 1, pp. 64-71, January 1988.

2.   N. H. Macdonald, L. T. Frase, P. S. Gingrich, and S. A. Keenan, "The Writer's Workbench: Computer aids for text analysis," *IEEE Transactions on Communications*, vol. COM-30, no. 1, pp. 105-110, January 1982.

3.   L. L. Cherry, "Writing tools," *IEEE Transactions on Communications*, vol. COM-30, no. 1, pp. 100-105, January 1982.

4.   L. L. Cherry and W. Vesterman, "Writing tools--the STYLE and DICTION programs," Comp. Sci. Tech. Rep. No. 91, Bell Laboratories, Murray Hill, New Jersey, February 1981.

5.   L. L. Cherry, "PARTS - A system for assigning word classes to English text," Comp. Sci. Tech. Rep. No. 81, Bell Laboratories, Murray Hill, New Jersey, June 1978.

6.   G. R. Klare, "Assessing readability," *Reading research quarterly*, vol. 10, pp. 62-102, 1974-1975.

7.   R. Flesch, "A new readability yardstick," *Journal of applied psychology*, vol. 32, pp. 221-233, 1948.

8.   E. A. Smith and P. Kincaid, "Derivation and validation of the automated readability index for use with technical materials," *Human Factors*, vol. 12, no. 5, pp. 457-464, October 1970.

9.   K. E. Keifer and C. R. Smith, "Textual analysis with computers: Tests of Bell Laboratories computer software," *Research in the teaching of English*, vol. 17, no. 3, pp. 201-214, 1983.

10. S. D. Richardson and L. C. Braden-Harder, "The experience of developing a large-scale natural language text processing system: CRITIQUE," *Proceedings of the Second Conference on Applied Natural Language Processing*, pp. 195-202, Austin, Texas, February 1988.

11. L. A. Miller, G. E. Heidhorn, and K. Jensen, *Text-critiquing with the EPISTLE system: an author's aid to better syntax*, IBM Thomas J. Watson Research Center, Yorktown Heights, New York, December 1980. IBM Research Report RC 8601.

12. G. E. Heidhorn, K. Jensen, L. A. Miller, R. J. Byrd, and M. S. Chodorow, "The EPISTLE text-critiquing system," *IBM Systems Journal*, vol. 21, no. 3, pp. 305-326, 1982.

13. K. Jensen, *PEG 1986: A broad-coverage computational syntax of English*, IBM Thomas J. Watson Research Center, Yorktown Heights, 1986.

14. R. Chandler, W. Creed, and S. Richardson, *CRITIQUE as a teaching tool for writing classes*. Presented at The Dynamic Text, Toronto, June 5-10, 1989.

15. C. R. Smith, "Text analysis: the state of the art," *The computer-assisted composition journal*, vol. 3, pp. 68-78, 1989.

16. C. R. Smith, *CRITIQUE at Colorado State*. Presented at CCCC '89, Seattle, Washington, March 1989.

Authorship Studies

A person familiar with the works of two writers, for example John Steinbeck and Graham Greene, can probably determine which of the two wrote a page of previously unseen material. There would be elements of the writing style that would suggest it was written by one and not the other. Aspects of the style of some writers, for example Ernest Hemingway and Edward Bulwer-Lytton, may be so distinct as to invite parody. Determination of the authorship of a text is of interest in cases where it is unknown or disputed. Examples of such cases are the letters attributed to St Paul, some of the Federalist papers, and some of the works attributed to Shakespeare.

Some techniques for authorship determination involve examination of an author's word choice, use of metaphor, phrasing and so on. However, others involve only statistical analyses and are well suited to computerization. In this chapter we look at some of the statistical techniques and examples of their application. An introduction to the area is found in Tankard [1]; a good survey of the current state of the art can be found in Smith [2]. Chapter 3 of Morton and McLeman [3] gives readable background to research on classical texts, particularly the authors' work on the Pauline letters.

It is probably not possible to have a program which says categorically: "this text was written by X". The best we can do is to have systems which say "this text has more in common with the works of X than it does with the works of Y" or "it is likely that texts P, Q, and R were written by the same person."

Evaluating tests Suppose we have developed a test that we think discriminates among works by different authors; how do we evaluate it? Morton [3 ch. 3] describes a method requiring the establishment of three groups of documents. One is a "white" group where the authorship is beyond doubt, a second is a "black" group where the alleged author is known to have had no connection with the text, the third is a "grey" group containing disputed texts. Our test may be considered reasonable as long as it does not cast doubt on the authorship of any document in the white group; it is desirable that it will reject most of the attributions in the black group. Now, when applied to the grey group, it should help us make decisions about that set of documents.

In the following sections we examine four tests that have been used. In 12.1 we look at techniques based on word-length frequency and in 12.2 at tests using the frequency distribution of sentence lengths. In 12.3 we examine a vocabulary characteristic devised by Yule. Finally, in 12.4 we examine some of the work of A.Q. Morton.

12.1 Word-length frequency

Williams [4] describes how Mendenhall [5, 6] proposed word-length distribution as a discriminator of authors. Mendenhall plotted graphs of relative word-length frequencies and termed the results the "characteristic curves" of composition of authors. Mendenhall's graphs included those for works of Dickens, Thackery, Shakespeare, Bacon and Marlowe. His most surprising result was the similarity between graphs for Marlowe and Shakespeare.

Since Mendenhall, there have been advances in the mathematics of comparing frequency distributions. Rather than plotting them and comparing graphs, a common technique is to compute the chi-squared value:

$$chi\text{-}squared = \sum \frac{(observed_i - expected_i)^2}{expected_i}$$

The premise behind examination of word-length distributions is that each text by a particular author is a sample from some fixed frequency distribution of word lengths.

The Quintus Curtius Snodgrass letters Ten letters signed Quintus Curtius Snodgrass (QCS) were published in the New Orleans Daily Crescent in early 1861. There is some interest as to whether they were written by Samuel Clemens (Mark Twain). If they were, it would strengthen claims that he served in a Confederate garrison in the city and would also illustrate his early development as a humorist. The first claim that they should be attributed to Twain appears to have been made by Brashear in 1934 [7]. The strongest claim may be that by Leisy [8] who edited the edition of the letters published in 1946. Wagenknecht [9], however, termed the attribution a "conjecture".

Brinegar [10] used word-length distributions and chi-squared values in comparing the QCS letters with pieces of text known to have been written by Twain. He first created a control group of known Twain writings from around 1861. This consisted of four samples of text totalling almost 11,000 words. The control group was compared with the QCS letters, with a sample from *Roughing It* (Twain, 1872) and with a sample from *Following the Equator* (Twain, 1897). Frequencies of words of lengths 1, 2, ... 12, 13 and over were counted by hand. The control group and the sample from *Roughing It* had a chi-squared value of 12.4. The control group and the sample from *Following the Equator* had a chi-squared value of 8.5. The chi-squared value of the control group and the QCS letters was 127.2.

Brinegar conducted a second test in which frequencies of 2-, 3-, and 4-letter words from eight control samples and the ten QCS letters were compared using a two-sample t test. The results of this test also suggested that the QCS letters were unlikely to have come from the same distribution that produced the Twain works.

The Federalist papers The Federalist papers, published under the pseudonym "Publius", were written in 1787-1788 by Alexander Hamilton, John Jay and James Madison. The authorship of twelve of the papers is in dispute between Hamilton and Madison. Mosteller and Wallace [11, 12] examined the papers using various statistical techniques.

For historical interest, they tried word-length distributions as a discriminator and, like Brinegar, counted the frequencies of words of lengths 1, 2, ... 12, 13 and over. Chi-squared values were computed for various pairs of text groups, for example, Hamilton's Federalist papers versus known Madison writings. Examination of the chi-squared values indicated that word-length distribution was a poor discriminator between Hamilton and Madison. The average chi-squared value when eight Hamilton papers were compared with Madison's total works was 29.0. This is almost the same as the average value when seven Madison papers were compared against the remaining Madison writings (29.8). The chi-squared value computed between Hamilton paper #72 and Madison's works is 15.0; this is a lower score than any obtained when seven of Madison's papers were compared with Madison's works.[1]

Hero and Leander Some claim that *Hero and Leander* [13] was written entirely by Christopher Marlowe. If this were the case, it would indicate that he was alive after 1593 (the generally accepted date of his death) and that he would be a candidate author for some of the later works attributed to Shakespeare. The prevailing view however, is that the last four sestiads of the poem were written by George Chapman after Marlowe's death.

---

1. Using methods that examined usage of particular words ("minor function words" such as "by", "to" and "that") rather than words in general, Mosteller and Wallace concluded that Madison is extremely likely to have been the author of all the disputed papers.

Smith [14] applied many stylometric tests to *Hero and Leander* and most of them showed the change of authorship. However, his analysis of the word-length results [2] shows that Mendenhall's method fails to distinguish the change.

Assessment of the word-length method Brinegar concluded that his test was comparable to a blood test in a paternity suit; it could exonerate but, by itself, could not convict. In other words it could strongly suggest that a piece was not by a particular writer but could not show that it was. Smith was more critical, concluding that the word-length method proposed by Mendenhall is "so unreliable that any serious student of authorship should discard it".

12.2 Sentence-length distribution

When considering sentence length, we are faced with the problem of determining sentence boundaries. This is much more difficult than determining word boundaries. We may be tempted to override printed punctuation which may, in any case, have been inserted by a compositor rather than by the author. Yule [15] relates how different editions of the same work have different punctuation.

The earliest published study of sentence-length distribution appears to be that of Sherman [16] who examined the development of the English prose sentence from Chaucer onwards. He computed the average sentence length of many writers and noted that, for most writers, average sentence length in large works was roughly constant. In addition, he observed that the average for some writers did not change much over periods of time as long as 30 years.

Because sentence length has a greater variety than word length, the frequency distributions have been compared differently. Statistics of a distribution, such as mean, first quartile and ninth decile, have been compared, rather than chi-squared values.

Figure 12.1 shows a Unix shell script that generates a frequency distribution of sentence lengths.[2] The parameter is the name of the text file, the output is a set of lines each containing two integers. A pair M,N indicates that there were M sentences of length N (words). The output is in ascending order of N. The script works as follows.

The *tr* program outputs the text one word to a line discarding characters that are not letters or sentence-ending punctuation (.!?). For those words terminated by a sentence-ender, *grep* outputs the line (now word) number

---

2. This script and others in this chapter were developed under Unix System V. They may require cosmetic changes in order to run under other versions of Unix.

Figure 12.1 Script for deriving sentence length distribution

```
tr -cs "[A-Z][a-z].!?" "[ 12*]" < $1 | \
grep -n "[.?!]$" | \
awk ' BEGIN { FS = ":" }
   { print $1-x
     x = $1
   }
 ' | \
sort -n | \
uniq -c
```

and the word. (It can thus be fooled by abbreviations and by insertions (?) like that.) The action of *awk* is to compute the differences between adjacent numbers output by *grep*; thus giving us sentence lengths. *Sort* and *uniq* compress the list of lengths into the form described above.

De Imitatione Christi Yule [15] used sentence-length to compare samples from Bacon's *Essays*, Coleridge's *Biographia Literaria*, Lamb's *Elia* and *Last Essays of Elia* and Macaulay's *Essays*. He computed the number of sentences of lengths 1-5, 6-10, 11-15 and so on. Because of the range of sentence length, he reduced the distribution to key statistics and computed estimates of mean, median, first and third quartile, ninth decile and interquartile range. Based on comparisons of these statistics for the sample texts, Yule concluded that sentence-length distribution was characteristic of an author.

One of the two cases of disputed authorship that he examined was that of *De Imitatione Christi*. This work is most usually attributed to Thomas a Kempis (1379-1471); the leading alternative candidate is Jean Charlier de Gerson (1363-1429). Yule computed the sentence-length statistics for four text samples: *De Imitatione Christi*, miscellaneous works by Thomas a Kempis, selected works by Gerson and randomly chosen text by Gerson. Based on a comparison of the statistics, Yule concluded that they were consistent with the view that Thomas a Kempis was the author of *De Imitatione Christi*.

Hero and Leander As noted in section 12.1, it is commonly held that the first two sestiads of *Hero and Leander* were written by Marlowe and the final four by Chapman. Smith [14] constructed sentence-length distributions for each sestiad and compared the same distribution statistics used by Yule. All the major measures (mean, median, first and third quartiles, ninth decile, semi-interquartile range) had higher values for the first two sestiads than for the final four.

Pericles Of the five acts in *Pericles, Prince of Tyre,* all or most of the last three are usually accepted as being by Shakespeare. He is regarded as having contributed little, if anything, to the first two.

Smith [2] formed sentence-length distributions for four extracts of *Pericles.* The first two were the Shakespearean and non-Shakespearean sections; each of the other two extracts was a mixture of Shakespearean and non-Shakespearean, each approximately half the size of the total text. In comparing the distribution statistics used by Yule, Smith found that for each statistic, the difference in the values for the first two extracts was greater than the difference in values for the last two extracts. He concluded that this was weak evidence that the play was the work of more than one author.

Assessment of the sentence-length method Sentence-length distributions appear to have greater discriminatory power than word-length distributions; although it is still weak evidence on which to base a claim of authorship. It is important to compare like with like, that is, poems with poems, prose with prose, and to compare documents with comparable punctuation history.

12.3 Yule's characteristic

In his investigation into the authorship of *De Imitatione Christi,* Yule [17] felt he needed some summary of an author's vocabulary. He derived a "characteristic" measure of an author's word distribution which was independent of the size of the text sample. The measure is derived from the frequencies of words in the text.

First, we build a frequency table of words and, from that, compute F_i, the number of different words each occurring exactly i times in the text.[3] Next we compute

$$S1 = \sum (F_i * i) \quad \text{and} \quad S2 = \sum (F_i * i^2)$$

Yule's characteristic (k) is now:

$$10,000 * \frac{S2 - S1}{S1^2}$$

The constant 10,000 is included in order to make the values of k more

---

3. In a large piece of text there is normally an inverse relationship between F_i and *i*. That is, there will be many words that occur only once, significantly fewer that occur exactly twice, fewer still occurring three times and so on. There will normally be one word occurring many times. Zipf [18] notes that the product of a word's frequency and its rank in the word list (most frequent = 1) is very similar for all words in a large text.

manageable. Normally k is in the range 50 to 250, though short documents, or subsets of a document (for example, nouns only) may have extreme values.

K is reasonable easy to compute. Figure 12.2 gives a Unix shell script for computing both k and a simpler measure based on the number of types (different words) and tokens (word occurrences) in a text.

The script starts by filtering out formatting directives (*deroff*), putting the words in the input one to a line (*tr*), and mapping everything to lower case (*tr* again). Hyphenated words are treated as separate words. The *sort* program sorts the word list alphabetically and *uniq* replaces a series of N occurrences of a word by a line containing N and the word. Finally, the *awk* program tallies the number of times each different value of N occurs and computes the text measures.

Figure 12.2 Script for computing Yule's k and type/token measure

```
deroff $* | \
tr -cs "[A-Z][a-z]" "[\012*]" | \
tr "[A-Z]" "[a-z]" | \
sort | \
uniq -c | \
awk '
   { f[$1]++; count += $1 }
   END { for ( i in f ) {
                  s1 += f[i] * i
                  s2 += f[i] * i * i
                  }
   printf "%8.2f", 10000 * (s2 - s1) / (s1 * s1)
   printf "%8.2f \n", NR/sqrt(count)
   }'
```

De Imitatione Christi Yule limited his measurements to nouns. He reasoned that prepositions, pronouns, articles, and so on, had little stylistic significance and thought that nouns would be more characteristic than adjectives and verbs. He computed statistics for *De Imitatione Christi* (using a concordance) and comparable samples from the works of Thomas a Kempis and Gerson (using the texts themselves). *De Imitatione Christi* contains about 8000 nouns. Yule took about 22 10-page samples from works by Thomas a Kempis and 25 samples each containing about 333 nouns from the theological writings of Gerson.

The value of k is 84.2 for *De Imitatione Christi*, 59.7 for the sample of Thomas a Kempis and 35.9 for the sample from Gerson. Part of the reason for the lower scores for the samples is the fact that they are less homogeneous than the single work. The score for the first quarter of the Thomas a Kempis sample is 73.8; the comparable figure for Gerson is 41.3.

In all major measures that Yule computed (for example, mean occurrences per word and percentage of words occurring only once) the value for *De Imitatione Christi* was closer to the value for a Kempis than it was to the value for Gerson. Yule's conclusion based on statistical evidence alone, ignoring the nature of the vocabulary, favors Thomas a Kempis over Gerson.[4]

Unix documents Table 12.1 shows the value of k for several Unix documents.[5] Documents were edited to remove non-narrative sections, for example, tables, sections in programming languages and bibliographies.

Table 12.1 Measurements of Unix documents (all words)

Doc.#	k	types/$\sqrt{tokens}$	Author(s)
5	245.39	11.54	Morris, Cherry
6	212.61	10.60	Bell
17	189.59	10.21	McMahon
4	188.35	11.75	Cherry, Morris
9	167.24	12.58	Ritchie
2	157.94	12.11	Ritchie
14	156.90	12.31	Feldman
15	154.69	11.84	Haley, Joy
12	148.20	11.61	Lesk
8	146.68	14.04	Thompson
10	145.47	13.41	Lesk, Schmidt
13	135.72	13.23	Kernighan, Ritchie
3	135.33	13.48	Aho, Kernighan, Weinberger
16	129.74	12.33	Bekins, Jolitz
7	123.70	13.46	Feldman, Weinberger
11	108.24	15.94	Johnson
1	90.32	16.42	Karels

There are probably not enough documents by the same author to draw firm conclusions as to the usefulness of k. In addition, the acknowledgements sections of some documents suggest that others may have had a

---

4. His conclusion, after taking the nature of the vocabulary into account, is that Gerson is almost excluded as the author of *De Imitatione Christi* while the results are consistent with the authorship of Thomas a Kempis.
5. Some of the supplementary documents for BSD 2.9. The document numbers have no significance.

hand in the writing. However, it is interesting to note that the two documents by Cherry and Morris both have high k values and the two documents written exclusively by Ritchie have similar scores. The two documents written in whole or in part by Lesk have similar scores as do the two co-authored by Kernighan.

The reader may have noticed that Yule's S1 is the number of tokens in the text. Yule also defined S0 as $\sum F_i$ (i.e. the number of types in the text). Thus, our second measure is $S0/\sqrt{S1}$. Morris and Cherry [19] report that with large files, for a given author, the number of types increases approximately as the square root of the number of tokens. In Table 12.1 this simpler measure appears to move inversely with k.

In his study of the vocabularies of Thomas a Kempis and Gerson, Yule limited himself to nouns. We can do the same. We can use the *parts* component of the Writer's Workbench [20] (see also Ch. 11) to filter all but nouns from an input file. Figure 12.3 shows a modified version of the Unix shell script of Fig. 12.2. The *parts* program strips out formatting directives and the -o flag causes it to put each word on a separate line preceded by its part of speech. Clearly the script can be modified easily to filter out other parts of speech.

Figure 12.3 Text measures script - nouns only

```
parts -o $* | \
grep "^noun" | \
awk '
    {print $2} '| \
tr -cs "[A-Z][a-z]" "[\012*]" | \
tr "[A-Z]" "[a-z]" | \
sort | \
uniq -c | \
awk '
    { f[$1]+ +; count + = $1 }
    END { for ( i in f ) {
                    s1 + = f[i] * i
                    s2 + = f[i] * i * i
                    }
        printf "%8.2f", 10000 * (s2 - s1) / (s1 * s1)
        printf "%8.2f \n", NR/sqrt(count)
        }'
```

How good a discriminator is k now? Table 12.2 shows the value of k for the documents of Table 12.1. There is a reasonable correlation between this ordering and the previous one; documents tend to be in the same third of the table in each case. Some of the earlier good results are preserved:

Table 12.2 Measurements of Unix documents (nouns only)

Doc.#	k	types/$\sqrt{tokens}$	Author(s)
6	156.27	8.43	Bell
17	155.11	8.25	McMahon
5	127.19	9.65	Morris, Cherry
4	123.15	9.89	Cherry, Morris
12	122.28	9.80	Lesk
14	111.40	11.20	Feldman
16	100.69	9.94	Bekins, Jolitz
9	91.74	11.26	Ritchie
15	87.38	10.50	Haley, Joy
8	85.28	12.43	Thompson
2	84.96	10.27	Ritchie
13	81.75	10.80	Kernighan, Ritchie
10	81.37	12.24	Lesk, Schmidt
3	76.67	11.78	Aho, Kernighan, Weinberger
7	61.14	12.78	Feldman, Weinberger
11	57.80	14.15	Johnson
1	32.94	17.05	Karels

consider the two documents by Morris and Cherry and the three having Ritchie as sole or joint author. The modified calculation of k is not completely satisfactory because of possible inaccurate word class assignments by the *parts* program. In addition, the results may not be comparable with those obtained by Yule who worked with large (2000 noun) samples.

Book chapters Table 12.3 shows the results of another test of k. Here we measured chapters of an introductory text on files and databases [21]. Each chapter had a principal author but both authors contributed to all chapters and the entire manuscript was copy-edited to even out style differences. These factors may account for the smaller range of scores compared with those for the Unix documents shown in Table 12.1. The results shown in Table 12.3 suggest that k is not a good discriminator between these two writers because, for example, Chapters 9, 10 and 11 had the same principal author.

Table 12.4 gives results when only nouns are considered. Note that Chapters 9 and 11 now have similar scores. There is not such a good correlation between tables 12.3 and 12.4 as between the two measurements of Unix documents (Tables 12.1 and 12.2). In general, considering only nouns produces a lower value of k. However, the score for Chapter 4 rose sharply. Examination of the word lists shows that the *parts* program assigned "noun" to some non-nouns in this chapter.

Table 12.3 Measurements of book chapters (all words)

Chapter	k	types/√$\overline{tokens}$
6	156.93	10.89
10	150.81	13.40
3	147.20	12.53
4	145.29	10.85
7	142.79	12.59
5	140.59	13.05
12	131.02	13.16
11	126.06	12.10
1	122.52	13.45
8	121.28	13.35
2	120.02	15.65
13	111.65	14.82
9	112.02	11.36
14	104.21	16.61

Table 12.4 Measurements of book chapters (nouns only)

Chapter	k	types/√$\overline{tokens}$
4	198.11	9.07
6	143.68	9.42
10	133.80	12.01
3	119.45	11.19
8	104.77	11.84
5	102.19	12.10
9	92.36	9.97
11	88.32	11.01
1	86.35	11.35
12	85.61	11.31
7	84.02	11.66
2	57.14	14.43
13	56.10	12.91
14	39.84	14.83

Assessment of Yule's k Reducing an author's vocabulary to a single number would not appear to be a promising strategy. However, Yule's results, and those presented here, show that it can be a useful authorship indicator. As with the other measures we have examined, the discriminating power of Yule's characteristic will depend on the authors among whom we are trying to discriminate.

12.4 Morton's methods

The discriminating methods devised by Rev. A. Q. Morton [22] include tests of word position, collocation and word pairs. Counts from the disputed text are compared with corresponding counts from writings known to be by one of the candidate authors. Morton advises caution when comparing texts from different literary forms, for example plays with sonnets.

Position tests include counting the occurrences of a word in certain positions, for example first in a sentence or last in a sentence, as well as its frequency elsewhere. Collocation tests count the number of times word X is followed immediately by word Y, is preceded immediately by word Y, and is used non-adjacently to word Y. Word-pair tests count the use of each of a pair of related words e.g. *up* and *upon*, *can* and *cannot*. Chi-squared tests are used to derive the significance of differences in the distributions.

Pauline letters There are fourteen letters attributed to St Paul in the New Testament.[6] Morton [3, 23] analyzed sentence length distribution, distribution of the Greek word *kai* and locations of other common Greek words. *Kai* accounts for about 5% of Greek prose. He tabulated the number of sentences with 0, 1, 2 and 3 or more *kai*s and found that the first four letters were consistent differed from the others. Differences between the four and the remaining ten, when observed in a range of texts, were found to be associated with different authorship. He concluded [23 p. 224] that "If Paul is defined as being the author of Galatians, then in the language of literature he also wrote Romans, 1st and 2nd Corinthians. The remaining epistles come from at least six hands".

More recently [24] Morton considered the *hapax legomena* (words occurring only once) in the letters and in various groupings of the letters.[7] In particular, he examined the positions in sentences of the occurrences and found, for example, that they were more likely to occur as the last word in a sentence than as the first. Morton compared figures for the four "genuine" letters with the others and concluded that comparing unique occurrences in first or last positions in a sentence can produce statistically significant differences between the two groups of letters.

---

6. Letters to Romans, Corinthians (2), Galatians, Ephesians, Philippians, Colossians, Thessalonians (2), Timothy (2), Titus, Phileman, and Hebrews.
7. As noted previously, this group of words tends to be larger than those occurring with any other frequency.

Elizabethan texts Elizabethan texts were often punctuated by an editor rather than the original author and different editors used different conventions. Because of this, in studying *hapax legomena* in Elizabethan texts, Morton [24] recorded positions relative to the most frequent words in the text rather than relative to sentence boundaries.

Morton computed statistics for four works of Shakespeare (*Titus Andronicus, Julius Caesar, Pericles, Comedy of Errors*) and two works by George Peele (*The Arraignment of Paris, David and Bathsheba*). Peele is sometimes proposed as the author of *Titus Andronicus*. On the basis of a study of words adjacent to occurrences of seven frequent words, Morton concluded that Shakespeare is consistent in the placing of *hapax legomena* relative to these words and that the pattern of words in Peele make it very unlikely that he wrote *Titus Andronicus*.

Assessment of Morton's method The validity of Morton's methods is controversial. Oakman [25 pp. 143-146] has a brief survey of some of the controversies. Morton's methods and conclusions have been attacked on both literary and statistical grounds. For example, Herdan [26] was very critical of Morton's analysis of Greek texts [23]. The application of Morton's methods to Elizabethan texts by Morton [22] and Merriam [27] is criticized by Smith [28, 29] who concludes that Morton's methods as applied by Merriam "cannot distinguish reliably between works of Elizabethan and Jacobean playwrights". Smith criticizes Morton and others who interpret chi-squared values as probabilities. He suggests that, as in sections 12.1 and 12.2, they be used as comparative measures and that an enlarged version of Morton's methods has potential as a weeding out process, reducing a field of candidate authors, prior to in-depth study.

12.5 Conclusions

There is currently no single technique which discriminates well between all pairs of authors. The test giving best results may depend on the authors being considered. For example, word-length distribution was not a good discriminator between Hamilton and Madison but was useful for the Quintus Curtius Snodgrass letters. Individually, the techniques described in this chapter are weak. However, they may be useful in support of more conventional evidence particularly if multiple independent tests point the same way.

Summary

Determining authorship through statistical means has been of interest for more than a century. Recently, computers have made it more convenient to test hypotheses.

The easiest general tests to implement are based on word and sentence statistics. While no such test by itself has proved to be an adequate discriminator, the results of several in combination may strongly suggest a particular attribution. More convincing results have been obtained in particular cases by examining the use of certain words. The words chosen for the tests typically depend on the authors and the material being tested.

Exercises

(1) What kind of text has a high value of Yule's k? Given a text, how could you edit it to (a) increase, (b) decrease its k value?

(2) Suppose we add a word of frequency X to a word list. What must X be to leave the value of Yule's k unchanged?

(3) Create text files each containing a sample of text from two of your favorite authors. Create four or five samples of each writer. How well do the tests described in this chapter distinguish between them?

References

1.   J. Tankard, "The literary detective," *Byte*, vol. 11, no. 2, pp. 231-238, February 1986.

2.   M. W. A. Smith, "Recent experience and new developments of methods for the determination of authorship," *ALLC Bulletin*, vol. 11, no. 3, pp. 73-82, 1983.

3.   A. Q. Morton and J. McLeman, *Christianity in the computer age,* Harper and Row, New York, 1964.

4.   C. B. Williams, "Studies in the history of probability and statistics: IV A note on the early statistical study of literary style," *Biometrika*, vol. 43, pp. 248-256, 1956.

5.   T. C. Mendenhall, "The characteristic curves of composition," *Science*, vol. 9, no. 214, supplement, 11 March 1887, pp. 237-249.

6.   T. C. Mendenhall, "A mechanical solution of a literary problem," *The Popular Science Monthly*, vol. 60, pp. 97-105, December 1901.

7.   M. M. Brashear, *Mark Twain, son of Missouri,* University of North Carolina Press, Chapel Hill, NC, 1934.

8.   Mark Twain, *The letters of Quintus Curtius Snodgrass,* Southern Methodist University Press, Dallas, Texas, 1946. Ed. E. E. Leisy.

9.   E. Wagenknecht, *Mark Twain: the man and his work,* University of Oklahoma Press, Norman, OK, 1961.

10. C. S. Brinegar, "Mark Twain and the Quintus Curtius Snodgrass Letters; a statistical test of authorship," *American Statistical Association Journal*, vol. 58, no. 301, pp. 85-96, 1963.

11. F. Mosteller and D. L. Wallace, *Inference and disputed authorship: The Federalist*, Addison-Wesley, Reading, Mass., 1964.

12. F. Mosteller and D. L. Wallace, "Inference in an authorship problem," *American Statistical Association Journal*, vol. 58, no. 302, pp. 275-309, 1963.

13. "Hero and Leander," in *The Works of Christopher Marlowe*, ed. C. F. Tucker Brooke, Oxford, 1910, 1966.

14. M. W. A. Smith, "A stylometric analysis of Hero and Leander," *The Bard*, vol. 31, pp. 105-132, 1982.

15. G. U. Yule, "On sentence-length as a statistical characteristic of style in prose, with application to two cases of disputed authorship," *Biometrika*, vol. 30, pp. 363-390, 1938.

16. L. A. Sherman, "Some observations upon the sentence-length in English prose," *University [of Nebraska] Studies*, vol. 1, no. 2, pp. 119-130, 1888.

17. G. U. Yule, *The statistical study of literary vocabulary*, Archon Books, 1968.

18. G. K. Zipf, *Human behavior and the principle of least effort*, Hafner, New York, 1965.

19. R. Morris and L. L. Cherry, "Computer detection of typographical errors," *IEEE Transactions on Professional Communication*, vol. PC-18, no. 1, pp. 54-64, March 1975.

20. L. L. Cherry, "PARTS - A system for assigning word classes to English text," Comp. Sci. Tech. Rep. No. 81, Bell Laboratories, Murray Hill, New Jersey, June 1978.

21. P. D. Smith and G. M. Barnes, *Files and databases: an introduction*, Addison-Wesley, Reading, Mass., 1987.

22. A. Q. Morton, *Literary Detection*, Charles Scribner's Sons, New York, 1978.

23. A. Q. Morton, "The Authorship of Greek Prose," *Journal of the Royal Statistical Society*, vol. 128 Part 2, pp. 169-224, 1965. Series A (General).

24. A. Q. Morton, "Once. A test of authorship based on words which are not repeated in the sample," *Literary and Linguistic Computing*, vol. 1, no. 1, pp. 1-8, 1986.

25. R. L. Oakman, *Computer methods for literary research*, The University of Georgia Press, Athens, GA, 1984.

26. G. Herdan, "[A contribution to a] Discussion on the paper by Mr. Morton," *Journal of the Royal Statistical Society*, vol. 128 Part 2, pp. 229-231, 1965. Series A (General).

27. T. Merriam, "The authorship of Sir Thomas More," *ALLC Bulletin*, vol. 10, no. 1, pp. 1-7, 1982.

28. M. W. A. Smith, "An investigation of Morton's method to distinguish Elizabethan playwrights," *Computers and the humanities*, vol. 19, no. 1, pp. 3-21, January-March 1985.

29. T. Merriam, "The authorship controversy of Sir Thomas More," *Literary and Linguistic Computing*, vol. 1, no. 2, pp. 104-108, 1986. (reply: M. W. A. Smith).

Abstraction

An abstract is a short accurate summary of a document. An abstract is useful because it reveals more of the content of the document than the title alone and yet is much shorter than the full text.[1] An abstract allows a reader to make a good decision as to whether the document as a whole is of interest. Abstracts rather than titles alone are the units of several information-dissemination services, e.g. Biological Abstracts, Chemical Abstracts and Psychological Abstracts.

In many cases, the author of a document is responsible for writing the abstract. On other occasions, someone else writes the abstract. In the latter case, abstracting is time consuming and expensive; the abstracter has to become familiar with the subject matter of the document in order to be able to abstract it. There is, therefore, an incentive to develop software which can input a document and output an abstract.

It would seem that a program would need to be "intelligent" and be capable of understanding what it is reading in order to produce an abstract comparable with those produced manually. While programs that produce summaries rather than abstracts have used an Artificial Intelligence approach (see for example Tait [1]), unintelligent programs can produce abstracts good enough for practical purposes.

Abstracting or Extracting? An extract of a document consists of one or more portions of it selected to represent the whole. Virtually all research in automatic abstracting has been concerned with selecting (possible non-contiguous) sentences from the document to form an extract. Some systems do a little editing on the extract but current abstracting programs do not create completely new sentences as a human abstracter can do. Abstracting/extracting programs vary in the ways in which they identify the

---

1. For example, *The Computer Journal*, in its Information for Authors, notes that the usual length of a paper is 4,000-5,000 words and that an abstract should be about 100 words long.

best sentences and deal with the problem of making the extract coherent.

Evaluation of automatic abstracts Pollock and Zamora [2] regarded the problem of evaluating an automatic abstract as being as difficult as the problem of generating one. Comparing an automatic abstract with a hand-made one is unsatisfactory because human abstracters are inconsistent and there may be many acceptable abstracts of a document. If the purpose of an abstract is to indicate the subject matter of a document, an appropriate test is to have it evaluated by someone who has read the complete document.

13.1 Early experiments

Early work in this area was largely concerned with developing criteria for extracting the most appropriate sentences from a document. The work of Edmunson [3] departs from earlier work in his use of syntactic and semantic information rather than purely statistical criteria. Edmunson devised four criteria for evaluating a sentence: cue, key, title and location. Details of the scoring methods are given in Ref. 3.

The cue criterion scored a sentence according to the presence in it of words in a 995-word dictionary. The dictionary contained 783 "bonus" words with positive scores; typical examples are superlatives, adverbs of conclusion and causality terms. The 73 "stigma" words had negative scores and included anaphoric terms, belittling and hedging words. The final list of 139 words did not affect the score of a sentence; articles, prepositions and pronouns were in this list.

"Key" words Edmunson's method were high-frequency content words. While the cue dictionary was common to all documents, a key list was document-specific. A word-frequency list was derived from the document then pruned of the words in the cue dictionary. The remaining words were weighted according to frequency.

Both title and heading words were deemed positive. Title words were given a higher weight.

Examination of many documents suggested that the location of a sentence was a good indicator of its importance. Sentences in the first and last paragraphs of a document and those under certain headings (e.g. "Conclusions") were weighted higher than others. High weights were also attached to the first and last sentences of a paragraph.

The four criteria could be given different weights in arriving at a total score for a sentence. An additional parameter to Edmunson's system was the size of the extract (expressed as a percentage of the number of sentences in the document).

Edmunson evaluated a computer-produced extract by comparing it with a target extract selected by hand from the document. For example, the number of sentences in common was computed. In addition, there was subjective comparison of the information content of the two extracts and consideration of the extract worthiness of the sentences selected by the program.

Edmunson determined that the best results were obtained from a combination of location, cue and title criteria and that the computationally expensive key criteria was not worth evaluating.

Chemical Abstracts has one of the highest rates of new articles. In the next section we look at automatic abstraction research at Chemical Abstracts Service.

13.2 Automatic Document Abstracting Method

The Automatic Document Abstracting Method (ADAM) tested at Chemical Abstracts Service (CAS) [2, 4] was tailored for a well-defined subject area and was designed to generate abstracts conforming to CAS standards. In contrast to Edmunson's system, ADAM focussed on excluding sentences from the abstract rather than including them. In sentence selection/rejection, ADAM used a Word Control List (WCL), information in the title, and frequency criteria. The latter two mechanisms were document-dependent; the WCL tended to be subject-specific.

The "dangling reference" problem plagues programs that abstract by extracting. Many sentences contain exophora - references to ideas or objects in preceding or following sentences. This sentence is an example of that phenomenon. A sentence with exophora cannot normally be included in an abstract unless the text being referenced is also included. Some of the problems in detecting and resolving exophoric references are very subtle (see 13.3). ADAM included a sentence with anaphoric (backward) references such as "these" and "this" only if it were possible to include the preceding sentence.

The WCL contained nearly 800 terms each tagged with a semantic and syntactic code. Examples of the semantic codes are shown in Table 13.1 and examples of the syntactic codes are shown in Table 13.2. Matches between terms and words in a sentence determined to a large extent whether the sentence would be excluded from the abstract. Elastic pattern matching was implemented so that up to three "noise" words in the document could be skipped between matched term words. For example "our most recent observations" matched the WCL entry "our observations".

The syntactic codes identified the part of speech of a term; many entries in the WCL had null syntactic codes. The syntactic codes were used to

Table 13.1 Example semantic codes used in ADAM WCL

Code	Meaning	Example(s)
M	Supernegative	Acknowledge, Appreciate
A	Very negative	Obvious, Previously
B	Negative	However
E	Intensifier	Many, Most
K	Positive	Noteworthy, Postulate
I	Very positive	Our work, Reported here

Table 13.2 Example syntactic codes used in ADAM WCL

Code	Meaning	Example
A	Article	The
C	Conjunction	And
N	Pronoun	Our
P	Preposition	With
Q	TO	

classify commas and enable introductory and parenthetical clauses to be deleted. In addition, the final abstract was screened to ensure that every sentence contained a verb.

Examples of WCL entries, taken from Table I of Ref. 2, are shown in Table 13.3. Most of the entries in the table had negative semantic codes. Many of the entries had null syntactic codes.

Table 13.3 Example WCL entries

Term	Semantic code	Syntactic code
Our experiments	I	
No accurate	A	
Noted	A	V
Our	K	N
On which	B	P
On the other hand	B	

In a preliminary pass, words occurring in the title were given a semantic tag (G) that caused sentences containing them to be included in the abstract in the absence of a negative term in the same sentence.

Frequency data was used to modify the weight given to some semantic codes. In general, if a term occurred frequently in the document, the strength of its semantic code was reduced.

ADAM differed from Edmunson's system in that it did some editing on the selected sentences. As noted above, parenthetical phrases were deleted. Non-substantive introductory phrases were also removed. Finally, some editing was performed so that the abstract conformed to CAS standards in matters such as spelling and abbreviation. The examples in Table 13.4, though not derived from actual ADAM documents, illustrate the kinds of editing it could do.

Table 13.4 Examples of abstract editing

Before	After
Our computation, performed on a VAX running VMS, shows no such convergence.	Our computation shows no such convergence.
An analysis of freshman transcripts shows that there is some correlation between verbal and math SAT scores.	There is some correlation between verbal and math SAT scores.
Sulphur at a concentration of approximately 29 parts per billion was found during the course of the experiment. This explains the behaviour of the sulphuric acid.	Sulfur at a concn. of approx. 29 ppb was found during the course of the expt. This explains the behavior of the H_2SO_4

Mathis *et al.* [5] outlined extensions to ADAM (as described in Ref. 4) that aimed to make abstracts more acceptable to readers. They outlined five ways in which the abstract could be changed.

First, appropriately constructed adjacent sentences could be combined using a coordinate conjunction, e.g. S1 and S2. Second, appropriately constructed adjacent sentences could be combined using a subordinate conjunction, e.g. S1 which S2. Third, graphical references could be transformed, for example "Table 2 shows ..." becomes "A table shows ...". Fourth, a sentence can be appended that reports the number of entries in the bibliography of the document. Such sentences were common in abstracts at one time. Finally, phrases such as "The third is that ..." would be deleted if sentences with appropriate smaller number ("first", "second") could not be located and included in the abstract.

ADAM suffers from two deficiencies. First, the WCL is subject specific; a variety of lists would be needed in a general abstracting environment, as well as a means for determining the most appropriate list to use for a specific document. The second deficiency, common to methods making a single select/reject pass over a document is that sentences selected for the abstract tend to be scattered in the original. The abstract reads like the set of disjointed sentences it is.

In the next section we look at an abstracting system that solves these two problems.

13.3 Indicator sentences

The system described by Paice [6] uses what he justifiably calls "the most obvious of all the indicators of sentence significance". His system searches for sentences that explicitly state that they have something important to convey about the purpose of the document. Examples of such sentences (from [7, 8, 9]) are shown in Fig. 13.1.

Figure 13.1 Examples of indicator sentences

This paper presents an Object-Oriented Data Model (OODM) for database modelling, implementation and access.

We describe a system called Exegis, through which integrity constraints may be specified and enforced over a relational database extended with a deductive component.

In this paper systolic arrays for computing the coefficient tables for commonly used difference techniques are considered.

It is difficult for most writers to avoid including somewhere in a paper a sentence or two describing what the paper is about. An examination of the 74 articles published in Volume 31 of *The Computer Journal* reveals that 69 of them contained some form of indicator sentence. Typically, indicators are found towards the beginning of a document.[2]

There are four stages by which the system of Paice produces an abstract. First, it finds the indicator sentences in the document and give each an appropriate weight. Sentences are locating by comparing the text to *templates* in a flexible way. Paice reports that in a sample of 80 documents, only 4 had no occurrence of any of the 7 basic indicator types used by his system. The weight of an indicator is a function of its length and content.

---

2. In Volume 31, 13 papers had their first indicator in the first sentence, 24 papers had it in sentences 2-10, and 19 had it in sentences 11-20. The most delayed first indicator was found in sentence 44.

Second, exophoric references in the indicator sentences are dealt with; typically by expanding the extract to include preceding sentences until there are no more unresolved references.

The third step is to select the extracts in order of weight until an abstract of the desired length is formed. The user can specify minimum, maximum and target abstract lengths. In contrast, a system selecting sentences in a single pass through a document may generate large abstracts. Those produced by ADAM tended to be about 10-20% of the document. In its final step, Paice's system performs cosmetic adjustments in order that the abstract read more like a coherent whole and less like the series of disjoint extracts it probably is.

Most effort has been expended on the first two steps, these are discussed in the next two sections.

13.3.1 Indicator identification
Identification of the indicator sentences in a document is non-trivial. It is complicated by two factors: first that words within sentences can exhibit a lot of variation (for example, "report", "paper" and "article" all mean much the same) and second that there may be "noise" words and phrases in sentences. Thus, all the sentence openers shown in Fig. 13.2 are variations on the same basic form.

Figure 13.2 Equivalent sentence openers

This article, simultaneously published in CACM, is concerned with ...
Our paper deals with ...
The present review concludes this series and concerns ...

No system can store every possible indicator and rely on exact matching. Paice's solution is to have templates in which each word is a *paradigm* and represents a group of words and phrases.[3] The current system has 7 templates. In order to skip over noise, the system performs elastic matching between the templates and document text. At some points in the template an arbitrarily long sequence of "noise" words may be tolerable. At others there may be a limit on the length of noise. Thus, in a template, a paradigm can be accompanied by a *skip limit* indicating the maximum number of words that may be skipped when searching for it.

A template may be non-linear, that is, it may have points where paths split and converge. Each template therefore represents a large set of indicators. Figure 13.3 (reprinted, with permission, from Ref. 6) shows an

---

3. For example the paradigm "paper" might represent the set [paper, article, report, review, study, analysis]

example template; skip limits are shown in brackets before the paradigms.

Figure 13.3 Example template. ₒ Butterworth and Co. 1981

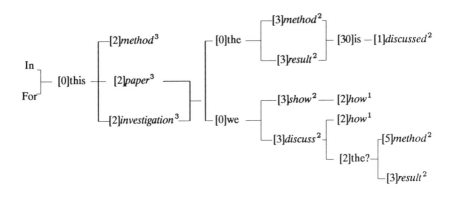

Sentences that match the template of Fig. 13.3 include the following

In this abbreviated paper the Kennedy-Long technique, named after two Kentucky chicken farmers, is briefly described.

In this article we describe how to catch sharks.

It is not likely that any template will be matched to completion, so weights are associated with template words. In Fig. 13.2 they are shown as superscripts following some words. The weight given to an indicator is the highest total weight it ever achieves along any branch of any template.

13.3.2 Extract formation and the problem of exophora
Having found one or more indicator sentences the system next attempts to make each the kernel of a self-contained extract of the text. An extract is self-contained if it makes no references to text outside itself. It must have this property if it is to be a candidate for inclusion in the abstract.

Exophora are elements of a sentence that refer to elements outside it. If they are backward references they are termed *anaphoric*; forward references are termed *cataphoric*. Figure 13.4(a) contains examples of anaphora and Fig. 13.4(b) has examples of the rarer cataphora. In both cases, the exophora are shown in bold. Note how none of the sentences could be included in isolation in an abstract because the reader would feel that something was missing. The system starts with an indicator sentence and attaches adjacent sentences until either every exophoric reference has

Figure 13.4 Examples of exophora

Our results have shown that **the stack** rarely overflows.

However, our conclusion is exactly the opposite.

We have shown that **this** is the case.

(a) anaphora

Firstly, we show that limited fusion is possible.

Our purpose in this paper is to refute **three** claims.

On the one hand we conclude that this is a very reasonable line of attack.

(b) cataphora

been resolved or the upper bound on the abstract size has been reached.

If there are unresolved references when aggregation finishes, the system tries to neutralize them by deleting or modifying them. For example, words such as "but" or "however" or "nevertheless" at the start of a sentence can be removed. A phrase such as "the precise form of storage is discussed later" can be neutralized by removing "later" or by changing the end to "also discussed". If the exophora cannot be resolved in this way then the extract is reduced a sentence at a time. As each sentence is discarded an attempt is made to resolve outstanding references. The extract may be discarded altogether if its length falls below some threshold.

If references are resolved before the extract reaches some desirable size other sentences are added. Exophora in the added sentences are resolved or neutralized. The order in which text is added is: following sentences in the same paragraph, preceding sentence in the same paragraph, following paragraphs, preceding paragraphs. Paragraphs are not added if they are in a different section than the indicator. The order of addition is designed to reflect the normal structure of a text in which a sentence is strongly related to others in the same paragraph and most strongly to its immediate neighbors. The links to adjacent paragraphs are weaker.

Exophora: recognition and resolution Potential exophoric references are easy to find, we can have a list of phrases and language constructions. The main problem is deciding whether or not the reference is really external to the sentence. Table 13.5 gives examples of exophoric and non-exophoric uses of *this* and *the*. Liddy *et al.* [10] studied the use of anaphor in

Table 13.5 Examples of words used exophorically and non-exophorically

Word	Exophoric	Non-exophoric
this	Our experiments have shown this to be true.	In this report we outline how the register allocation algorithm can be eliminated and show that this leads to no loss of efficiency.
the	The index was small enough to fit in memory.	The President talked about the future of the world.

abstracts. They listed 142 potentially anaphoric words and phrases, grouped them into 10 classes and devised rules for determining if a potential anaphor is actually being used anaphorically. In an examination of 600 scientific abstracts they found that 95 of the terms in their list occurred and that, on average, a potential anaphoric term was truly anaphoric about a third of the time.

Unfortunately, the rules devised by Liddy *et al.* were designed for humans to interpret and are very difficult to program. Paice and his co-workers incorporated necessarily less sophisticated rules in their abstracting program. The following example is taken from the lengthy discussion of the problem in Ref. 11:

"then" is:-

non-anaphoric if "if" occurs earlier in the same sentence;
external if no later than the fifth word of the sentence;
internal otherwise.

Having identified what we think is an exophoric reference, how do we resolve it? The resolution technique depends on the direction (forwards or backwards), range (short or long) and precision of the exophora. For example, *below* is an imprecise long-range forward reference whereas *the index* is a precise backward reference the distance of which depends on the location of the concept.

A word such as "better" used anaphorically is resolved by prepending the previous text unit (sentence or paragraph as appropriate). If this is not possible (e.g. upper size bound reached) then the sentence is discarded. Finding the antecedent of a phrase such as "the transformation algorithm" involves searching back through the text for an appropriate match. Cataphoric references such as "the following three reasons" require searching

for three identifiable labels such as "First", "Second" and "Finally" or "(a)",
"(b)" and "(c)".

13.3.3 Passage selection
The aggregation process is designed to find tidy extracts and then put them
together into an abstract. The length may not fall between the user-
specified word limits because there may not be enough sentences to reach
the lower limit or the limit may be reached in the middle of a sentence.

13.3.4 Cosmetic adjustments
Cosmetic adjustments are only vaguely defined in published reports on the
system. The goal of this final step is likely to be similar to that of the
ADAM system, namely to increase the cohesiveness of the abstract. For
example, two short sentences could be joined by ";". In addition, anaphoric
references could be introduced. For example, if two successive sentences
were "The organization we present ..." and "The organization was
developed ..." the second occurrence of "The organization" could be
replaced (with care) by "It".

13.3.5 Miscellaneous
Corresponding to the negative terms in Edmunson's cue method and the
negative semantic codes of the ADAM system, the program of Paice also
detects features in a sentence that make it less likely to be an acceptable
part of an abstract. Examples of such features are references to figures,
diagrams, tables, and so on, and references to other documents. Some
care is needed in detecting inappropriate references. While we want to
remove a sentence containing " ... as shown in figure 3." (because the
figure itself cannot appear in the abstract) we do not necessarily want to
discard a sentence ending with " ... reduce to an acceptable figure". Some
negative features are neutralizable; for example in "We make use of a B-
tree [Bayer72]", the citation could be eliminated.

13.4 Future directions

Paice [11] describes his system as a linear descendent of ADAM (see 13.2)
and notes that such systems have limited potential. He describes ways in
which the structure and balance of automatic abstracts might be improved.

Structure can be improved by a move away from free-form abstracts to
structured ones in which one or two sentences appear under such headings
as "Goals", "Methodology", and "Findings". In this way, the reader is made
aware of the role of each of the extracted sentences. The abstracting program fills in slots in an *abstract frame*. In doing this, it needs to be able to
classify text sentences - using headings and word clues and then to select
from among the appropriate class.

The balance of an abstract can be improved if it accurately reflects the document itself. Headings and sub-headings guide the abstraction process to the various sections of the document to ensure that all parts are represented. If there is orientation material in which the author gives a preview of the text to come, this can also be used to direct the program.

Summary

An abstract is such a useful component of a document that if a text does not have one, it may be worth creating it. It reveals more about the content of a document than does the title and takes much less time to read than the document itself. Manual abstracting can be tedious. At first sight, abstracting appears to be a task requiring some intelligence, or at least knowledge of the topic area. However, reasonable abstracts of documents can be obtained by extracting passages from the text, if these are carefully chosen. Early automatic abstracting systems selected sentences based on the words they contained but concatenations of such sentences tended to read poorly. Recent experiments use sentence structure in an effort to detect sentences that indicate the content of a document; such sentences then form kernels of coherent extracts. We looked at the problem of dangling references that such systems have to deal with.

Exercises

(1)   Implement Edmunson's four sentence-scoring methods. See how good each is at identifying the most important sentences in a document.

(2)   Examine a number of documents and identify the indicator sentences. Try to cluster them in different categories.

References

1.   J. I. Tait, "Automatic summarising of English texts," Technical Report #47, University of Cambridge Computer Laboratory, December 1982.

2.   J. J. Pollock and A. Zamora, "Automatic abstracting research at Chemical Abstracts Service," *Journal of Chemical Information and Computer Sciences*, vol. 15, no. 4, pp. 226-232, 1975.

3.   H. P. Edmunson, "New methods in automatic extracting," *Journal of the ACM*, vol. 16, no. 2, pp. 264-285, 1969.

4.   J. E. Rush, R. Salvador, and A. Zamora, "Automatic abstracting and indexing. II. Production of indicative abstracts by application of

contextual inference and syntactic coherence criteria," *Journal of the American Society for Information Science*, vol. 22, no. 4, pp. 260-274, July-August 1971.

5.   B. A. Mathis, J. E. Rush, and C. E. Young, "Improvement of automatic abstracts by the use of structural analysis," *Journal of the American Society for Information Science*, vol. 24, no. 2, pp. 101-109, March-April 1973.

6.   C. D. Paice, "Automatic generation of literature abstracts--an approach based on the identification of self indicating phrases," in *Information retrieval research*, ed. R. N. Oddy, S. E. Robertson, C. J. van Rijsbergen and P. W. Williams, pp. 172-191, Butterworths, London, 1981.

7.   L. Zhao and S. A. Roberts, "An object-oriented data model for database modelling, implementation and access," *The Computer Journal*, vol. 31, no. 2, pp. 116-124, April 1988.

8.   C. Small, "The implementation of the Exegis system," *The Computer Journal*, vol. 31, no. 2, pp. 125-132, April 1988.

9.   G. M. Megson and D. J. Evans, "The unification of systolic differencing algorithms," *The Computer Journal*, vol. 31, no. 1, pp. 125-132, February 1988.

10.   E. D. Liddy, S. Bonzi, J. Katzer, and E. Oddy, "A study of discourse anaphora in scientific abstracts," *Journal of the American Society for Information Science*, vol. 38, no. 4, pp. 255-261, July 1987.

11.   C. D. Paice, "Constructing literature abstracts by computer: techniques and prospects," CS-NL-1-89, Department of Computing, University of Lancaster, Lancaster, England, 1989.

Translation

We are concerned in this chapter with the computer-assisted translation, from one natural language to another, of technical and business documents. For such documents, accuracy and timeliness of translation is important. In contrast, in producing a translation of ancient Greek poetry, for example, a translator is allowed some license in the translation, speed is not usually of the essence and a computer would not normally be involved.

In 1984, worldwide expenditure on translation was estimated to cost up to $20 billion a year [1]. In Canada, the Translation Bureau of the Secretary of State is responsible for translating about 300 million words a year between French and English. A considerable portion of the budget of the European Community (EC) is spent on translating documents between the languages of the member countries. In 1982 more than one million pages were generated by approximately 1100 EC translators and over a third of the administrative budget went to the translation division. Since that time, Portugal and Spain have joined the community, adding two more languages, and Turkey is waiting to join. Expenditure on translation is likely to grow as more documents are produced in native languages.

Translation is a skilled job; the translator not only has to be familiar with the source and target languages but also with what might be termed "the domain of discourse", that is, the subject matter of the document. A skilled translator working with typewriter and dictionary will translate only about 1500 words a day. Clearly there is potential for computer assistance. In this chapter we look at the development of computer translation systems and some of the problems.

The required quality of a translation varies. For example, an information-gathering application that scans abstracts of scientific papers, need only produce rough translations sufficient to indicate the contents of the papers. On the other hand, an information-dissemination application, for example one that translates maintenance manuals for use by non-native customers, needs a much higher quality of output.

There is a range of possibilities for computer assistance in translation. At one end of the scale is autonomous machine translation (MT); at the other end is the use of on-line dictionaries and thesauri. In between are computer-assisted human translation (CAHT) and human-assisted computer translation (HACT). Completely autonomous translation in unrestricted domains is probably an unrealistic goal. Because the output from most human translators is subjected to post-editing by senior translators, a more realistic target is to have a program produce output of the same quality as the regular human translators. If the senior translator is unable to distinguish the work of machine from that of a human, it suggests that the computer has passed a test analogous to Turing's test for intelligence in computers.

In section 14.1 we look at some approaches to MT and at some of the apparent obstacles. Computer translation was one of the first well-funded non-numeric applications of computers; however, the ALPAC report in 1966 [2] was very critical of MT research at that time and its publication is a watershed in the field. Federal funding in the USA dried up after its publication. In section 14.2 we look at some pre-ALPAC systems and in section 14.3 at some of the work in the years following 1966. In section 14.4 we examine the current status of and future prospects for the field.

This chapter is necessarily very selective; a comprehensive survey of Machine Translation with an extensive bibliography can be found in Hutchins [3]. Reference 4 contains papers describing the status of several current systems.

14.1 Approaches and obstacles

Approaches to MT can be classified broadly as *direct*, *interlingual* or *transfer*; though recently, distinctions have become blurred as systems begin to contain elements of more than one method. Figure 14.1 illustrates the differences in the approaches.

A direct system is designed for a particular source-target language-pair. The source is analyzed only to the extent necessary to be able to generate the output. For example, translating the French *son oncle* into the Spanish *su tío* requires little analysis of the source. However, translating it into English requires the program to determine if the output should be *his uncle* or *her uncle*.

In an interlingual system, the analysis of the source text is independent of the synthesis of the target text and the goal is to extract all the meaning from the input. Rather like some computer language systems, there is a language independent intermediate form into which the source is translated and from which the output is generated.

Figure 14.1 Approaches to translation

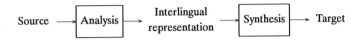

Direct system

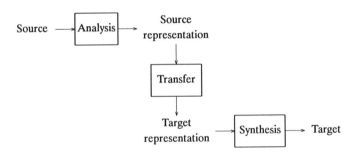

Interlingual system

Transfer system

In a transfer system, there are two internal forms and three stages in translation. The source is analyzed into one internal form, then there is a transfer into a second internal form followed by generation of the output. Some of the problems that the interlingua method needs to tackle in the analysis phase are handled during transfer.

Obstacles Translation is not a simple matter of parsing an input sentence and generating a corresponding output sentence. As examples of some of the problems encountered during translation, consider idioms, "untranslatable" concepts and the width of view of the translator.

An idiom can be defined as a phrase the meaning of which is not derivable from the meaning of its elements. Figure 14.2 contains examples of English idioms. While idioms are not generally a problem in technical documents, the translator has to be on the look-out for them.

Figure 14.2 Idioms

You are pulling my leg.
She let the cat out of the bag.
He has a frog in his throat.
He is leading them up the garden path.

   Some languages have words for ideas that are not as succintly expressible in other languages. For example, the Welsh *hwyl* is poorly represented by the dictionary definition - "emotional fervor". Rheingold [5] has many examples of similar words including *Schaddenfreude* (German - delight in the misfortune of another) and *attaccabottoni* (Italian - bore who buttonholes people and tells sad, pointless stories). Perhaps the most succint word listed is *mamihlapinatapei* from Tierra del Fuego meaning "looking into each other's eyes, each hoping the other will initiate what both want to do but neither chooses to commence". Some languages have a richness in certain areas; for example, native languages in polar regions have words corresponding to several types of ice and snow. Thibert [6] lists the snow words shown in Table 14.1; translating the English "snow", which do you use?

Table 14.1 Some snow words

snow (spread out)	aput
snow drifting (it is drifting)	perksertok
snow is hard	sitidlorak
snow (for melting into water)	aniuk, anio
snow (like salt)	pokaktok
snow (is soft)	mauyak, mauyao^lertok
snow (mixed with water)	massak
snow (on clothes, boots etc.)	ayak
snow (first snow fall)	apingout
snow (newly drifted)	akelrorak

   Early MT systems took little more than a word-by-word approach. Such a local view has problems with words such as *pen* and *bar* that have many meanings. The second edition of the Oxford English Dictionary, for example, lists more than two dozen meanings for *bar*. Each of the examples in Fig. 14.3 translates to a different word in French.
   When reading a sentence, it may be necessary to look outside it in order to determine its meaning. For example, resolving pronoun references may require information from a previous sentence. In some instances, significant knowledge of the real world appears to be necessary in order to make the correct reference. Consider the pairs of sentences in Fig. 14.4.

Figure 14.3 Different meanings of *bar*

The window could not be opened because of the bar across it.
The professor ate the bar of chocolate.
The landlord wiped the beer off the bar.
The child chewed on the bar of soap.
The soprano held the note to the end of the bar.

Figure 14.4 Sentence pairs with pronoun references

The men shot at the women. They fell down.
John drank the whisky from a glass. It felt warm in his stomach.
The councillors barred the demonstrators. They feared revolution.
The councillors barred the demonstrators. They advocated revolution.
The missile struck the target. It shattered.

Translation may require the correct reference to be determined; for example, when translating the first sentence into French, *they* becomes *ils* or *elles* depending on whether the women or the men fell down. A human translator knows that things shot at are more likely to fall down than things shooting. In addition to the basic approach, the width of view of the translator is another way in which MT systems can be classified.

14.2 Pioneering systems

Almost as soon as computers became widely available in the 1950s, there was interest in using them for translating natural languages. Translation research was one of the few well-funded non-numeric areas; the governments of both the USA and USSR were financially supportive. In the USA, the main efforts were in translating Russian, French and German into English. In the USSR, interest was in translating a variety of languages to and from Russian, though there were few computers available at the time and a lot of the work was hand simulation. Important systems in the USA in the first 15 years included those at Georgetown University and the Linguistic Research Center at the University of Texas.

Work at Georgetown University started soon after a landmark MT conference at MIT in early 1952. The Georgetown system (GAT) was a direct system designed to translate Russian physics texts into English. It took a very narrow, word-by-word, view of the text and the output quality was poor. However, it was sufficiently good for information gathering. The system was developed in an *ad hoc* fashion with little theoretical foundation, being modified as required to deal with the input. A 1954 demonstration of GAT sparked public interest in MT and helped obtain US government funding for the field. A version of GAT was delivered to Oak Ridge National Laboratory in 1964, where it was used for at least 15 years, and to EURATOM in Italy, where it was replaced by SYSTRAN in 1976.

Research at the Linguistic Research Center of the University of Texas was not confined to MT but included a German to English translation system (METAL). Work on METAL started in 1961 and was thus able to benefit from the experience gained with earlier systems such as GAT. More theoretically sound than GAT, it used Chomsky's ideas on transformational grammar, though some compromises were necessary in order to make an operational system.

The ALPAC report [2] focussed primarily on the economics of translation, particularly from Russian to English. The committee looked at the demand for translation and at the supply of human translators and concluded that the demand was being met. The report was critical of the fact that MT output had to be post-edited, even though most human output was also subject to such review. The report recommended a reduction in the support of MT because "there is no immediate or predictable prospect of useful machine translation". However, the report was in favor of support for research in computational linguistics.

14.3 Post-ALPAC

In this section we look at some of the work in the years following ALPAC: TAUM at Montreal, the work at Grenoble University and at an AI system of the period.

TAUM While the ALPAC report caused a dearth of funding in the USA, research continued elsewhere. With government funding, a research center in computational linguistics was established at the University of Montreal in 1965. About five years later, it narrowed its focus to MT and was retitled Traduction Automatique de l'Université de Montreal (TAUM). Its goal was to produce an operational English-French system; it was the first to take a strictly transfer approach.

TAUM-METEO was a spin-off of the TAUM project, apparently the result of a chance remark by a bored human translator. In daily operation since 1977, it processes an average of 25,000 words a day and is still the only fully automatic MT system. Input, over communication lines, is scanned for weather forecasts in English; French translations are transmitted. Its input uses a limited vocabulary and a small number of syntactic forms; parts of only about 20% of the forecasts are diverted to human translators and most of the diversions are because of errors in the input. The introduction of TAUM-METEO greatly reduced the high turnover of translators. Hutchins [3 p. 230] gives an example of a TAUM-METEO translation.

Following the success of TAUM-METEO, the Translation Bureau of the Secretary of State contracted for TAUM-AVIATION [7]. The goal was to provide a system to translate 90 million words of aviation maintenance manuals from English to French within three years; at the end of that period the aircraft in question were due to be delivered. TAUM devoted its efforts exclusively to this project.

As an information-dissemination project, it was essential that TAUM-AVIATION produced high-quality output. Like TAUM-METEO, if TAUM-AVIATION could not parse an input sentence, it left it for human translators to process rather than produce a possibly erroneous translation. At time of project evaluation, output was high quality but 20%-40% of input sentences produced no output. Taking post-editing needs into account, TAUM-AVIATION proved not to be cost effective averaging 18.3 cents (Canadian) a word versus 14.5 cents for human translators. It was rejected not for quality reasons (Ref. 7 gives example translations) but because of the time and money needed to make it operational. Researchers thought that termination was premature and that another 12 person-months of work would have resulted in significant improvements.

The cancellation of TAUM-AVIATION left TAUM with no funding and it was disbanded in 1981.

CETA Grenoble University is one of the principal European MT research sites; the Centre d'Études pour la Traduction Automatique (CETA) was established in 1961. Researchers concentrated on translating from Russian to French using basically an interlingual approach; they learned from experiences at Georgetown and took sentence-wide views of the input. The CETA system used a pivot language, primarily a common "deep syntactic" base, for various source and target languages.

In the period from 1967 to 1971 the translation system was tested on 400,000 words of Math and Physics texts. An evaluation of the system in 1971 classified 42% of the output sentences as correct and 61% as comprehensible. While the researchers felt that over half the errors were fixable, others were due to limitations of the basic method. Like TAUM-AVIATION, CETA had no fail-soft mechanism: if it could not completely analyze a sentence it did not generate any output.

A hardware change in 1971 led to a rethinking and the winding-up of CETA. It was replaced almost immediately by GETA (Groupes d'Études pour la Traduction Automatique) using a transfer rather than an interlingual approach.

Stanford MT Project In the post-ALPAC USA, machine translation research was kept alive as a by-product of work in natural language understanding systems. One way of testing if a program has "understood" a text is to have it translate the text into another language. Such a system from this period is the Stanford Machine Translation Project.

Wilks [8, 9] developed a program that analyzed English and generated French. The text was broken into fragments at sentence boundaries, prepositions and pronouns and the system used "preference semantics" to resolve anaphoric references, interpret propositions, and handle compound nouns. Preference semantics aimed at understanding the text only to the extent necessary to translate it.

Knowledge of the domain of discourse was represented in template form and templates were used, for example, to create chains from unknowns (pronouns) to possible referents. The preferred interpretation was the one that satisfied the preferences of neighboring fragments to the greatest extent. As an example, consider the analysis of the following sentence:

John drank the whisky from a glass and it felt warm in his stomach.

This was broken into four fragments, thus:

John drank the whisky | from a glass | and it felt warm | in his stomach.

Candidates for the pronoun reference are "whisky" and "glass". From the sentence, the system makes extracts, each of which contains either a candidate word or the pronoun. In our example, this yields:

> [whisky in John part]   from the 1st fragment
> [whisky to John part]   from the 1st fragment
> [whisky from a glass]   from the 2nd fragment
> [it in his stomach]   from the 4th fragment.

For example, the first extract is derived from the first fragment because the system knows about drinking; a representation of its formula for the action *drink* is shown in Fig 14.5. The formula indicates that drinking is an action, preferably performed by an animate being, that causes a liquid to be moved from a container into the animate being. (Though we can think of instances of "drink" that do not match this model.) Now the system can make the link between the first and fourth extracts and thus link "it" and "whisky".

Wilks' system made no distinction between syntax and semantics. It used exclusively semantic features in "parsing", built no syntactic structures and was notable for solving problems by semantics that might be difficult to solve through syntactic analysis. The French dictionary used to generate

Figure 14.5 Formula for *drink*

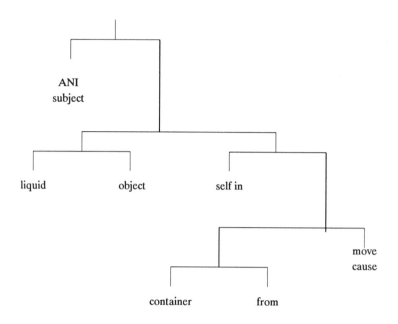

output was a list of pairs of the form:

(semantic formula, French "stereotype")

where the stereotype consisted of generator rules and French words. The rules test case conditions e.g. masculine/feminine.

14.4 Current systems and future prospects

Machine translation has seen something of a renaissance and is the subject of much research; the discussion in this section is likely to be out of date by the time it is in print. Current investigations range from knowledge-based MT systems that aim to produce automatic translations in limited domains, to commercial machine-assisted systems that are more general in application but require more human intervention. We look at the EC EUROTRA effort, research sponsored by the Japanese government, at a knowledge-based system and at a commercial product.

EUROTRA Because it was designed from the outset to be a multi-lingual system, EUROTRA is probably the most ambitious current MT project. Initial work was with the 42 language pairs resulting from the seven official languages of the EC: Danish, Dutch, English, French, German, Greek and Italian. The system was intended to help the EC reduce its translation mountain.

EUROTRA uses the transfer approach with individual countries responsible for analysis and synthesis of particular languages. The 42 transfer modules are developed by groups; with the addition of Spanish, Portugese and Turkish, the number of modules will more than double. To minimize the size of the transfer components, input representations are made as close as possible to an interlingua and all possible meaning is extracted from a source text. A transfer module inputs and outputs dependency trees [10]. The goal of EUROTRA is to produce output of sufficient quality for information-gathering applications and output suitable for post-editing for other applications.

Japanese government translation project Machine translation is one of the main objectives of the Japanese government's fifth generation computer project; initial efforts are directed towards translation between Japanese and English. The project began in 1982 and work is distributed over several organizations. MT software, for example, is the responsibility of Kyoto University and the Electrotechnical Laboratory. The scope of the project is to demonstrate the feasibility of translations between Japanese and English of abstracts of scientific and engineering papers. It is expected that private industry will then continue the development.

A transfer rather than an interlingual approach is being used because of the nature of Japanese and English; for example, the two languages have different types of classifications for verbs. Three dictionaries are employed: one for analysis, one for transfer and one for synthesis. Translation is essentially lexicon-based and, initially, uses independent transfer rules for the two directions. Nagao *et al.* [11] present the results of some evaluations. It is expected that post-editing will be required for the foreseeable future.

KBMT KMBT-89 [12] is an example of a knowledge-based machine translation system. Using an interlingual approach, it is able to translate between Japanese and English, individual sentences in the domain of personal computer installation and maintenance. The domain model contains about 1500 concepts; each of the analysis and generator lexicons contains about 800 Japanese lexical units and 900 English lexical units.

The analyzer contains two components: a parser that produces a syntactic structure (an f-structure) and a semantic interpreter that maps source lexical and syntactic units onto their interlingual representations. The interlingua captures the meaning of an input sentence and can be regarded as a type of semantic net.

Before the generator is called to generate the target sentence, the augmentor arranges the interlingua in canonical form and attempts to remove any ambiguities. This latter may require interaction with the user.

The generator is similar in form to the analyzer. The semantic component selects target language lexical components and syntactic structures. It creates an f-structure of the target language sentence from which GENKIT [13] generates the output text.

The report on KMBT-89 gives a very detailed description of the way in which the system operates and, unusually, examples of some of the problems encountered and solved during design and implementation. Possible future developments include extensions to handle running text with inter-sentence references.

Weidner Communications Corporation A typical commercial translation system is the one produced by Weidner Communications. It is a computer-assisted translation (CAT) package that the company claims does about 85% of the job of translation. It currently handles about two dozen source/target pairs, including, for example, English into about eight other languages, French to Arabic, and Japanese to English. The company has two products: MicroCAT and MacroCAT.

MicroCAT 20 is a single user system running on IBM PC/XT. It handles only Roman characters and processes up to 3000 words an hour. The cost, including hardware, is about $20,000. For each source-target pair it uses a core dictionary, typically about 9,000 words. A split screen allows the translator to see both source and translation.

MacroCAT 20 is a multi-user system for a PDP-11 or a VAX. More than one language pair can be handled simultaneously. The system needs 1MB main memory and 20MB of disc but can process up to 8,000 words per hour per user. Non-Roman alphabets are handled by Weidner terminals that have 128 programmable characters.

Software Though details of the translation process are secret for commercial reasons, the company does reveal the broad schematic shown in Fig. 14.6.

The *input handler* breaks text into words and *dictionary lookup* gives the corresponding target-language words, thus proving a rough word-for-word translation. The *idiom converter* finds idioms by pattern matching and the correct equivalent phrase can then be generated.

Weidner has devised a "Linear Compaction Grammar" (LCG). The LCG method breaks down a sentence and groups elementary parts of speech into clauses and phrases. For example, nouns and adjacent adjectives are

Figure 14.6 Weidner translation strategy

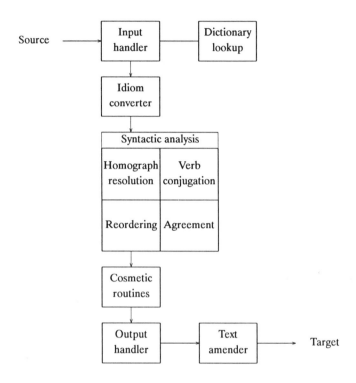

linked to form noun phrases. *Syntactic analysis* marks each word according to its function and relationship to other sentence elements. This information is used in *homograph resolution, verb conjugation, reordering* and *cosmetic routines*.

Homograph resolution determines which of several meanings of a word such as "bond", "pen" and "light" is being used. Verb conjugation determines the tense, number, gender and person of each verb and determines the appropriate output form. Reordering positions adjectives correctly with respect to the noun and reorders subjects and verbs where necessary.

Finally, cosmetic routines make small adjustments to the output, for example, replacing "a" with "an", eliminating double negatives, inserting/deleting articles and special punctuation. The *output handler* formats the target text for display and the *text amender* enables the user to edit the translation.

Summary

The first phase of machine translation was marked by a lot of hope and comparatively unsophisticated direct systems. Expectations were perhaps unrealistically high. While research continued abroad, the ALPAC report almost killed MT research in the USA. Interest was kept alive mainly as an offshoot of some AI systems. Indirect systems replaced direct as the preferred method of operation. Recently, MT systems have begun to be used in day-to-day operations and commercial systems are available even for personal computers. There is likely to be continued growth in the use of MT systems, particularly interactive ones, and the emergence of translator's workstations.

Exercises

(1)   How would you detect idioms in an input text? How could your proposed method be fooled?

(2)   Recipes are a limited domain of discourse with few basic sentence types. Investigate the problems of translating recipes between two natural languages with which you are familiar.

References

1.   E. Myers, "Speaking in tongues," *Datamation*, vol. 30, no. 1, pp. 78, 82-84, January 1984.

2.   J. R. Pierce (chair), *Language and machines: computers in translation and linguistics,* Automatic Language Processing Advisory Committee, Division of Behavioral Sciences, National Academy of Sciences, Washington, D.C., 1966. National Research Council Publication 1416.

3.   W. J. Hutchins, *Machine translation: past, present, future,* Ellis Horwood, Chichester, England, 1986.

4.   J. Slocum (editor), *Machine translation systems,* Cambridge University Press, 1988. Updated versions of papers in Computational Linguistics, Vol 11, No. 1-3, 1985.

5.   H. Rheingold, *They have a word for it,* J. P. Tarcher, Los Angeles, 1988.

6.   A. Thibert, *English-Eskimo, Eskimo-English dictionary,* Canadian Research Centre for Anthropology, Saint Paul University, Ottowa, Canada, 1970. Revised edition.

7. P. Isabelle and L. Bourbeau, "TAUM-AVIATION: its technical features and some experimental results," in *Machine translation systems*, ed. J. Slocum, pp. 237-263, Cambridge University Press, 1988.

8. Y. Wilks, "An artificial intelligence approach to machine translation," in *Computer models of thought and language*, ed. R. C. Schank and K. M. Colby, W. H. Freeman, San Francisco, CA, 1973.

9. Y. Wilks, "An intelligent analyzer and understander of English," *Communications of the ACM*, vol. 18, no. 5, pp. 264-274, May 1975.

10. R. Johnson, M. King, and L. des Tombe, "EUROTRA: A multilingual system under development," *Computational Linguistics*, vol. 11, no. 2-3, pp. 155-169, April-September 1985.

11. M. Nagao, J. Tsujii, and J. Nakamua, "The Japanese government project for machine translation," in *Machine translation systems*, ed. J. Slocum, pp. 141-186, Cambridge University Press, 1988.

12. Center for Machine Translation, *KMBT-89 Project Report,* Center for Machine Translation, Carnegie Mellon University, Pittsburgh, PA, 1989.

13. M. Tomita and E. Nyberg, *Generation Kit and Transformation Kit Version 3.2 User's Manual,* Center for Machine Translation, Carnegie Mellon University, 1988. Technical Memo.

Appendices

Mar 19 12:19 1990 PROOFR OUTPUT FOR gopher Page 1

***************************** SPELLING *****************************

Possible spelling errors in gopher are:

ashpalt   barrier   enviorment

If any of these words are spelled correctly, later type
              spelladd word1 word2 ... wordn
to have them added to your spelldict file.

***************************** PUNCTUATION *****************************

The punctuation in gopher is first described.

0 double quotes and 0 single quotes
1 apostrophes
2 left parentheses and 1 right ones
Because of the unbalanced parentheses, the following check for mistakes
may make errors.

The program next prints any sentence that it thinks is
incorrectly punctuated and follows it by its correction.

line 15
OLD: one theory for gopher damage is that the animals believe
NEW: One theory for gopher damage is that the animals believe

For more information about punctuation rules, type:
              punctrules

***************************** DOUBLE WORDS *****************************

For file gopher:

and and appears beginning line 23 gopher

***************************** WORD CHOICE *****************************

Sentences with possibly wordy or misused phrases are listed next,
followed by suggested revisions.

For file gopher

beginning line 19 gopher
P Because of gopher damage experienced on less important cables
the first Bell System coaxial cable was protected
[by means] of .

Mar 19 12:19 1990 PROOFR OUTPUT FOR gopher Page 2

beginning line 28 gopher
Because of this experience, tests with live animals were conducted
by Livingston, to *[hopefully]* find what thickness of material
would prevent penetration, and in addition be corrosion resistant.

beginning line 31 gopher
These tests *[which]* used the cables as a barrier
*[indicate]*d that a .

beginning line 33 gopher
This material was first *[utiliz]*ed on Bell's Dallas - Los Angeles
coaxial toll cable.

beginning line 39 gopher
Jute or polyethylene-covered thermoplastic-flooded steel has been
*[utiliz]*ed for the cables while wire products were protected
with polyvinyl chloride (PVC jacketed galvanized steel.

file gopher: number of lines 42 number of phrases found 6

Please wait for the substitution phrases

------------------ Table of Substitutions -------------------

PHRASE   SUBSTITUTION

by means: use "with, by, through" for " by means of"
hopefully: use "hopefully means full of hope" for " hopefully"
indicate: use " indicate" for " give an indication of"
indicate: use "show, suggest" for " indicate"
utiliz: use "use" for " utilize"
which: use ""that" when clause is restrictive" for " which"
which: use "of which" for " of that"
which: use "when" for " at which time"

----

    * Not all the revisions will be appropriate for your document.
    * When there is more than one suggestion for just one bracketed
      word, you will have to choose the case that fits your use.
    * Capitalized words are instructions, not suggestions.
    * To find out more about each phrase, type "worduse phrase."

NOTE: If you want this program to look for additional phrases
      or to stop looking for some, for instance to stop
      flagging "impact," type the command dictadd.

************************* SPLIT INFINITIVES *************************

For file gopher:

Possible split infinitives:

Mar 19 12:19 1990 PROOFR OUTPUT FOR gopher Page 3

to hopefully find

For information on split infinitives type:
                    splitrules

Mar 19 12:20 1990 prose -mm -li -l -tm gopher Page 1

BECAUSE YOUR TEXT IS SHORT (< 2000 WORDS & < 100 SENTENCES),
THE FOLLOWING ANALYSIS MAY BE MISLEADING.

NOTE: Your document is being compared against standards
derived from 30 technical memoranda, classified as good
by managers in the research area of Bell Laboratories.

READABILITY

The Kincaid readability formula predicts that your text
can be read by someone with 14 or more years of schooling,
which is a good score for documents like this.

VARIATION

Variation in sentence length, type, and openings
prevents monotony. More importantly, a lack of such
variation suggests that every topic and every sentence has
equal weight, which makes it difficult for the reader to
pick out the important points.

In this text 62% of the sentences are complex and 23%
are simple. These percentages should be closer together.
The difference between these percentages, here 39, should be
less than 24.

While the readability score predicts that your paper is
readable, it contains many more complex sentences than is
common for this type of text. (Complex sentences are
sentences containing an independent clause [a sentence] and
a dependent clause [an incomplete sentence], e.g., "After
the rain fell, the plants grew.") One way to improve this
text then, would be to rephrase the most important ideas in
simple sentences, which will give those ideas additional
emphasis.

SENTENCE STRUCTURE

Passives

This text contains a much higher percentage of passive
verbs (36.0%) than is common in good documents of this
type. The score for passive verbs should be below 28.6%.
A sentence is in the passive voice when its grammatical
subject is the receiver of the action.

PASSIVE: The ball was hit by the boy.

When the doer of the action in a sentence is the subject,
the sentence is in the active voice.

ACTIVE: The boy hit the ball.

The passive voice is sometimes needed

Mar 19 12:20 1990 prose -mm -li -l -tm gopher Page 2

1. to emphasize the object of the sentence,

2. to vary the rhythm of the text, or

3. to avoid naming an unimportant actor.

EXAMPLE: The appropriations were approved.

Although passive sentences are sometimes needed, psychological research has shown that they are harder to comprehend than active sentences. Because of this you should transform as many of your passives to actives as possible. You can use the style program to find all your sentences with passive verbs in them, by typing the following command when this program is finished.

style -p filename

Nominalizations

You have appropriately limited your nominalizations (nouns made from verbs, e.g., "description").

Expletives

In this text, a higher percentage of sentences begin with expletives (8.0%) than is common in good documents of this type, which usually have no more than 4% of their sentences beginning with expletives. Expletives are words that have no content. For instance, "it" and "there" are often used as expletives in sentences such as "It is dark" and "There are three solutions to this puzzle." In these sentences, "it" and "there" have no content; they are simply linguistic placeholders.

Expletives are sometimes necessary, e.g., "It is raining." Often, however, they add unnecessary words to a sentence: "There are three solutions to this puzzle" can easily be shortened to "This puzzle has three solutions."

To find all the expletives counted by this program, type the following command after this program is finished.

style -e filename

PROSE OUTPUTS

Options

You can request that your document be compared against different standards; typing -t with the prose command, e.g.,

prose -t filename

will compare your text against training documents.

Mar 19 12:20 1990 prose -mm -li -l -tm gopher Page 3

A -s option will provide a very short version of the
prose output.

> prose -s filename

If you already have a style table in a file, you can
save time by using it as the input to prose rather than the
textfile. To do this, precede the style table filename with
a -f, e.g.,

> prose -f styletable-filename

All the options can be selected at the same time and
listed in any order.

> prose -f styletable-filename -s -t

Statistics

The table of statistics generated by the program style
can be found in your file styl.tmp. If you want to look at
it type:

> cat styl.tmp

You can also use the match program, which provides a better
format, type:

> match styl.tmp

If you are not interested in the file, remove it by typing:

> rm styl.tmp

ORGANIZATION

The prose program cannot check the content or
organization of your text. One way to look at the overall
structure of your text is to use grep to list all the
headings that were specified for the mm formatter. To do
this, type:

> grep '^.H' filename

You can also use the organization program, org, to look
at the structure of your text. Org will format your paper
with all the headings and paragraph divisions intact, but
will only print the first and last sentence of each
paragraph in your text so you can check your flow of ideas.

> org filename

Chapter 3   Some more adventures with macros

This is the introduction, it comes before all the text in the chapter. It should be quite long enough now to test the macros.

1.1 Part 1

This is a section of text. We might need quite a lot of text to test the macros, at least so one of the headings appears on page 2. Not much of it will make any sense at all though.

1.1.1 Level 2 sub-head

This is really just filler to make sure that we don't have 2 headings next to each other. Nothing bad happens if we do, it just doesn't look good.

Level 3 sub-head

We can define the XX macro to do anything we like with the parameters it is given. One possibility is for it to put only the first 2 levels of sub-heading into the table of contents.

1.1.2 Level 2 sub-head

Some more filler. What more can I say. Hope we

are getting close to the bottom of the page now.

Level 3 sub-head

This is text following another third level
header. By now we must be on the second page so
let's throw in one last top level header

1.2 Part 2

Just a couple of lines here just so that we
don't end with a header. Then we can invoke the
macro (CO) we have been appending text to all this
time. And see what's in it.

Table of Contents   Page

Some thoughts on teaching night classes

Peter Smith

Department of Computer Science
C.S.U.N., Northridge, CA 91330

ABSTRACT

Some advantages and disadvantages of night classes are presented and some conclusions drawn.

1.   Introduction

CSUN offers many sections of courses at night. This is so that students who work during the day can come to school. In addition, it gives people a chance to teach part-time.

2.   Some advantages and disadvantages of night classes

2.1.   Advantages

2.1.1.   Parking

Parking is usually easier than during the day (the most difficult time to find a parking place is in the morning). The campus police are less likely to come round and check decals in the dark.

2.1.2.   Students

Students tend to be sleepier at night and not give you such a hard time. However, this may mean that classes are not as lively as those during the day.

2.2.   Disadvantages

2.2.1.   Candy

The store in the student union closes around 7pm which may make it difficult to get a quick fix of candy. Machines are available but charge outrageous prices.

January 12, 1990

- 2 -

2.2.2. Mountain lions

The existence of mountain lions on campus has
not been proven. It is likely that this rumor ori-
ginated in one of the local colleges wishing to
attract our better, but more timid, students.

3. Summary

On balance the availability of parking and the
comparatively quiet atmosphere at night outweighs
the threat of attack from wildlife.

January 12, 1990

Arthur O'Connor

18111 Main Street
Northridge, CA 91324

(818) 555-1264 (home)
(714) 555-7681 (work)

EMPLOYMENT
OBJECTIVES

Leading position in a venture capital organization, preferably one with profit-sharing and own penthouse.

EMPLOYMENT
HISTORY

July 1985
to
Present

Timmy's Burgers
Roscoe Blvd
Sepulveda, CA

Duties included maintenance of the chili recycling equipment. Also helped administer emergency first aid to customers unfamiliar with our products.

August 1983
to
June 1985

Joe's Lo-Loss Diamond Cutting Company,
Reseda Blvd
Reseda, CA

Duties included cleaning the sledgehammers and sweeping up bits of diamonds after precision cutting operations.

September 1980
to
July 1983

Happyworld Amusement Park,
Anaheim, CA

Duties included ensuring that the amount of lost property met daily quotas established by management. Occasional responsibilities as Ricky Rat stand-in.

EDUCATIONAL
BACKGROUND

1981-87

California State University Northridge. BS 1987.
Major: Computer Science. GPA 3.6 (out of 4.0).

1980

Graduate of Granada Hills High.

REFERENCES

Available on request

THE AUTOLOGIC HYPHENATION PROGRAM

The hyphenation program described herein is used in both the Autologic Newspaper and Commercial Printing (APS-COMP) photocomposition systems. In order to optimize accuracy and effeciency an exception word dictionary is used in conjunction with an algorithm to obtain hyphen points within a word. The exception word dictionary, the algorithm, and their use will be hereinafter described.

In a test of 94,566 words of the English Language the algorithm alone has proven to be 71% accurate and 58% efficient, i.e.,of the 94,566 words tested, the algorithm produced an accurate subset of hyphen points for 71% of the words and accurately reproduced all possible points for 58% of the 94,566 words.

The natural fall-out of these test rendered an initial exception word dictionary of 39,455 words, i.e., words for which the algorithm could not accurately determine all of the possible hyphen points. Thus by using the algorithm and the exception word dictionary in conjunction with each other, the program is capable of but not limited to 100% accuracy and efficiency in the hyphenation of more than 94,566 words of the english language. Utility programs available to the system are capable of adding more words to the exception word dictionary as may be required. The number of words that may be added is limited only by the amount of available system disk storage.

In the process of program hyphenation with an exception word dictionary it is always necessary to search the dictionary first and then proceed to the algorithm in the event that an entry is not found. It is for this reason that the organization of the dictionary and its directory must be highly efficient inorder to minimize the number of disk accesses required to either find or eliminate the possibility of finding a word therein. Also to be considered is the ease of maintenance of the dictionary. For example, any scheme for building or adding words which would require the sorting or sequencing of input data should be avoided. Thus in the autologic system, words may be added to the dictionary in any random sequence.

EXCEPTION WORD DICTIONARY ACCESS AND FORMAT

The initial exception word dictionary and its directory requires 1103 contiguous sectors of system disk storage. To allow for reasonable expansion it is recommended that 1200 sectors be allocated on the system disk. The dictionary directory is contained in the first two sectors and contains a possible 390 entries to the dictionary. All entries are relative to the directory itself, the dictionary may therefore be located on either platter of the system disk drive and at any location where 1200 contiguous sectors are available.

THE DIRECTORY

The directory consist of 390 possible entry points to the dictionary. Words to be hyphenated are first converted to the numeric equivalance of each character, i.e., since there are 26 characters in the alphabet each character will have some numeric value between 1 and 26. The entry point is determined by the first alphabetic character of the word (1-26) and the number of characters in the word, with the restriction that no entry shall have less than 4 characters and all words having in excess of 18 characters shall be filed asthough it did have 18 characters. This allows the directory to be organized into 15 groups of 26 entries each. To determine the correct entry point for any given word:

[(number of characters −4) X 26] + value of first character −1 = relative directory entry

The real sector address = sector address of the directory + the relative sector address of the directory entry.

Example:

Given: Beginning sector address of directory = 2000
Given: Relative directory entry 130 = 109
Find: Start search sector for the word **ALGORITHM**

$$[(9-4) \times 26] + 1\text{-}1 = 130$$

Thus the entry 130 of the directory gives the relative sector address to start the search i.e., start the search for the word ALGORITHM at disk sector address 2109.

If there are no entries in the dictionary for a particular category of words, the relative sector address in the directory will be 0 and the program will proceed immediately to process the input word by the rules of the algorithm.

DICTIONARY WORD AND HYPHEN POINT FORMATS

Since the program is only concerned with alphabetic characters and a number of hyphenation points less than 30, all items in the dictionary may be uniquely expressed in 5 bits. Thus in a 16 bit word macnine it is possible to pack 3 items per word and use bit 16 to distinguish alphabetic characters from numeric hyphen point positions.

The words and their respective hyphenation points are packed into 199 words of a disk sector. Word 200 of the sector is used a pointer for any necessary continuation records of the file. This pointer is also relative to the disk sector address of the directory. A value of 0 for this pointer or any other word in the sector signifies the end of that particular file. The format of the dictionary may be better understood by the following example:

Relative Buffer Address	Record Octal Content	Encoded Character Equivalent	Hyphenated word
191	003143	asc	as-co-spor-ic
192	037160	osp	
193	037111	ori	
194	006000	c	
195	120202	842	
196	002642	amb	am-bu-la-to-ry
197	052601	ula	
198	050762	tor	
199	000301	⇐	Relative sector address of continuation record

Continuation Record
Relative Sector Address 0301

000	062000	y	
001	120304	864	
002	104000	200	
003	000000	⇐	End of file for 10 character words beginning with the character A

THE NO ENTRY CONDITION

In the event that the input word cannot be found in the dictionary, the program will proceed to process the word using the rules of the algorithm. These rules are described in detail in the following pages.

AN ALGORITHM for ENGLISH HYPHENATION

The rules of the algorithm are seperated into two parts. The first part, called the **LAST CHARACTER** rules, are the rules used to find a hyphenation position from the end of a word. The second part, called **OTHER TIMES** rules are the rules used to find a hyphenation point in the remainder of the word after the **LAST CHARACTER** rules have been used.

The first step is to strip the word of all non alphabetic characters. The last character of the word is then tested for a **D,E,G,R,S, or Y**. If it is one of these, the appropriate **LAST CHARACTER** rules are used, the **OTHER TIMES** rules are used to find the hyphenation points in the remainder of the word. The **OTHER TIMES** rules consist of scanning the word from right to left for a vowel. (If the last character of the word is an **E** it is skipped.) After a vowel is found, the scan continues to find a consonant. When a consonant is found, it is tested for a **H,K,L,N,P,R,S,T,W** or **X**. If it is one of these, the appropriate **LAST CHARACTER** rule is applied. If it is not, a hyphen is placed preceding the consonant (**B,C,D,F,G,J,M,W,V,** or **Z**) unless the consonant is preceded by a vowel. This proceedure is continued until the beginning of the word has been reached. The following paragraphs give a detailed description of the **LAST CHARACTER** and **OTHER TIMES** rules that will be used.

LAST CHARACTER RULES

D (D-D, T-T) ED, r(D,T) -ED
 CL-LED, r-KLED
 -(B,C,D,F,G,P,T,Z) LED
 ʦɪʀ(D,ED)

If the last character in the word is a **D**, the previous character is tested for an **E**. If it is not an **E**, the end of the word cannot be hyphenated. However, if it is an **E**, and the previous two characters are a **DD** or a **TT** the word can be hyphenated between the **DD** or **TT** (**D-DED,T-TED**). If it is not a **DD** or **TT**, the character before the **E** is tested for a **D** or a **T**. If it is a **D** or **T** the word can be hyphenated after the **D** or the **T** (**D-ED,T-ED**). If the character before the **E** is not a **D** or a **T**, it is tested for an **L**. If it is not an **L**, the end of the word cannot be hyphenated. If it is an **L**, the previous character is tested for a **K**. If it is a **K**, the word can be hyphenated before the **K** (**-KLED**) except if the **K** is preceded by a **C**, the word is hyphenated after the **K** (**CK-LED**). If the **L** is not preceded by a **K**, but preceded by a **B,C,D,F,G,P,T,** or a **Z**, the word can be hyphenated before the afore mentioned characters (**-BLED,-ZLED**).

E -(B,C,D,F,G,P,T,Z) LE
 ʦɪCKLE, r-KLE
 ʦɪʀ(E,LE)

If the last character in the word is an **E**, the previous character is tested for an **L**. If it is not an **L**, the end of the word cannot be hyphenated. If it is an **L**, and the character preceding the **L** is a **B,C,D,F,G,P,T,** or a **Z**, the word can be hyphenated before the afore mentioned characters (**-BLE,-DLE**). If the character before the **L** is not one of these characters, it is tested for a **K**. If it is not a **K**, the end of the word cannot be hyphenated. If it is a **K**, and the character preceding the **K** is not a **C**, the word can be hyphenated before the **K** (**-KLE**).

G (B-B, D-D, G-G, M-M, N-N, P-P, R-R, T-T)ING
 (ING) CK-LING, r-KLING
 -(B,C,D,F,G,P,T,Z)LING
 (r-rL) -ING
 ʦɪʀ(G,NG)

If the last character in the word is a **G**, the previous two characters are tested for an **IN**. If they are not **IN**, the end of the word cannot be hyphenated. However, if it is an **IN**, and the two characters before the **IN** are **BB, DD,**

GG, MM, NN, PP, RR, or TT, the word can be hyphenated betweeen one of the afore mentioned pair of characters (B-BING,T-TING). If the two characters before the ING are not one of these pairs, the character before the
I is tested for an L. If it is an L, and the character before the L is a K, the word can be hyphenated before the K
(-KLING), except if the character before the K is a C, then the word is hyphenated after the K (CK-LING). If the
character before the L is not a K, it is tested for a B,C,D,F,G,P,T, or a Z. If it is one of these, the word can be
hyphenated after the L (L-LING). If the character before the I is not an L,the word can be hyphenated before the
I (-ING).

R (B-B, D-D, G-G, M-M, N-N, P-P, R-R, T-T)ER
-(B,C,D,F,G,P,T,Z)LER
vS-TER, c-STER
ᵥₑᵢEVER, r-EVER
ᵥₑᵣ(R,ER,TER)

If the last character in the word is an R, the character before the R is tested for an E. If it is not an E, the end of
the word cannot be hyphenated. If it is an E, the two characters before the E are tested for BB, DD, GG, MM,
NN, PP, RR, or TT. If they are one of these, the word can be hyphenated between the character pair (B-BER, D-
DER). If the two characters before the ER are not one of these pairs, the character before the E is tested for an
L. If it is an L, and the character before the L is a B,C,D,F,G,P,T or a Z, the word can be hyphenated before one
of these characters. If it is not one of these, the word cannot be hyphenated at this point. If the character was not
an L, the previous two characters are tested for a ST. If they are a ST, the word is hyphenated before the ST if
the character before the ST is a consonant (c-STER) or after the S if the character is a vowel (vS-TER). If the two
characters are not an ST, they are tested for an EV. If they are an EV and the character before the EV is not an
I, the word can be hyphenated before the EV.

S -(LES, NES)S

If the last character in the word is an S, the three characters before the S are tested for an LES or NES. If they
are an LES or NES the word can be hyphenated before the LES or NES (-LES, -NES). Otherwise, the S is dropped
and the LAST CHARACTER check is started with the letter before the S.

Y -BLY
G-GLY, r-GLY by ING rules
r-LY
ᵥₑᵢHTY
r-TY
ᵥₑᵣY

If the last character in the word is a Y, the character before the Y is tested for an L. If it is an L, the character preceding the L is tested for a B. If it is a B, the word can be hyphenated before the B (-BLY). If the character before
the L is not a B, it is tested for a G. If it is a G and the character before the G is not another G, the ING rules
above are then applied to the end of the word. If the G is preceded by another G, the word is hyphenated between
the GG (G-G). If the character before the L is not a G, the two characters before the G are tested for a DD, MM,
NN, PP, RR, or TT. If the two characters are one of these pairs, the word is hyphenated between the two characters
(D-DLY, M-MLY). If the two characters preceding the LY are not one of these pairs, the word is hyphenated before
the LY (-LY). Finally, if the character before the Y is not an L, it is tested for a T. If it is not a T or it is a T preceded
by an H, the word cannot be hyphenated at this point. If it is a T and the T is not preceded by an H, the word
can be hyphenated before the T (-TY).

OTHER TIMES RULES

H -(C,P,S,W) H (G,T) H-, -vH, r-H

If the consonant is an **H**, and the character before the **H** is a **C,P,S,** or **W**, the word is hyphenated before the **C,P,S,** or **W** (-CH, -PH). If the **H** is not preceded by a **C,P,S,** or **W**, but is preceded by a **G** or **T**, the word is hyphenated after the **H** (GH-, TH-). If it is not one of the previous cases the word is hyphenated before the **H** (-H) unless the **H** is preceded by a vowel.

K CK-, r-K

If the consonant is a **K**,it is hyphenated before the **K** (-K) except if the **K** is preceded by a **C**, then the word is hyphenated after the **K** (CK-).

L -(C,F,P) L, -vL, r-L

If the consonant is an **L**, and the character before the **L** is a **C,F,** or **P**, then the word is hyphenated before the **C,F,** or **P** (-CL, -FL). If the **L** is not preceded by a **C,F,** or **P**, a hyphen is placed before the **L** unless the character before the **L** is a vowel.

N vN, r-N

If the consonant is a **N**, the word is hyphenated after the **N** if the **N** is preceded by a vowel, and before the **N** if it is not.

P (DIS, MIS) -P, r-SP, -vP, r-P

If the consonant is a **P**, the three characters before the **P** are tested for a **DIS** or **MIS**. If the three characters are **DIS** or **MIS** the word is hyphenated before the **P** (DIS-P, MIS-P), If the three characters are not **DIS** or **MIS**, the character before the **P** is tested for a **S**. If it is a **S**, a hyphen is placed before the **S**. If the character before the **P** is not an **S**, the hyphen is placed before the **P** unless the character before the **P** is a vowel.

R (v or c) vR-
vS-TR, c-STR, GHT-R, r-TR
(DIS, MIS) -CR, r-SCR, r-CR
-(B,D,F,G,P)R r-R

If the consonant is an **R**, the character before the **R** is tested for a vowel. If it is a vowel, the word is hyphenated after the **R** (vR-). If it is not a vowel, the two characters before the **R** are tested for **ST**. If they are **ST**, the word is hyphenated between the **S** and the **T** if the **ST** is preceded by a vowel (vS-TR) and before the **S** if the **ST** is preceded by a consonant. If the two characters are not **ST** but the last three characters before the **R** are **GHT**, the word is hyphenated after the **GHT** (GHT-R). If the three characters ane not **GHT**, preceding the **R** is a **T**, the word is hyphenated before the **T** (r-TR). Now, if a **T** did not precede the **R**, the character before the **R** is tested for **C**. If it is a **C**, and the three characters before the **C** are **DIS** or **MIS** the word is hyphenated before the **CR** (DIS-CR, MIS-CR). If the three characters before the **C** are not **DIS** or **MIS**, the word is hyphenated before the **C** (r-CR) except if the **C** is preceded by a **S**, then the word is hyphenated before the **S** (r-SCR). If the character before the **R** is not **C**, then it is tested for a **B,D,F,G,** or **P** If it is one of these, the hyphen goes before the ,**D,F,G,** or **P** (-BR, -DR). If it is not a **B,D,F,G,** or **P** the hyphen is placed before the **R** (r-R).

S DIS, MIS, (rl, r) -S

If the consonant is a **S**, the hyphen is placed after the **S**, if the previous two characters are a **DI** or **MI** (DIS-, MIS-). If it is not a **DIS** or **MIS**, the hyphen is placed before the **S** (r-S).

T v-ST, c-ST
GHT-, rH-T
r-T

If the consonant is a **T**, the character before the **T** is tested for a **S**. If it is an **S**, the word is hyphenated after the **S**, if the **S** is preceded by a vowel (**vS-T**), and before the **S**, if it is preceded by a consonant. If the **T** is not preceded by an **S** it is tested for an **H** preceding the **T**. If it is an **H**, the word is hyphenated between the **H** and the **T** (**H-T**) except if the **H** is preceded by a **G**, and then the word is hyphenated after the **T** (**GHT-**). If the **T** is not preceded by an **S** or **H**, the hyphen is placed before the **T**.

W ʜ₁(v,T)**W**, r-**W**

If the consonant is a **W**, the word cannot be hyphenated if the **W** is preceded by a vowel or a **T**. If it is not preceded by a vowel or **T**, the hyphen is placed before the **W**.

X X-

If the consonant is an **X**, the hyphen is placed after the **X** (**X-**).

c -(**B,C,D,F,G,J,M,Q,V,Z**)

If the consonant is a **B,C,D,F,G,J,M,Q,V,** or **Z**, the hyphen is placed before the character (**-B, -C**), unless the character is preceded by a vowel.

In the above rules, the rule that is underlined signifies that after the hyphen point is found, a specisl check is to be made. If the letter preceding the hyphen is a **G**, the ING rules will be applied. If the two letters preceding the hyphen are **EX**, they will be bypassed before going to the vowel check.

Also, in order for a hyphen to be placed in a word, the hyphen point must be preceded by at least one vowel.

Index